PRAISE FOR

The W

MW00974469

∞

"With this little book, *The Wealthy Physician*, Chase Chandler has done an exceptionally good job of producing an essential outline for all professionals as they develop their financial future. This work can be equally valuable to those who have been led astray by the conventional wisdom that has plagued mankind since the beginning of time. I encourage all to study the wisdom that Chase has incorporated here."

—R. NELSON NASH
Austrian Economist, Best-Selling Author of *Becoming Your Own Banker* and *Building Your Warehouse of Wealth*

"The busy, hard-working professional will be well served to read and learn the truth in *The Wealthy Physician*. Chase Chandler has respectfully, succinctly and precisely given the reader the opportunity to understand traditional financial planning and to realize the incredible power of using properly designed life insurance to finance lifestyle and business expenses as well as conventional investments. This book will guide the reader into a better or new financial advisor relationship. You and your family will receive incredible value from this book and the references therein. I am a finance educator. Every one of my clients will receive a copy of *The Wealthy Physician*."

—DICK J. DIJKMAN, D.D.S., M.S.
Leading Orthodontist, Bullmoose Orthodontics

"Teaching at the university level, I am always looking for sources to use with my students. Your book will be one I use in my administration class for health care professionals and I will highly recommend it to my students as a helpful source as they deal with personal

finance issues. I sat down and read it through as soon as I got it. It is easy to understand and gives sound advice that even someone that is not into finance will find helpful. I look forward to others in the series. A job well done!"
—RANDY LAMBETH, ED.D., ATC, LAT

"Chase and his book have been indispensable resources for our financial strategy. When my wife and I married and I finished Pharmacy school in more debt than we care to share, we started doing what most professionals do, taking every extra penny and paying down student loans, mortgage payments, debt in general. This was advice we had received from trusted sources but not from sources that shared our "responsible type of debt" and earning ability position. This is not a bad idea but not the best either in our situation. Over the course of working with Chase, through assigned readings, conferences, working with independent CPA's and seeing the lack of understanding my previous financial institution had, we are in the process of securing a greater financial future for ourselves and our family."
—JARED BROWN, PHARM.D. &
TAYLOR BROWN, CPA

"I believe *The Wealthy Physician* addresses pertinent planning issues more concisely than any book I have read. As an entrepreneur I have found that the idea of having liquidity, use, and total control of my dollars is the best way for me to achieve my long-term goals while at the same time capitalizing on any opportunities that may arise in the meantime. My hope is that those who read this book will find it as enlightening as I have."
—JAY GENTRY
Managing Director & Principal, Chandler Advisors

"*The Wealthy Physician* is a must read for anyone in the medical profession. Chase Chandler does an excellent job explaining the correct way to grow your wealth. Chase uses examples, facts, and historical documentation to support his position."
NEIL DENMAN, CPA

"*The Wealthy Physician* is a great book for anyone wishing to enhance their financial situation and become educated on the strategies the truly wealthy are implementing. Chase has done a fantastic job revealing the truth about planning and he understands the needs of his clientele. As someone who works a great deal with medical professionals I know this is a book my clients will enjoy and benefit from reading!"
—MATTHEW L. ALLEN
Top Financial Professional, MDRT®

"Congratulations to you, the reader, for keeping an open mind and continuing to learn. Reading Chase's book was a great reminder to me about WHY we practice Prosperity Economics (my word for what Chase and his team do) and we love having other authors out there telling the WHOLE truth."
—KIM D. H. BUTLER
Best-Selling Author, President of Partners for Prosperity, Inc.

The Wealthy Family

The
Wealthy
Family

BREAK THE CYCLE OF
MEDIOCRITY

B. Chase Chandler

#*TWF*

EIII
PUBLISHING
COMPANY
NASHVILLE

FOR KATE

My hope is that you grow up to be just like your mother.

A portion of all profits from this book go to Purple Door Coffee. To learn more about this incredible organization visit Purple-DoorCoffee.com.

PURPLE DOOR
★ COFFEE ★

CONTENTS

Part III

Rising Above Mediocrity *187*

"In a time of universal deceit, telling the truth is a revolutionary act."

GEORGE ORWELL

INTRODUCTION: MORE THAN MONEY

"*Wealth is the ability to truly experience life.*"
HENRY DAVID THOREAU

THIS BOOK IS, FOR THE MOST PART, about money; finance as it relates to the family and, in many ways, the business. However, in reality, it is about much more than that. It's about making prudent decisions. It's about rising above the median. It's about doing things because they are right and honorable rather than acting out of habit or convenience. In summation, I suppose the central question of my book is this: **How can we optimize our financial lives while properly integrating other areas of our life?** It's a two part answer.

In many ways, I feel as though I've bitten off more than I can chew. I still have a lot to learn. However, I believe that statement can be made by any individual, regardless of age or circumstance.

The learning should never stop, and we should never come to a point at which we think we've got everything figured out—or even one specific thing figured out. And I suppose that this simple recognition is the first step to achieving financial and life optimization: **to truly succeed, we must commit to continuous life-long learning and improvement**. That is the first and most fundamental part of the process.

My wife recently introduced me to a uniquely intriguing podcast, *Serial*. Some of you may have already listened to this 12 series podcast from the producers of NPR's *My American Life*. If you haven't yet, I'm torn between recommending it versus suggesting you flee from it. It's about a 1999 case where a man was convicted to life in prison for the murder of his ex-girlfriend. The only problem is that the evidence clearly isn't as clear as they once thought it was. Sarah Koenig, the host and producer, tells the story so well that I don't think I could do it justice by summarizing further—and I don't want to ruin it for you. The point Koenig makes, though, is one that you will see throughout this book. In one of the episodes she makes reference to *"...how easy it is to throw stereotypes in with facts."* Enter the first of many *pedagogical paradoxes*: We are often certain about things we should not be so certain about. Our certainty is, more than we realize, grounded in little. It is often the product of false confidence instead of concrete knowledge—a flaw that we must admit in order to move forward. The fact is, we must admit to not knowing in order to gain true knowledge.

∞

The second step is no less important: we must realize and display our belief that life is not about money. At its deepest core, life is about faith, family, and selflessness. It is about integrating (rather than balancing) work and family life. It is about controlling what we have the ability to control and making smart decisions with the information we have. **Life is about knowing yourself— your limitations as well as your potential—and eventually coming to the conscious understanding that your limitations are only those that are set in your own mind.**

Money is a significant resource. It can open doors, reduce stress, save time, and alleviate discomfort. It can create massive opportunity to teach and help others. We cannot refute the power of money. We enter dangerous territory, though, when we make money our end goal. Money itself is never the main objective. This is not a new truth; even the least observant of us can see that many of the world's wealthiest people are living lives of utter emptiness. We watch their reality TV shows and stand by as the sadness of their existence is laid bare behind all of their shiny possessions. We *know* this to be true. Why, then, do we continue to see them as sources of fascination? Why do we idolize them and the materials they possess? If we recognize that these things do not lead to happiness, satisfaction, joy, or fulfillment – then why do we chase them? One word: **feelings**. Our intellectual knowledge is overcome by the idea that these things are going to make us feel good. Our subconscious seems to believe that material possessions and shallow praise from others will lift us to a better place. This is not so. As Einstein once remarked, *"A life directed chiefly towards the fulfillment of personal desires sooner or later always leads to bitter disappointment."*

Maybe some of this "stuff" does provide happiness, but it is short-lived. It certainly does not lead to deep-rooted contentment or fulfillment. Like I said before, this is a truth we all recognize. However, syncing intellectual understanding with the emotional desire for short-term satisfaction is no easy task. It is so difficult, in fact, that most people never do. And so the question becomes this:

how do we separate ourselves from the majority—the popular opinion of the day which threatens to drag us into (or keep us in) generality? A question that many have asked, many have answered, but few have mastered.

Herein lies *the* intrinsically vital notion; in truth, a law which, on its face, seems illogical. Yet this law is the seemingly enigmatical key to the aforementioned separation, the less taken path that leads to place we desire to go. I speak of a process enlightened and illuminated upon me by the works of R. Nelson Nash, Mark Spitznagel, Robert Murphy, Carlos Lara, Henry Hazlitt, Friedrich Hayek, the great Ludwig Von Mises, Eugen von Böhm-Bawerk, and the few others who have subscribed to the Austrian school of economics. I do not claim to hold a candle to these men. And, in fact, I do not consider this work you currently hold in your hands commensurate to the works of them; rather, this is a moderately comprehensive entry point for the family looking to sustainably and substantively improve their economic situation. One which should, I believe, substantiate this—the intrinsically vital notion: **flee the convention of the masses, immediately and swiftly—be a contrarian with a purpose.**

Overstated? Perhaps. But if so, only faintly.

A good portion of this book will challenge conventional wisdom, specifically the way you have likely learned to make financial and other life decisions. And not in the *Okay good! I want to learn...* kind of way. More in a slightly exasperated *Why doesn't everyone understand this?* or *Why haven't I learned this before?* or *What is the world is everyone else thinking!* kind of way. Probably, at some point, you will be tempted to disregard or even stop reading because some of the information is so different than what you've heard in the past. It may cause friends, family, or colleagues to question you. They won't understand. You may be tempted to question my analysis and conclusions at times. I encourage you to do so.

The preponderance of accepted wisdom has historically been dubious, a little off at best. Our current situation is no different, difficult as it may be to accept. I hope though, as read this book, you will be reminded of Sarah Koenig's line in which she refers to the ease of "throwing stereotypes in with facts." I hope you will recognize in yourself, as in all the rest of us, the tendency to make decisions for reasons we do not really or fully understand; a natural human flaw which leads to lack of prudence followed by less than desired results. And I hope you will be encouraged, principally by virtue of manifesting a knowledge and belief that a grander life is there for the taking.

This is a far cry from claiming that richer is better. As we progress to further appreciate *The Wealthy Family* it will become clear that money for the sake of money is more than a fool's errand—it is a life wasted. So many are chasing it not knowing why. Actor Jim Carrey, not the philosopher we might think of, may have put it best when he said, "I think everybody should get rich and famous and do everything they ever dreamed of so they can see that it's not the answer."

Rather, the epicenter of focus, for our purposes, is significance, meaning, and freedom. Simply put, the derivative of productivity (economic relevance and value creation) is financial gain. The combination of productivity and purpose; this is the aim of *The Wealthy Family*.

∞

What you now hold is a product of my research inside and outside the field of personal (and business) finance. It is the current integration of this research and of my time, introspection and experience. There are countless other publications that can give you wisdom about the world of financial success. However, I believe that this book will take you on a unique journey, and by the end you will have a solid understanding of what it will take to be financially free. As you will read, much of the "conventional wisdom" that is tossed around in the financial world today, in fact, comes from the intense desire of major financial institutions to meet quarterly earnings projections. This is not always bad, but it has reached a point in which Americans are being deprived of potential wealth, and that wealth is instead shifted to Wall Street and Washington. Much of the propaganda thrust upon Americans today arises from a hidden agenda that seeks to continue massive profits in a cut-throat economy; all the while benefiting many, with the exception of the customer.

Whether they know it or not, American families have been hustled, specifically since the mid 1970's. Over the past forty years, they have seen the value of their dollar take a massive decline. Simply put, money does not buy what it used to buy (think in terms of college, cars, housing, and medicine). Today, the Fed is printing money like it's going out of style. Our country is addicted to low interest rates and Federal Reserve manipulation. The government has an obsession with stiffening overregulation – just look at the cost of medicine 20 years ago in contrast with the prices of today. The rich are certainly getting richer; some are doing so because of their contrarian thinking and entrepreneurial creations. However, most of the wealthy become so by cozying up to and getting special deals from Washington bureaucrats. The middle class, on the other hand, is getting squeezed. From the upper middle class to the lower middle class and everywhere in between, Americans are being swindled by Washington and the self-serving relationships on Wall Street. Hurt worst of all are those who are older and living on fixed incomes. They were promised social security as a "benefit," and now they are only receiving a slight portion of what they were sold.

The Occupy movement wanted to blame it all on Wall Street, and the Tea Party movement wanted to blame it all on Washington. In some sense, they were both right, even though most of them didn't fully understand why. It is not a Republican issue or a Democrat issue. It's an American issue.

Most of financially affluent are not conforming to the so-called "conventional" ways of managing money. In reading this book, you will come to understand why traditional financial planning is not working, how to protect your assets from economic catastrophe, what the most efficient strategies for managing money are, and why it's important to spread this word to those you care about the most. It takes a certain level of financial sophistication to be successfully prudent with your God given resources. You will learn the whys and the hows.

∞

This book has three main sections: **Part 1: How We Think**, **Part II: The Fall of Logic**, and **Part III: Rising Above Mediocrity**. Part one, *How We Think*, addresses our natural tendencies to think and act in a defective manner. We consistently and unnecessarily doubt ourselves, we take things out of context, we rationalize our poor decisions, we make excuses, and we accept conventional wisdom at face value simply because it is conventional. Each of these human flaws contributes to the results we get, which—whether we want to admit it or not—have been less than decent. But don't worry. It's all uphill from there.

Part two, *The Fall of Logic*, focuses more on this "conventional wisdom" or common sense that, as Jim Rogers once put it, is not so common. I address specific financial issues related to modern financial planning, mutual funds, rates of return, qualified plans, debt reduction strategies, and understanding time value of money principles. The combination of part one and part two give you the context that I believe you absolutely must understand in order to make truly pragmatic financial (and other life) decisions.

Part three, *Rising Above Mediocrity*, is all about strategies and solutions that will help you and your family to better manage your money. From wealth building to asset protection to prudent management to giving with passion—this is culmination of expansive research. The data and research of the most successful families in the U.S. all point in one direction, and it is a direction that can help you to increase your income and protect your family from devastating financial events. But keep in mind, you have to appreciate and internalize parts one and two to in order to fully understand part three.

It is best to read the book in sequence to understand the full context. Focus on the idea, the concept, and the message of each chapter and section. Certain philosophies and analysis are repeated a decent amount. This is not to exasperate, but to reinforce some of the more imperative matters of this text. Matters that we all struggle with. Matters of human nature. Matters that we must be fully aware of to progress.

In order to fully understand some of the more in-depth concepts of this book, you will need to have some level of financial and mathematical understanding. You will need to learn to think in probabilities—to think statistically. This may be the most difficult section for the many, but I am confident that you can get through it and even enjoy it.

As an aside, I make an attempt at humor to make some of the more mundane reading of financial analysis and strategy more enjoyable. Whether or not it works, well, only you may judge. If you read something that seems to be completely out of left field and makes little sense, forgive me; for it is likely an attempt. My dryness takes its toll on paper, as it is not always the easiest to grasp. If you do not find it humorous then you'll be in shrewd company—with my wife. If you do find certain sections or footnotes humorous you'll be in my company. May the *force* be with you.

∞

A DECISION OF ACTION

If you're willing, make a single promise. Promise yourself that you will try to analyze your situation as it pertains to the information and recommendations of this book. Promise yourself that you will not fall into what Daniel Kahneman[i] calls the *"law of least effort"* which *"asserts that… laziness is built deep into our nature."* The outcome of your decision is too dire to be lazy. You might be reading this for your family. You might be reading this for you. You might be reading this for your business. Any or all of the above call for full attentiveness and engagement. The first decision that you can make is one of action. A decision that you will study and you will learn. You will let nothing hold you from knowing what is going on and what the options are.

I believe life is meant to be exhilarating, not mundane. We were created to live a life of meaning, of significance—not to just survive. **We do not know what tomorrow will bring. But we do know that we have today. We must make the most of what we have today.** The great tragedy, as will be a central theme of this book, is our human inclination to go for what is easiest. Our subconscious desire to avoid discomfort at all costs has made us into a dull and mediocre people. And modern society only perpetuates the problem

---

[i] From the book *Thinking, Fast and Slow*

by telling us that possessions will make us happy. The truth is that growth only occurs via struggle or study. And for some of us study is struggle. When you make an intentional decision to take the path less traveled, it tends to lead you to a better place—a place where the majority is not.

The end of each chapter concludes with a section called '*Questions to Contemplate.*' The purpose of this is to get you to consider matters related to finance and life—and specifically the integration of the two. These are not questions that you must immediately have an answer for; in fact, it would be better if you elude trying to think of an immediate and absolute answer. The most effective outcome will result from pondering many different possible answers. And maybe, for some of them, absolute answers do not exist. However, they are questions that will help you to think more critically about your decision-making process and how you should manage your money. My hope is that these questions will revolutionize the way you think, act, and decide— culminating in new learning around how to manage life and money.

Wishing you more than financial prosperity,

B. Chase Chandler
Proverbs 12
12/5/2014

"Inaction breeds doubt and fear. Action breeds confidence and courage. If you want to conquer fear, do not sit home and think about it. Go out and get busy."

DALE CARNEGIE

PART I

HOW WE THINK

Ascending to a Higher Level of Consciousness

"Intellectual honesty is an applied method of problem solving, characterized by an unbiased, honest attitude, which can be demonstrated in a number of different ways, including but not limited to: One's personal beliefs do not interfere with the pursuit of truth..."

http://en.wikipedia.org/wiki/Intellectual_honesty

1

OBJECTIVITY, HONESTY, & INTELLECTUAL INTENSITY

"Most people do not listen with the intent to understand; they listen with the intent to reply."
STEPHEN R. COVEY

IN HIS BOOK 'THE CASH RESIDENCE,' author David Saucer tells the parable of a man who has a heart attack. While eating dinner with his wife, the man collapses holding his chest as he falls. His wife calls 911 in a panic, explaining what has just occurred. She fears the worst. Within minutes, the volunteer paramedics show up. The wife is flabbergasted at the promptness of the medics. They rush him to the hospital. Because of her swift call and the paramedic's rapid response, the man is going to make a complete recovery after having just one heart stint. The physician prescribes a few meds and a healthy diet, and then he turns to the wife. He tells her that she should be thankful the paramedics got them to the hospital so quickly—another ten minutes and the man may not have made lived.

As the man is wheeled out of the hospital with his family, the wife sees one of the paramedics standing a short distance away. She thanks him for his efficiency but notices something a bit odd. The ambulance, rather than looking normal, is lime green with pink letters—something she hadn't noticed during the rush to get her husband to the hospital. She remarks, "*That's odd. I've never seen a green ambulance before.*" The paramedic replies, "*Neither had I. But it was the fastest, most affordable ambulance we could find. And the lime green paint is actually lighter and more aerodynamically efficient than normal white and red paint.*" Did the wife care that the ambulance was so unconventional? **I think not.** The wife and the rest of the family were focused on what mattered—the health of their husband and father. The fact that the ambulance looked odd and abnormal had no impact on the validity of the aid he received.

Imagine, if only for a moment, that the family (for whatever foolish reason) had only accepted and endorsed a traditional white and red ambulance. Well, of course, the man would not have made it. He may have passed on simply because of the family's previously held view of what was right and acceptable. That single view could have contributed to the death of their husband and father. *Logically*, they didn't care. The color of the vehicle was of no consequence.

Let's consider another version of this story.

A few days earlier, the same man goes to his doctor after feeling chest pains and shortness of breath. The doctor examines the patient by asking a plethora of questions and running a few tests. A few minutes later, the physician enters the patient's room and explains that he is showing signs of heart disease and potential blood clots. The doctor tells the man that he needs to quit smoking, stop drinking so much, eat more vegetables, and lose about 30 pounds.

The man responds, *"I'm too busy to exercise. I've got a wife, three kids, and five grandkids. I'm an executive at IMC[i], and I've got a few big reports due this quarter. I just can't do it."* The doctor says, *"Well, it is really important to exercise. If you can't change your lifestyle now, then you may not have it at all in the near future. Can you at least eat better and stop smoking and drinking?"* At this, the man becomes angry, saying, *"Do you not understand? I have to drink with my co-workers - it's how we bond. I have to smoke. It's how I cope with stress. I have to eat fast food because my schedule is so busy. Why don't you just give me medication? I see all sorts of commercials for this kind of thing. Just give me some pills and I'll be fine!"*

The doctor, becoming a bit impatient, tells the man that medication won't fix the problem. It will merely cover it up for a short while. The long-term fix is to make a few lifestyle changes right now; otherwise, the result could be dire. The physician goes on to explain that we have to make choices in life and that everything is a trade-off. We can choose to experience the short-term pleasure of certain futile decisions today, but those decisions may cause severe pain in the future. Or, we can choose to feel an amount of discomfort today by making tough choices, from which the long-term result will likely be meaningful and pleasant. The man doesn't take too well to being told these things that he clearly doesn't want to hear. He leaves the doctor's office with a prescription for blood thinners. He changes nothing. He still drinks often, smokes daily, and eats mostly fast food. The man has a massive heart attack four months later and dies.

---

[i] For the record – I made up "IMC" which stands for Incoherent Mail Company. It doesn't actually exist... or does it?

∞

The moral of these stories are simple, yet profound: **if we want to optimize the results of our personal, professional, and financial life, we must focus on what matters.** Not only must we focus on what matters, but we must also mitigate distractions, habits, and beliefs that either do not matter or prove to be misguided. We must learn the practice of *intentional apathy* towards that which is fruitless. And, in order to accomplish this, we must put aside our preconceived notions and opinions—not of what is inherently and morally right or wrong, but of what we rationalize as not really being 'that big of a deal.' These are the life decisions that we make every day that will have an impact on our future well-being. Decisions such as: how much we spend on this or that, what kinds of food we eat, whether or not we grow our minds, how much time we spend with our families, and, *get ready…* what our decision-making process looks like. For the most part, right and wrong is easy. Don't steal. Don't murder. Don't hurt others. **It's the seemingly smaller internal decisions, the ones that appear to have little immediate consequence in our lives, that we miss. These unseen components can make the difference between average and significant futures.**

Take the story of the green ambulance from just a moment ago. Because we probably won't see many lime green ambulances in our lifetime, let's imagine a more pragmatic, real-life example. (While this example is not clear-cut, it is real and powerful. So pay attention.)

You probably know someone whom does something that you don't understand, and it frustrates you. You know that the belief or action of this person is wrong, and you understand why they believe or do this thing—whatever it is. It could be how they communicate, whom they vote for, how they raise their kids, or what they post on Facebook. Fill in the blank. And for the sake of this point, you're absolutely right. We are assuming that the flaw in this person is just plain wrong, and everyone sees it but them. Now, this begs the question:

Why do they do it? Why does this person continually do this thing that irritates and baffles everyone around them?

If any of us could answer this question with total accuracy, we wouldn't need this book or any book like it (and we'd give Dr. Phil a run for his money). The reality is that there are many reasons why people do what they do—and not all of it has to do with our mothers. A complex situation can only be answered by God.

However, maybe we do know, at least in some cases, why people act foolishly: because either no one has alerted them to their ill-informed behavior, or someone has and they just refuse to listen. In large part, this book is about listening and learning—becoming self-aware enough to know what we do know and what we do not know... as well as how to improve on what we absolutely need to know.

It is likely that you and I are both, in some small way, similar to the person of whom you were just thinking. That person who always did that thing that annoyed you and everyone else. A recent New Yorker article summed it up nicely[1]:

"Perhaps our most dangerous bias is that we naturally assume that everyone else is more susceptible to thinking errors, a tendency known as the "bias blind spot."

> *This "meta-bias" is rooted in our ability to spot systematic mistakes in the decisions of others—we excel at noticing the flaws of friends—and inability to spot those same mistakes in ourselves."*

If we're honest—if we take a moment of deep introspection—we can probably think of a time or two when we were *that person*. We're all guilty of it. Unfortunately, we can't force *that person* to change. **We can't control the decision-making process of others. However, we can control our own. And herein lies the difference between massive success and massive failure.** Our willingness and ability to enhance our own financial decision-making process (i.e. our cognitive financial skills), followed by taking action on those process enhancements, is key. We make decisions in one of two ways: with our conscious mind or our subconscious mind[2]. First, we need to become aware of the fact that neither mind is all-knowing. However, we can improve our conscious knowledge in certain important areas—faith, family, financial strategy, exercise, and so on. The accumulation of these "little" things is what will make all the biggest difference over time.

We are going to primarily discuss a type of financial cognitive improvement that can help you to *think differently*—although I believe this applies to the professional and personal arenas as well. In chapter three, I am going to discuss this human issue of people thinking they know things that they actually don't (or in some cases, things that used to be true that have changed). I do not claim to be a social psychologist, but when it comes to money, I think we can agree that people make unwise choices. Sometimes they consciously know that what they are doing makes no sense, and sometimes they are completely unaware. And when I say they, I really mean *we*. Each of us has made and continues to make financial decisions that are questionable. Oftentimes, these questionable decisions don't actually make us *feel* better. So then, why? Why do we do it? Before you move on, think about these questions for just a few moments:

How do you make financial decisions?

Why do you make decisions in that manner?

WE DON'T KNOW WHAT WE DON'T KNOW

Ask yourself if you agree with this basic premise:

We all have problems, difficulties, and blind spots.

There are things that we don't know that we need to know.

One of the differences between generally successful people and unsuccessful people is how they react to (or deal with) these problems.

There are things that we think we know that in reality, we do not know. It is likely that we will discover them to be false sometime in the future.

There are things that we don't know right now that, in the future, we will wish we had known.

If you agree with these statements[ii], then you may also agree that ignoring problems, difficulties, and blind spots is not the best solution.

> *" Men are anxious to improve their circumstances, but are unwilling to improve themselves; they therefore remain bound."*

> JAMES ALLEN

If you do agree with the aforementioned premise and conclusion, then why do you and I continually ignore issues that need to be addressed? It is likely that we just don't want to deal with it. We don't want to have to think about it. We already have so much going on in our lives. The easy solution, whether consciously or subconsciously, is just to remain ignorant. **Ignoring the issue, therefore, is nothing more than a coping mechanism. It's a coping mechanism that can payoff in the short-term, but will do damage in the long-term.**

Stop and listen. Stop thinking you know. Be open to new thoughts, to new possibilities. Close your mind to the judgment mentality by which you've been trained. Open your mind to equitable critical thought. Ponder the 'seeing mind' and the 'unseeing mind.'

[ii] If you do not agree with them, then you may put down this book and continue with your (likely mediocre) life.

"Two people can see the same thing, disagree, and yet both be right. It's not logical; it's psychological."

"We see the world, not as it is, but as we are——or, as we are conditioned to see it."

STEPHEN R. COVEY

The overarching theme of this book is truth. But truth—while in and of itself is easily defined—can be quite ambiguous and eso-teric. Ministers, doctors, lawyers, and politicians constantly argue about how they interpret the facts—their version of the truth. And, as much as some want to believe that there is only one version of the truth, in many cases there is substantial ambiguity. We have to be okay with that. In order to become better, to become more ef-fective, we must realize that alternative opinions matter. Just be-cause we have believed this or that, just because our parents believed this or that, does not make it right today. Circumstances change. Economies change. People change. We have to integrate the data of the past, present, and future to make the best decisions for today. If we want to be successful, especially financially, we must think differently. We must, in some ways, mitigate our opinions—our versions of the "truth."

While there is so very much that we really don't know—there are a few things that we can know. There are principles, as the late Stephen Covey[iii] put it, which do not change. For instance, we can know that the world is round. We can know that consistent exercise and healthy eating will statistically lead to a healthy life. And, I be-lieve, we can better know what to do financially with logic, proper

---

[iii] As you will see throughout this book, I really like Stephen R. Covey and his book The 7 Habits of Highly Effective People. I admit, reluctantly, that I may have used his too much in this introduction. However, if you haven't read his book, please read it now. Do it for me. Do it for you. Do it for everyone around you. Please. Right now.

analysis, and by looking at what has and has not worked over the past few hundred years.

For the purpose of this book, when I use the word *truth*, I actually mean objectivity, honesty, and the purposeful desire to approach topics with intellectual intensity. Let me briefly describe what I mean.

Objectivity is the ability to be impartial when viewing or analyzing a subject. In order to be impartial, we must be open to new learning. We must be open to the fact that we could be wrong (or that what we've been taught could have been wrong). And, most importantly, we must be open to the fact that people you have trusted (parents, close friends, etc.) may be wrong.

Honesty, in this book, is the ability to look at situations and to be honest with ourselves. Part of honesty is admitting internally that we do not know everything. In fact, the first step of honesty is acknowledging to ourselves (and, of course, to your spouse[iv]) that you have blind spots.

Intellectual Intensity (I.I.) is a term I like to think that I coined on my own. However, I'm sure someone coined it before me. I.I., as I'll call it from here on out, is the commitment to understanding things you need to understand (i.e. things that are important in your life). Why and how did this term come about? Mainly from a constant habit that I saw in people. A habit that is often built over years of the exact opposite, which is intellectual laziness. This is the habit of not wanting to learn; of not wanting to take the time to gather, accept, and analyze data, even if it is immensely relevant to family and future. I.I., on the other hand, is the conscious choice to study

---

[iv] If you're married and you haven't done this recently, I recommend you haul it to wherever your spouse is right now and tell him or her that you fully realize and understand you don't know everything. Then tell them you read that in a wonderful new book that you picked up and they should begin reading it ASAP.

and think intently on those aforementioned topics in order to make a positive difference.

Each of these internal development areas (*Honesty*, *Objectivity*, and *I.I.*) involves analyzing issues with the intent to understand, rather than looking at them with the intent to judge based on current (or previously learned) understanding. Then, once we do understand, we can judge and, if necessary, implement. Go forth. Learn. Judge. Implement. Continue reading.

QUESTIONS TO CONTEMPLATE:

WHAT MOTIVATES YOU?

WHAT ARE THE FINANCIAL PROBLEMS YOU NEED TO ADDRESS?

WHAT ARE THE PROFESSIONAL ISSUES YOU NEED TO ADDRESS?

WHAT ARE THE FAMILY ISSUES YOU NEED TO ADDRESS?

IF YOU DIED TOMORROW, WHAT WOULD YOU BE REMEMBERED FOR?

2

ARE WE ALL DESTINED FOR GREATNESS?

"There comes a time in the lives of those destined for greatness when we must stand before the mirror of meaning and ask: Why, having been endowed with the courageous heart of a lion, do we live as mice?

We must ask if our desires to feel safe and accepted are in fact enslaving us to popular opinion—and to boredom. We must ask: When will we be ready to ascend to another level of existence?"[3]

BRENDAN BURCHARD

CAN WE ALL BE DESTINED FOR greatness? Well, if you must ask, yes… and no. In order to make true headway, we must first define the term "greatness" (primarily so that you and I are on the same page). The word is generally defined as something of "exceptionally high quality[4]."

Similar terms could be distinction, perfection, preeminence, superiority, supremacy, faultlessness, flawlessness, impeccability, perfectness, goodness, value, and worth[i].

Greatness has two meanings from the same definition. In one sense, we all can and should aim for distinction, value, and worth. We should all aim to be of "exceptionally high quality." However, none will hit perfection or flawlessness and, in the sense that one sees himself as "great" conceitedly, he is only hurting himself. The reality is that, with the right mindset, we can "ascend to another level of existence.[5]"

While there are many antonyms for greatness—two very simple, yet powerful, words strike me as most relevant:

AVERAGE

MEDIOCRE

Most of us will never run a four-minute mile. We won't play in the NBA. However, I believe that we can reach greatness in an even grander sense. Author Brendon Burchard gives us a good explanation of how to seek and think about greatness. Burchard asks directly, *"Why, having been endowed with the courageous heart of a lion, do we live as mice? We must look squarely into our own tired eyes and examine why we . . . consent to play small. We must ask why we participate so humbly in society's . . . mazes of mediocrity. We must ask if our*

---

[i] As can be found here: http://www.merriam-webster.com/thesaurus/greatness

desires to feel safe and accepted are in fact enslaving us to popular opin-
ion—and to boredom. We must ask: When will we be ready to ascend to
another level of existence?"

To ascend to another level of existence is to rise to a greater
level of purpose and to a higher level of consciousness. Purpose, in
that we know what we are living for, and we have decidedly made it
known, first in our own minds, what we will accomplish in life. Consciousness, in the sense that we become so aware of our thoughts,
actions, and words that we know they align with our purpose. We
ascend to a greater level of living by persistent intention, not by
default.

There will consistently be people in your life who have their
own goals and desires for you. **There will be those who want you
to play small and safe—maybe a family member or a boss or a
friend. That is for their benefit, not yours.** Other people will
always want you to play by their rules. They fear that, one: you
could be hurt if you shoot to high and fail or, two: that you will
achieve some level with which they could never keep up. Why do
they have such fears? It is their own insecurity. It is their own regret. It is their desire to keep you at their *mediocre* level. **Let me
reframe the situation for them and for you. Number one**, fail-
ing is not and has never been a bad thing. In fact, it is the only way
to achieve any level of success. The only sense that failure is a bad
occurrence is in our head and in our emotional inability to handle
failure. Assuming that we have mental toughness and intestinal for-
titude, failure is a great thing. Failure is the only way to success.
Number two, reaching great levels of success is great, as long as
we keep a level head, as long as we preserve our humility. They
don't want you to try because you might fail. You might fail because
you are human, and you must fail in order to learn. You have to
learn if you want to reach any level of significance. **Therefore, fear**

of failure and a desire to "play it small" are, at their cores, illogical.

Many of you have already achieved this other "level of existence." You have lived intentionally and you will never stop living that life. This book may help you recommit to that calling and, at least financially, enhance your learning. Most of you have not. Most of you are playing small—playing by someone else's rules. You are letting others tell you what you can and cannot accomplish—personally, professionally and financially. All you need to break out of this place that you're in is a belief: a belief that you can truly change things for the better. You can change your family, your finances, your industry, your spiritual life—all for the better. You don't have to have some spry level of over-the-top artificial motivation to do this. You just have to sync your intellectual understanding with your emotional desire. You have to find what creates a deep level of internal drive and external enthusiasm for you. This isn't some "wish upon a star." It is reality. It is reality for those who have done it—young and old. Moreover, it can be reality for you and your family. Take a page from the book of Walt Disney and Steve Jobs.

"To some people, I am kind of a Merlin who takes lots of crazy chances, but rarely makes mistakes. I've made some bad ones, but, fortunately, the successes have come along fast enough to cover up the mistakes. When you go to bat as many times as I do, you're bound to get a good average." – WALT DISNEY

"Life can be much broader once you discover one simple fact. And that is: everything around you that you call life was made up by people that were no smarter than you. And you can change it. You can influence it... Once you learn that, you'll never be the same again." – STEVE JOBS

∞

Consider the story of Dr. Loray Rector. Dr. Rector, by an outsider, would perhaps be considered an above average dentist, nothing more. However, to those who knew him, Loray was more than a little above average. He was remarkable. He was selfless. He was a giver of everything God had given him. He was a husband, a father, a grandfather and a leader.

On December 1st, 2014, Dr. Rector was killed while riding his bike with the youth minister of his church. This isn't some sappy story of the local doctor who is remembered, mainly only after his passing, as having been a good man. This is a different story. This is the story of a man who gave and gave and gave. Whatever was needed, he gave. Just a few weeks before Dr. Rector's heartbreaking death, his son was in a horrific motorcycle accident. Evan, his son, lost an arm and a leg. My wife and I were in college with Evan. My brother-in-law is the preacher at Evan's and the late Dr. Rector's church. One of my finest mentors in the financial services industry, Joe Bedwell, is a member of that church and was Dr. Rector's financial advisor. Joe's son-in-law, David, is a member of my organization. I never knew Dr. Rector. However, I know one thing: he gave. He cared so much for others that he forsook himself. He became great, not in a prideful way, but in the impact that he left on so many. Moreover, he thought with prudence and intelligence. I know that he made decisions with foresight, not considering how those decisions would make him *feel* in the moment, but what impact those decisions would have in years to come. His focus was that which mattered—that which was noble. As one friend put it: "He helped a lot of people behind the scenes. He was not one to be showy about what he did. He just wanted to help people and to serve.[6]" He had the confidence to think differently and look at situations and at new ideas without judgment.

Again, ask yourself what matters. What really and truly matters. Is it material? Can any possession satisfy you? Can your faulty insecurities or your worldly pride protect you? Insecurity and fear hold us back—our fear of failure, rejection, uncertainty, and other people's opinions of us. Pride and narcissism are nothing more than defense mechanisms born out of a desire for others to think that we are important—for others to find us fascinating and successful. And in the end, other's views simply do not matter. We must move past our irrational fears, and we must learn to focus on what matters.

"*As I grow older I pay less attention to what men say. I just watch what they do.*"

ANDREW CARNEGIE

∞

It's all about what you do. Words mean (almost) nothing. We have all heard this countless times. However, it remains easy to find people who will talk, and difficult to find people that will do. So stop talking... and just do. I know—there's more to it than that. There are many psychological components involved in taking action, and I know not a soul who has mastered the art. However, you can consistently improve. Early in my career I had a business coach that taught me the 'because' exercise. This strategy changed the way that I think, and it took my thinking to a higher level. The basic premise of the 'because' exercise is to finish this statement until you get down to the deepest possible level: I _____ BECAUSE _____. An example might be:

I *didn't pay the bill* BECAUSE I *forgot*.

I *forgot* BECAUSE I *didn't put it on my schedule*.

I *didn't put it on my schedule* BECAUSE I *was too busy*.

I *was too busy* BECAUSE I *didn't intentionally manage my time*.

It sounds simple—and it is. However, whenever you can't figure out why you, your spouse, or your kids are thinking a certain way, try it. I think that you will find it to be an effective way to get to the real issue. Actions tell us where our priorities lie. If we want badly enough to improve, then we will find a way to make it happen. Too often we 'let life get to us,' and we decide to give up and settle. Not that we shouldn't be content in all situations—we most certainly should. However, I don't think we were meant to go through life just trying to get by. Life is so much more than that. It can be so much more than that. We must know ourselves and we must focus on objectivity, honesty, and intellectual intensity.

Becoming A 10 Talent Person

20 "So he who had received five talents came and brought five other talents, saying, 'Lord, you delivered to me five talents; look, I have gained five more talents besides them.' 21 His lord said to him, 'Well done, good and faithful servant; you were faithful over a few things, I will make you ruler over many things. Enter into the joy of your lord.'

Matthew 25 (NKJV)

My central point is this: our duty is to make the most with what we've been given. Our calling is to be as productive and effective as we can be. Like the parable of the talents, we want to turn our '5 talents' (or bags of gold) into five more. **We can reach higher levels of significance if we have a strong understanding of where we are going and why we're headed in that direction.**

The integration of our financial strategy is relevant to what we will be able to accomplish. For some, much of their impact will be through monetary means. For others, their impact will be even greater by utilizing those monetary means. Either way—our level of financial understanding in the modern world matters. Our ability to be prudent, to plan and make decisions with foresight, is somewhat contingent on our understanding of financial issues. Financial education is paramount.

Let us first dig in the depth of our minds, thinking intensely about meaning and significance. What do you want? *Not*, what do you kind of want right now, in the present? *Not*, what would you like to have in the next five minutes, or the next day, or even the next week? What do *you* really want?

When asked to think about what they truly want out of life, most people come to an answer that involves comfort or security; some object of their desires that will grant them peace, pleasure, or—the often overused term—happiness. Over the last few decades in the United States, an idea of how life "should be" has emerged: the idea that comfort and security are the chief goals in life. Perhaps it has been that way since the beginning of time. Karl Marx said, in a letter to his father, that "...experience acclaims as happiest the man who has made the greatest number of people happy."[7] Presumably, we must first define the term. In this context of happiness, I am referring to the natural human desire for immediate comfort, security, and gratification. That is, the inherent emotion that is the initial driver of most of our decisions. It is securely focused on the short-term result, the instantaneous feeling that results from choices. Current culture is a bursting populace searching for some esoteric level happiness. A mysterious and controlling force lies within them, creating an overwhelming sentiment that they should be—that they deserve to be—happy right now; right this very moment. And if not now, no later than next week or next month.

Marketers have preyed on this longing and have convinced us that we need *this* or *that* product because it will make our lives easier. Now, do not misunderstand me. This is not always a detrimental pattern. I say this simply to point out that we, as consumers, have been trained to think in terms of what is going to make life simpler and easier. Much of this is very good. In fact, this pattern has catapulted society to levels of extreme proficiency. However, the overfocus on ease and comfort can be dangerous. Over time, our minds are conditioned to the idea that "easier" is synonymous with "better" – and it most certainly is not. We are also trained to believe that security is attainable, and this lie is the very crux of consumerism. Contrary to what marketers tell us, security is no more attainable than the wind. You can think, in one fleeting moment, that you have it – that you have reached a state of security. But alas, the great paradox of life: **security and comfort are rarely found when searching for security and comfort.** This is not to say that working towards security is a completely worthless pursuit. Should we be prudent in our decision-making? Of course. As this book points out repeatedly, we should make decisions today that will make our lives easier and better in the future. However, the irony lies in the fact that most of the decisions our brains want us to make are counterproductive to this goal. As Dan Ariely put it in his best-seller *Predictably Irrational*[ii], *"But because human beings tend to focus on short-term benefits and our own immediate needs, such tragedies of the commons occur frequently."*

> *"Security is mostly a superstition. It does not exist in nature, nor do the children of men as a whole experience it. Avoiding danger is no safer in the long run than outright exposure. Life is either a daring adventure, or nothing."*
>
> HELEN KELLER

The pursuit of happiness, or rather—our pursuit of *instantaneous* happiness, inadvertently generates more lasting pain and struggle than not. Therefore, by seeking that which is most desired, the least desirable is actually acquired. We wonder why we are not where we thought we would be, or why we haven't exactly achieved our goals, never realizing the exact origin. This is a principle that will be extensively examined and further validated throughout this book.

You see, the human brain lies to us. The brain seeks comfort primarily through the path of least resistance. Think of a time you witnessed a person who made a decision because it would make things easier in that moment. Chances are, you can think of a time when you have done this. Did it lead to value in the future? I doubt it. In fact, it's far more likely that it led to excessive difficulty later on. Think of when you...

... took out more debt than you could handle.

[ii] For a comprehensive list of books you should read – please visit www.TheWealthyFamily.com/readinglist.

. ... chose apathy instead of sympathy or thoughtfulness.

... stopped exercising.

... stopped reading and growing your mind.

... gave someone a pass because you feared and uncomfortable confrontation.

... bought something you didn't need and regretted it later on (even though you knew you didn't need it at the time of purchase[iii]).

When we seek immediate comfort, it almost always leads to the opposite result over time. We must, therefore, ignore our brain's natural tendency to take the path of least resistance.

This book will help you avoid that path of least resistance, and take the more challenging path, when it matters most. You will learn to make wiser and more beneficial financial decisions. Whether you are the CFO of a Fortune 100 company, just entering the workforce, or anywhere in between, I believe this book will be of value to you. For some of you, it will enhance your already astute financial sophistication. For more of you, it will help you develop a strong level of financial skill and competency—to realize potential.

[iii] I do this often. Thank you modern consumerism.

QUESTIONS TO CONTEMPLATE:

WHAT IS YOUR MISSION IN LIFE?

WHY DO YOU DO WHAT YOU DO?

DO YOU DO WHAT YOU SAY YOU'RE GOING TO DO?

DO YOU SPEND TOO MUCH TIME TALKING ABOUT
WHAT YOU'RE GOING TO DO?

HOW DO YOU MANAGE AND ORGANIZE TIME AND
TASKS? WHY?

3

WHY WE'RE BLIND TO OUR BLINDNESS

"The difference between stupidity and genius is that genius has its limits."
ALBERT EINSTEIN

"Our comforting conviction that the world makes sense rests on a secure foundation: our almost unlimited ability to ignore our ignorance."
DANIEL KAHNEMAN

THE FIRST STEP IN REALIZING OUR FULL potential is to acknowledge the fact that *we don't know what we don't know*. Let's start with a simple example. Have you ever looked back at a decision you made—maybe something you said or did or thought that was out of character—and wondered how you could have been so irrational? Think of the last time you disagreed with someone. Think of the last time you were told that you were wrong. How did you respond? What about the last ten times you were told you were wrong (if you can think back that far) — how did you respond? Daniel Kahneman has some incredibly intriguing insight into what we might be missing. Larry Swedroe of CBS News said of Kahneman's book *Thinking, Fast, and Slow*, "He [Kahneman] clearly shows that while we like to think of ourselves as rational in our decision making, the truth is we are subject to many biases." Dr. Steven Pinker, professor of psychology at Harvard, said that Kahneman's "...work has reshaped social psychology, cognitive science, the study of reason and of happiness, and behavioral economics." Before I read his book I was much more inclined to give myself the benefit of the doubt—to think that I was probably in the right in most situations, as I think most of us do. Now, not so much.

For many years, Kahneman has been at the forefront of behavioral economics research. His findings have sparked a great deal of interest in the field of (what I call) "blindness to blindness" — simply put, we don't know what we don't know. This term came from a section in *Thinking, Fast, and Slow*, where Kahneman says, "we can be blind to the obvious, and we are also blind to our blindness." Meaning, we can be and, in fact, are often completely unaware of our mental deficiencies in judging situations and making intelligent decisions. Again, go back to the thought of *that person* who did something that you just couldn't understand. It's easy to see that person's "blindness to their blindness." Again, as we discussed earlier, *that person* doesn't know what he doesn't know, and you've determined that his not-knowing is a detriment to him—at least in this particular example.

In short—we repeatedly judge too quickly, which inevitably leads to faulty decision-making. While it's easy to see this in others, it's immensely difficult to see our own blind spots. Similarly, in his book *How We Know What Isn't So*, Thomas Gilovich writes, "*When examining evidence relevant to a given belief, people are inclined to see what they expect to see, and conclude what they expect to conclude. Information that is consistent with our pre-existing beliefs is often accepted at face value, whereas evidence that contradicts them is critically scrutinized and discounted. Our beliefs may thus be less responsive than they should to the implications of new information.*" Therefore, we must make an effort be extremely open to alternative ideas.

I often think of my business as it relates to these ideas from Kahneman and Gilovich. When I first entered the financial services industry, I thought I could figure out how to be successful on my own (i.e. do it my "own way"). After a few months, I luckily concluded that I was dead wrong. I had no earthly idea what I was doing, and any idea I thought I had was based on no hard evidence. Today, as I'm running a mid-size consulting firm, I repeatedly see new consultants come in and initially think that they know something about what they should be doing. It seems that it is difficult to function if we "don't know," so instead of working extremely hard to figure out what we need to know, we make up what we "think we know" even though there is little to back up our belief. Over time, these new consultants typically come to the conclusion that they didn't know what they were doing, at which point they latch on to the hard and often counter-intuitive evidence they hadd been taught on day one. The difference between the average ones and the great ones is how quickly they figure out that they don't know what they don't know and—more importantly—how quickly they can live by that new learning.

∞

On some level, there's another issue here. I certainly don't want to be blind to *my* blindness. I'd rather know what I need to know. However, I was reminded of my primary issue—and it's probably yours too—time. We only have a certain number of hours in the day, and we have to determine how many hours will go to family, work, hobbies, thinking, planning, and learning. Personally, it has been easy for me to claim that time is the issue, and it certainly is. But what if it's deeper than that? What if I am lying to myself?

Recently, I was sitting in a *terribly* (imagine a slightly satirical tone) stimulating conference call on estate planning, gifting limits, portability, probate, grantor and defective trust rules and incapacity. As the words might delineate, this call was less than riveting. It took all I had just to pay attention. However, as I was thinking about my thinking (which I try to do often)—I concluded that I was doing exactly the opposite of what I preach. Naturally, my brain didn't want to pay attention because the conversation wasn't immediately pleasant. Even though this information was incredibly relevant to me and what I do, and even though this was information that I needed to know, my subconscious' preferred inclination was to day-dream, to look for other things to do, and to tell myself that I would just study the material later. In this case, the issue wasn't time—it was the lack of intellectual intensity (i.e. Kahneman's "law of least effort").

So, even when we comprehend our own human fallibility, (and attempt to find our blind spots) we must then fight our mind's natural tendency to want to primarily do things that we find enjoyable.

∞

As we'll see, financially speaking, the majority are exceptionally "blind to their blindness." It's common to see a person, no matter the age, who is unwilling to accept or even look at the data. Generally, people who refuse to look at the facts are dealing with some sort of bias. The first step is to be aware of what types of bias you (or anyone around you) may be experiencing. For our purposes, there are three types of biases of which you'll want to be aware: status quo bias, outcome bias and confirmation bias.

Status Quo Bias is fairly straight forward. It is the desire to stay where you are and to stay with the crowd. It is the default position, and it's often based on simply continuing to do what everyone else is doing.

Outcome Bias is also fairly straight forward, although a little harder to spot. This is the notion that because a decision created a positive result, then you must have made the right decision. Its focus is the *outcome* (of course) rather than the accuracy of the decision-making process. It's essentially a false affirmation that you did well, when you really just got lucky.

Confirmation Bias is the most difficult to spot and change. For honest people like you and me, it is also the most common bias that I see when people are making financial decisions. This is the tendency to search for, interpret, or remember information in a way that confirms one's beliefs or hypotheses[8] (Thank you Wikipedia). You can probably spot other people selectively interpreting information they receive in order to *confirm* their beliefs—but we are not focused on other people right now. We are focused on you.

As we move on, it is imperative that we remember the impact of biases on our own behavior. When *we* take responsibility for our own actions, we consciously remove that responsibility from others. This then, for all logical purposes, eradicates our capacity to make excuses. Taking these steps is what will allow you to reach for your full financial potential. There are two primary factors:

1. *Being aware of our blindness and taking full responsibility (i.e. Living a life of no excuses)*

2. *Committing to our own financial education and continuous learning*

Do this to give yourself the best chance for financial success. Do not do this and, one day, you'll likely wish that you had.

"*The truth is rarely pure and never simple.*"

OSCAR WILDE

"*The truth will set you free, but first it will make you miserable.*"

JAMES A. GARFIELD

"*Facts do not cease to exist because they are ignored.*"

ALDOUS HUXLEY

QUESTIONS TO CONTEMPLATE:

WHEN WAS A TIME YOU THOUGHT SOMETHING TO BE
TRUE, AND THEN LEARNED THAT IT WAS DIFFERENT
THAN YOU'D BELIEVED?

WHAT BELIEF DO YOU HAVE THAT MIGHT NOT BE
THE WAY YOU THOUGHT IT WAS?

WHEN HAVE YOU DISPLAYED STATUS QUO,
OUTCOME, AND CONFIRMATION BIAS?

4

THINKING BEYOND TOMORROW

"There's a need for accepting responsibility—for a person's life and making choices that are not just ones for immediate short-term comfort."

BUZZ ALDRIN

ASSUMING KAHNEMAN IS RIGHT, there is a grave need to analyze the way we think through and rationalize situations. In finance and financial planning, there is one particular human urge that seems to trump all others—**the desire to make decisions for the short-term.** Our subconscious mind yearns to make the quick and easy choices that will satisfy us today or tomorrow, rather than in the distant future, even though most times we do not recognize it. Five or ten years, and especially twenty or thirty years, seems so far off. In the context of making financial decision-making, our brain seems adequately able to ignore the future implications of our immediate decisions. You may even think that you're making a decision for the future when, in fact, you're actually making that decision for today.

There are a few reasons for this. First, simply making a decision is a challenging task. In today's economy, we have so much information coming at us so quickly. It is hard to process all of this information, much less to process it in context. (We'll discuss context more in the next chapter.) Dan Ariely's eye opening book *Predictably Irrational* is full of research on how difficult it is for us to make a decision. Ariely's eventual conclusion is that we would rather not make a decision than have to contemplate the ramifications of all the options. While this might be okay when it comes to opting in or out of organ donor programs[i]—the, financial areas of our life deserve our full attention.

This, our financial decision-making process (I'll use the abbreviation *DMP*), is the first financial area where status quo, outcome, and confirmation biases become quite noticeable. It is much easier to just stay put and do what everyone else is doing, financially. It's comfortable, and we don't have to put a lot of thought into it. Then, if the outcome happens to turn out decent, we tell ourselves that we've made a good or intelligent choice. Our DMP has been confirmed to be satisfactory. If the outcome turns out not so favorably, we still usually tell ourselves that we made the right choices—and we confirm those choices by conveniently noting that others made the same choices and had the same fate. We fail to realize that we really haven't made many (or any) decisions, but have opted for the default options that someone else chose for us.

---

[i] Google "Dan Ariely Ted Talk" to learn more about opting in or out of organ donor programs.

You may be thinking that this is not true. You may be thinking that you thoughtfully and deliberately make decisions on a daily basis. In fact, you're right. You do. Most of us do. However, in good conscience, ask yourself this: *are those thoughtful, carefully considered decisions made because of short-term needs and pressures?* When you're deciding on whether to buy this or that car; when you're determining cell phone A vs. cell phone B; when you're discussing whether your kids should go to a private school or a public school—those decisions are made because you *have* to make them right now. Of course, they may have long-term impact; however, we are not inherently making the decisions because of their long-term impact. We're making them because we are in a position in which we don't have the option to not make them.

Our subconscious and involuntary desires will instinctively lead us to focus on the here and now. It is how we deal with all of the thousands of potential decisions that we have each week. And that is not all bad. Our instinct is what keeps us alive and well, in the Darwinian sense. Yet, in this complex world, we will have to take a step back and learn to make decisions, or at least form our DMP. Our DMP should be determined before we ever enter most situations in which we would be forced to hastily choose. We also must begin to look into the future and attempt to figure out which decisions we should begin to think through and act on now, instead of waiting.

DMP

Our Decision Making Process from which we, intentionally or by default, reach our internal conclusions.

ADMITTING MISTAKES

In their book *Mistakes Were Made (But Not By Me)*, Carol Tarvis and Elliot Aronson explain why humans make and justify absurd and foolish beliefs and decisions. I found their book to be very interesting in my research of 'blindness to blindness.[ii]' In chapter one, Tarvis and Aronson state, *"The engine that drives self-justification... is the unpleasant feeling that Festinger called 'cognitive dissonance.' Cognitive dissonance is a state of tension that occurs whenever a person holds two cognitions (ideas, attitudes, beliefs, opinions) that are psychologically inconsistent..."*

The authors go on to explain why it's so difficult for us to admit when we're wrong. Society (and likely our human nature) has trained us to believe that being wrong is not just a bad thing, but a terrible thing. When we get two or more pieces of inconsistent information—for example, your parents taught you something to be obviously true and you come across information that contradicts that "truth"—we are more likely to mentally throw out the contradicting data than empirically analyze our belief.

A few years ago, I left the traditional financial planning world (which I will talk more on) after extensive research of mutual funds, qualified plans, and other conventional financial planning schemes. My departure was quite an experience. Luckily, I've still got a few friends in that world, and many of them have begun to see the light. I vividly remember sharing some of the reasons I was leaving this world to an executive at a large company. This gentleman had been a client for about a year, and I logically explained the ins and outs of my decision. I also thought it important to tell him that I thought I owed it to him to admit when I was wrong. I presumed he and

---

[ii] See Appendix A for books related to 'blindness to blindness.'

every other client would rather have an advisor who would be fully open with them. Most of my client relationships responded well. However, a few did not. This guy's first reaction was horrific. His response was a mixture of confusion and distrust—it was as if he thought that, because I was admitting a mistake, I must have been a moron.

Another client threatened a lawsuit. After which I was advised to avoid admitting and explaining my "mistake." It's a bit ridiculous that we humans have created an environment in which we cannot be honest with each other. Moreover, I'm sure I am just as guilty as anyone else is. This experience (and others) make it easy for me to see why it is so difficult to admit faults, flaws, mistakes, and wrong-doings. Our subconscious mind eventually takes over and averts us from taking responsibility, for if we do we may be chastised by our peers.

Give this book to everyone you know[iii]. Maybe it will help them to see that we must be okay with the fact that people make honest mistakes. We must create a more empathetic environment for open dialogue about what we have or haven't believed that may have been wrong. We probably won't sway everyone we know; however, we can sway ourselves. **We can accept the fact that we have, at one time or another, been wrong. Then, only after we've accepted our potential faults, we can accept the can move towards embracing our wrongness—for it is the only way to grow.**

[iii] This is a shameless plug for you to promote my book, hopefully because you find it interesting. Still, if we want to change the world, we need people to read my writings.

THE EVOLUTION OF THINKING

Sometime in 2010 or so I attended a series of private seminars given by, what I consider, one of the top financial strategy and planning minds in the country. We'll call him Thomas (for the sake of privacy, I'll only use his first name). I had paid a lot of money to hear this guy speak, and I knew because I'd heard him before that he would be good... but I didn't know how good. Thomas was one of the top financial advisors to Fortune 500 executives and as well as other top professionals. However, Thomas was different from other successful people. He was utterly humble—probably one of the most articulate and intelligent people I had ever met, but he didn't care for others to praise him or tell him how great he was. He did not, as many people in the financial and banking industries do, boast about how important he was, or how much money he had made last year (think *Glengarry Glen Ross*). Thomas knew that those things didn't matter, and people loved him for it.

At this series of seminars, he taught a principle that is likely the most vital general philosophy to reaching financial success—and, more importantly, to becoming a financially prudent person. The principle is directly related to knowing and controlling our DMP. Thomas said that **we shouldn't focus so much on how today's decisions will impact us today. Rather, we should focus more on how today's decisions will impact us in 20, 30, or 40 years.** Although simple, this will be a key principle to which we will return as we discuss family financial decision-making and planning. In many ways, we've already hit on this idea. However, let me tell you how and why this is so relevant to your financial situation.

∞

Thomas called this process the *Evolution of Thinking*, meaning that over time, there is an evolution of thinking that occurs. The way we think shifts as years pass. You can almost certainly understand that on an intellectual level—but what we have [iv] found is that most people can't deal with it on an emotional decision-making level. Let me first describe what the *Evolution of Thinking* is. Specifically in financial strategy and planning, it's not uncommon to hear a tenured person—somewhere between the age of 60 and 85—discuss what they "wish they would've done" or what they "wish they would've known" twenty or thirty years ago. Consistently, we hear older people proclaim their mild regrets. I have established that we need to think and plan with foresight. Therefore, it would be advantageous to know what a person might have "wished" they had known when they were younger. In fact, that is the main value of what these more mature-in-life individuals are sharing.

I am sure you can think back to times in your life when you wish you had taken advantage of something. Specifically, think about something that you wish you would have done or known. Think of something that was in your control, something you could have reasonably done back then, but for whatever reason, you didn't do it. Not a stock you wish you had bought. You couldn't predict a certain stock to rise. Rather, an event. If you have been able to objectively think through a decision you could have (or should have) made, then you have just demonstrated to yourself that your *thinking* has *evolved*.

The *Evolution of Thinking* is not about trying to predict the future. It is about making prudent choices today that will likely produce effective outcomes in the future. It's about thinking in proba-

---

[iv] When I say "we" I mean my research team and I.

bilities. The example Thomas gave was of an entrepreneur and successful business owner, Steve, with whom he had worked for many years[v]. Steve had built a great business from the ground up. I don't remember the exact details, but it was some type of manufacturing business, and the revenues over 30+ years had risen to something close to $200 million. Steve had always been risk seeking, and it had paid off. He had built up a liquid net worth north of $50 million and a total net worth (including the business and other non-liquid assets) of over $300 million. Needless to say, Steve had done very well.

Steve was getting ready to retire on June 30 and move on to charitable work, spending more time with family and sailing. He was going to live exclusively from the income he could generate from his vast assets. An outsider would imagine that Steve was in a good position, which of course he was. At the date of his departure, he would have $50 million liquid and another $50 or so million coming from the sale of his ownership shares. That retirement date came and went. One would imagine that Steve was enjoying his mission work, grandchildren, and passion for sailing.

Only a few short months after the retirement date, Steve and Thomas were reviewing the asset distribution plans. Steve proclaimed that he'd had an epiphany. The epiphany came to him after lots of thought while sailing up the Pacific Coast. He'd been having a nervousness unlike other anxieties he had ever felt. Steve had experienced much anxiety while running his company. He'd built a business which required sixty plus hours per week, even into his final year. He had led more than one thousand employees and dealt

---

[v] Many of the exact details have been changed – one to protect privacy and then, two, because I can't remember. ☺

with all of the badgering issues from the human resources, marketing, sales, and accounting departments. He had spent an increasing amount of time with uptight regulators, making sure his factories were up to OSHA standards. As Steve put it, he thought, *"I've built up all of this wealth and now I believe I can do a lot of good with it. My concern is not the money itself—it's not having enough money. My concern is 'what do I now do with the money.' How do I keep it safe?"*

Steve went on to explain that he'd always been fine with risk, predominantly because he understood risk as it related to his business. He understood how to analyze various economic conditions and make precise decisions. However, when it came to his money being outside his sphere of expertise, he was not so fine. He passionately said:

"On June 29 I was fine with risk. I loved it. That 'risk' was my business. The next day, June 30, I despised risk. All the sudden risk, for me, took on a whole different context. It was no longer my business. It became stocks, bonds, and such. I hate volatility. Can't stand it now. I want safety and security. I want to know what [my money] is going to do. Why didn't I think about that years ago?"

Steve was communicating that, before his retirement date, he intentionally took financial risk and he embraced that type of risk. After his retirement date, all he wanted was safety, security, and protection. Steve's *thinking* had *evolved*. If he had recognized that he would value his safer dollars earlier, then he could have protected some of the anxiety he was feeling about no longer being okay with 'risk'—specifically this type of risk that he had no control over. Steve's retirement was in 2010. Interest rates on fixed income investments (i.e. safer dollar assets) like CD's, money markets, and investment grade bonds were headed toward all-time lows. Additionally, Steve would have to pay taxes at his highest marginal bracket on the interest earnings of those safer dollar assets.

Fortunately, Thomas, brilliant as he was, had recognized Steve's need two decades before. With great foresight, Thomas and Steve had allocated a large portion of the liquid $50 million into a safer, more efficient asset[vi]. Steve had forgotten. As Thomas re-explained the value and the power of what they'd set up more than twenty years ago, Steve melted with gratefulness.

Steve's story changed the way I thought about planning. The first time I heard the story, I thought it was just a neat thing that Thomas had done. I thought it was simply further proof that Thomas was a great strategic thinker. However, it was so much more than that. Throughout the series of lessons, Thomas, from time to time, referred to Steve's story. He reiterated to us that, at some point, our most precious dollars become our safer, more secure dollars. And, over time, that message began to sink in.

In Part III, I will describe the model for the *Evolution of Financial Thinking*. When you get there, you will see how powerful this way of thinking really is. (That doesn't mean you should skip there right now... more context is still needed!)

Unfortunately, many people will hear Steve's story and then go about their lives never realizing the significance of the *Evolution of Thinking* mindset. Even still, some will read it and comprehend, in the moment, the brevity, and importance of the message, but they'll forget when, how, or why it was important. Moreover, they'll fail to become aware of and implement their new learning.

[vi] We'll further discuss the strategies Thomas used in Part III.

Certain decisions you will make this year will play a large roll in defining who you are, what you do, and how you live in twenty years. **It doesn't matter if you're 25, 37, 54, or 65. Even if you're 60 or 70, your thinking will still evolve. You already recognize some of the things that you wish you would've known 'back then.' In twenty years, when you're 80 or 90, you'll come back and say, "*I wish...*" this or "*I wish...*" that.** Due to modern medicine, we're living longer. Our [potential] longevity can be a pro or a con. When people do not comprehend the brevity of the message (and/or forget the message), it is because of those human tendencies to think short-term. It is because they haven't yet overcome their human nature.

I know it's repetitive, but it's important. After reading this, many people of all ages will continue to make the same mistakes over and over again—then they'll continue to rationalize those mistakes. Our human nature is motivated by what *immediate feeling* we'll receive after a given action. For instance, a 62 year old man might have read Steve's story and thought, "*That is great advice. It really makes wonderful sense. I wish I'd read that thirty years ago. I sure hope all the younger people out there get the message.*" Never did that man realize that he would likely, if he were in good health, live another twenty or thirty years. Meanwhile, the 71 year old woman thought, "*Wow. I've never thought about it that way before. I should think long and hard about what I'm going to need and want when I'm 90. What should I be doing today—what decisions should I make this year to be most prudent for the future?*" Meanwhile, the 35 year old is thinking... "*Sheeessshhhh. This 'Evolution of Thinking' thing never ends.*" That 35 year old would be right. However, it does become fun—trust me.

QUESTIONS TO CONTEMPLATE:

DO YOU THINK, BEING HONEST WITH YOURSELF, THAT YOU MAKE MOST DECISIONS BECAUSE OF SHORT-TERM PRESSURE?

IN WHAT AREAS OF LIFE SHOULD YOU FOCUS ON MAKING IMMEDIATE DECISIONS THAT WILL HAVE A LARGER LONG-TERM IMPACT?

HOW MIGHT YOU REMEMBER STEVE'S STORY AND THE '*EVOLUTION OF THINKING*' PRINCIPLE?

5

THINKING IN CONTEXT

"Judge a man by his questions rather than by his answers."

VOLTAIRE

MANY OF THE SMARTEST PEOPLE I know are the exact same people who have made some of the dumbest decisions. It seems to be a constant theme that people who have shown exceptional intelligence in one area of life (or in their professional specialty) often make very bad decisions in other areas of life. Of course, there is not a causal relationship. Their intelligence in one area doesn't necessarily cause them to be faulty in another area... I hope. Rather, it is common for a person who has proven aptitude in his field to slowly begin assuming his intellect will translate into another field. In other words, he takes his intelligence out of *context*. In many cases, he forgets how much time and effort he has devoted to learning his area of expertise. Moreover, when he does make a mistake, it's often magnified because that competence has led to success. That success has led to capital. And when he puts that capital to use in the wrong speculation, it can go from bad to worse in a flurry.

Consider the story of Rico Thompson.[i] Rico had two engineering related graduate degrees and had been a mechanical engineer for twenty or so years. Earlier in his career, he invented a modern packaging technology and received a few hundred thousand dollars per year from the licensing fees. Needless to say, Rico would be considered, in most circles, very sharp. Technically, he was a genius. Rico also did some consulting. All sorts of Fortune 500 companies regularly hired Mr. Thompson to come in for $2,000 an hour and help them with their engineering processes. From the licensing deal, consulting, and a few scattered speaking engagements, Rico's income was well above the mean. By most respects, he would have been the financial model for others to follow. He had a wonderful wife, two kids doing well in college, a good amount of money saved up, and what seemed to be the perfect career.

When I first met Rico, he had just invested about 75% of his liquid cash in a group of local restaurants. Rico's reasoning, as he explained it, was this:

- He had invested in multiple engineering companies and products, one of which was his revolutionary packaging technology.
- He wanted to focus on one investment or business at a time so he could give that one thing his undivided attention. This is how he had operated with the other investments as well.

---

[i] Name and profession changed to protect the innocent. However, in case you were wondering, it's pronounced *ree–ko*.

- Because he only focused on one deal at a time—and he would work on that deal for sometimes five plus years—he had put the vast majority of his cash into that one deal. Rico thought this was a better strategy then attempting to juggle a few deals at once.
- A friend from grad school had left the engineering business and gone into real estate. That friend ended up running a research division for a large fast-food chain.
- After close to a decade, this fast-food friend left the chain and began buying franchises with a few other chain restaurants. Eventually this person built a portfolio of more than 200 restaurants.
- Rico, rightfully assuming that he was just as smart as his college friend, decided that he could do the same.

Rico came to me to discuss what he should do with the other 25% of his capital. He really didn't want my thoughts or advice on the restaurant investment—that was already a done deal, and he felt that he and his partners had it covered. Rico and I had multiple conversations over the next year. He was on the west coast and I was in Little Rock, so most of our conversations and meetings occurred via webinar. The two times I met Rico in person established why he'd had so much success. He was a well-dressed, charismatic man who immediately made you feel at ease. His perspective on life was refreshing. Initially, Rico was a happy-go-lucky, down-to-earth guy who happened to be extremely intelligent and wealthy. In addition, he seemed to be quite financially sophisticated.

Over the course of that year, though, I watched Rico's stress level escalate to the height of Mount Everest. The food business hadn't quite turned out as the other deals of which he'd been a part.

There were numerous circumstances and complexities he had never expected. A few months in, Rico's highest revenue restaurant lost half their wait staff to some other fine-dining establishment a couple miles north. That experience alone catapulted Rico's diner into the red, losing substantial money and having to subsidize operations from the other restaurants' revenues. It was a long and hard year for Rico, and in the end, he decided he couldn't take it anymore. He sold his interests and lost about 72% of his investment.

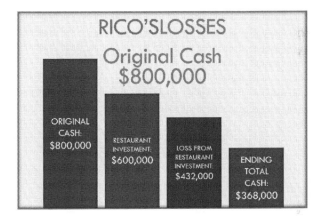

The fundamental problem here was the *context* in which Rico made the decision to invest in the food business. His friend from college, the one who owned all of those franchises, had spent nearly ten years in the industry before he ventured into investing his money in stores. He knew the ins and outs of the business and likely made very data-driven decisions because he was head of research for the large chain before. Rico, on the other hand, had very little understanding of the restaurant business. However, he thought that just because he was a smart guy, he could figure it out. He thought to himself, "*How hard could this be?*"

This is a common issue with smart and successful people. Each of Rico's previous investments were in the engineering field. He presumed that success would translate into another business. What he neglected to remember was how much time and energy he'd put into learning and mastering his craft. And herein lies the issue of successful people: they take their knowledge and their success out of context. They take their specialty out of context. When I originally began meeting with Rico, he was extremely confident that his technical engineering skills would translate well to the restaurant business. He didn't leave room for any doubt. However, over time that confidence turned into humiliation.

This is not at all to say that failures are bad. In fact, many failures are good. However, in this case, Rico failed to see the lack of context in his decision-making sequence. His success had made him overconfident and, on some level, led him to failure. In fact, his extraordinary success in his sphere of expertise caused him to fail on a larger scale. The combination of confidence from previous successes and the amount of money he'd put into those deals—that's what eventually created disaster[ii].

THE SIMPLEST ANSWER IS (NOT) USUALLY THE RIGHT ANSWER

"Occam's Razor" states that the simplest answer is usually the right answer. Maybe that's true in many areas of life, but not so much when it comes to finance. I think the statement has gained so much traction because our brains, whether we know it or not, strive for the simplest and easiest solution. The solution that requires the least effort. Smart people often assume they should be able to fully

---

[ii] A quick update on Rico is at the end of this chapter.

comprehend complex topics too easily. In many ways, we've bought into this notion that if we can't understand something in a short period of time, then it's too complicated. This will, on its face, hurt you financially.

Cognitive neuroscientist Chris Chatham, Ph.D., in a 2007 article[9], wrote about the subject: "*Simple theories have many advantages: they are often falsifiable or motivate various predictions, and can be easily communicated as well as widely understood... However, there are numerous reasons to suspect that this simple "theory of theories" is itself fundamentally misguided... The continuing use of parsimony in modern science is an atavistic practice equivalent to a cardiologist resorting to bloodletting when heart medication doesn't work.*"

Aside from his intricate wording (he was writing this mainly for other scientists to read), Dr. Chatham is arguing something quite compelling. With the advances of modern science and philosophy, there's not a lot of weight behind the 'simplest answer is the right answer' approach. After all, Occam's Razor is what told us (or our ancestors) that the earth was flat and stagecoaches would never move without horses. Certainly there are areas where the principle still applies—maybe in terms of just generally being a good person (be nice) or why a tire is flat (it has a nail in it) or why a student failed a test (he didn't study). However, research[iii] and my own experience[iv], I believe, demonstrate Occam's Razor to be false—at least in a certain context of finance and science.

LOGICAL FALLACIES

[iii] Mainly referring to the *thinking* and *decision-making* research of Daniel Kahneman's book, *Thinking, Fast and Slow,* and Dr. Chatham's work.

[iv] I'm trying not to fall into confirmation bias. Feel free to send me your thoughts or disagreements at TheFallofLogic.com. I might read them.

Most of us, many times unknowingly, use syllogisms in our everyday life. A syllogism is a logical argument that utilizes deductive reasoning to reach some conclusion. It's a basic way to find truth and to come to an agreement based on a set of premises. For instance, if we agree that (1) most people who exercise and eat well are healthy and (2) that our friend Joe exercises regularly and eats right, then it would make sense that Joe would be healthy. Another example might be, "People who do not work hard are not successful. Some people are successful. Therefore, some people work hard."

SYLLOGISM → A LOGICAL ARGUMENT USING DEDUCTIVE REASONING BASED ON AT LEAST TWO PREMISES.

EXAMPLE → Premise #1: ALL MEN ARE MORTAL
Premise #2: ALL GREEKS ARE MEN
CONCLUSION: ALL GREEKS ARE MORTAL

Syllogism fallacy is when there is either a false premise or when the premises do not exactly match the conclusion. For example, "All crows are black and the bird in my cage is black. So, the bird in my cage is a crow." In the financial world, people use false syllogisms every day. A typical person begins to interweave status quo, outcome, and confirmation bias with these false syllogisms, leading to all sorts of rationalized chaos. A common syllogistic fallacy, for instance, is, "My mutual funds went up. I made the decision to put money in those mutual funds. I must have made a good financial decision." Or, better yet, a subconscious fallacy: "I bought a bunch of stuff I didn't need. I didn't go bankrupt. Therefore, I can go on buying whatever I want." However, oh, my all-time favorite (and the one that's used most often) is this: "John is smart. John makes money. So, John is smart with money." In this case, there is no relationship between John being smart in general, John making an income, and John being smart with money. It's a solid premise which ends with a totally out-of-context conclusion. Whereas, if we say, "All men are mortal. John is a man. John is mortal"—that would be a concrete relationship. Yet, people use this logical sequence every day, never realizing (or never admitting to themselves) the evidence that their family member, friend or co-worker isn't necessarily a great financial decision maker.

The complexity of financial decisions, large and small, is not to be taken lightly. Some things are simple—budgeting, paying your bills on time, having a cash buffer—but others are not. Finance, both planning and strategy, is multifaceted. **Once you reach a certain level of investment, risk management, and financial strategy, there are many variables to be considered—and context is key.**

∞

A QUICK NOTE

For those of you who were wondering, Rico is doing just fine today, although he did ratchet up his consulting and speaking efforts following the major loss. He is focusing on his sphere of expertise and has developed a DMP that's second to none. We'll discuss DMP formulation in part three.

He actually played quite an important role in certain parts of this book and has been a great friend and client. Simply put, Rico thinks at a higher level and, while I don't think he'd do it again, he learned quite a bit from the 'restaurant' experience. He's hoping others will learn the lesson from his blunder.

*All names and quite a few details were changed for privacy… and to confuse you if and when you decide to seek Rico out.

QUESTIONS TO CONTEMPLATE:

HAVE YOU EVER ENTERED A SITUATION THAT WAS OUTSIDE YOUR SPHERE OF EXPERTISE? WHAT WAS THE OUTCOME?

DO YOU HOLD OCCAM'S RAZOR TO BE TRUE? WHY OR WHY NOT?

WHAT IS AN EXAMPLE OF A SYLLOGISTIC FALLACY YOU HAVE USED BEFORE?

6

COGNOSCO, PRUDENTIS & OUR DMP

" It is good to learn what to avoid by studying the misfortunes of others. "
PUBLIUS SYRIUS

AS TEDIOUS AS IT MAY SEEM BY NOW, THINKING at a higher level is imperative to our success on every level. Yet, it is so difficult to find a man who does. In many ways I attribute this to our educational system—not that I am an expert on the American (or any other country's) education system. I am not. But I do know that in most schools, listening, self-awareness, and effective personal finance are not taught (or not taught extensively and consistently)—both in the public and private system.

The first step to thinking at a higher level is to become self-aware. The English word aware comes from the Latin term *cognosco* and *prudentis*, meaning "to recognize" and to be farseeing and prudent.[10] Aristotle said, *"The ultimate value of life depends upon awareness and the power of contemplation rather than upon mere survival."* To know ourselves is to be aware of who we are, what we are doing, how we communicate, and how decisions affect our lives. To be aware *is not* to be omniscient. To be aware is to make a conscious decision to make conscious decisions—to be aware of our awareness. Ascending to a *higher level of consciousness* is the integration of *striving for significant impact* and *the art of thinking at a higher level* (i.e. studying to mitigate relevant blind spots, thinking in context, and controlling the process). Our basic premises must be accurate to make good decisions. In essence, *cognosco* and *prudentis* are the aggregate of what we have to this point discussed.

On the contrary, thinking at a lower level would be the act of making decisions that do not direct our lives towards significance or impact. I am sure that most people do not make a conscious choice to live a life of mediocrity. No, it is most often done by default in the subconscious. Mediocrity it often achieved because our emotional and mental state is striving for what is easiest or what feels best in the moment. It is a lack of studying to mitigate relevant blind spots. It is the failure to think in context. Mediocrity comes to those who focus on the results rather than the process.

An example might be a person who believes that if he purchases flamboyant jewelry for his wife and designer clothes for his kids, it will show how much he loves them. He knows these things will make his family feel good now. And, in truth, this is the easiest decision he could make. It will also give him short-term pleasure to see his wife and kids happy, and they'll adore him for the moment. His motivation is present pleasure. This entire act is based on a false premise, one that assumes material possessions will make them truly happy. Yet we know through biblical study and modern research that possessions do not make one happy. Money and things work only so far as to allow one to buy the necessities. After a modest level of income (enough to make ends meet), little happiness is gained.[i] In essence, the conventional wisdom that we are naturally motivated by money and things is wrong.

Rather, significance and autonomy and mastery and meaning are what we really desire.[11] Scientific research about what makes us happy is confirming what religion has taught for centuries. It is confirming that those who give more money away are happier than those who don't, and that lottery winnings help people short-term but hurt them long-term.[12] This is not to say that we should not have nice things or buy gifts for our families. However, it is the context in which we do those things that makes the difference. Maturity, in the family and financial sense, is our ability to intentionally and effectively think through the rationale of our actions and the long-term effects of those actions. We must make our conscious consistently aware of the fact that our natural desires are often wrong. We must shift our being from seeking *easy* and *pleasure* to seeking *significance* and *integrity*. Our thinking and decision making process (DMP) must be rooted therein. We can't be perfect. We won't always get it right. But we can improve. We can get better, primarily through being aware of this process.

> "*Until you make the unconscious conscious, it will direct your life and you will call it fate.*"
> C.G. JUNG

---

[i] I encourage you to watch Daniel Pink's Ted talk and read his book *Drive*.

It is only when we can make decisions for the right reasons and by the right process that we can be assured that we have done what we needed to do. As we begin to discuss our DMP and the importance of it, please ponder the relevance. In the next section I will delineate what I call *the fall of logic*, or what I believe to be the massive swindling machine that has become the modern personal finance industry. You will find that many of the problems that have arisen are primarily from a lack of context and DMP. Most of the people who are giving traditional financial advice (and I used to be one) are not bad people. They believe they're honest, good people, just like you and me. But they've built their world view around a flawed methodology. And once we build our world view, it is difficult to change. It is hard to be open to new ideas or to the fact that we might be wrong.

In Part III, you will see the relevance of building an adequate DMP for making decisions and breaking away from the problems discussed in Part II. The most important takeaway, my primary goal in this writing, is for you to see (mainly financial) matters more clearly. The foundational component is your DMP. Until now we have primarily discussed the philosophical elements of effective financial and life decision-making. While subjective, these philosophical components lay the groundwork for systems and processes—the objective and precise components of our DMP. Let us then harmonize reason and application.

∞

OUR DECISION MAKING PROCESS

Over the past few years I have developed a framework for my own DMP. I have worked to make *cognosco* (awareness) and *prudentis* (experience and foresight) the tenets. But, of course, my DMP will likely evolve and improve over time. Your DMP doesn't have to be the same as mine. Rather, mine is an example for you to use and, if you like, build from. The following will give you insight into my DMP.

The Importance of Framework

A few years ago a professor from graduate school helped me see the importance of thinking and decision-making frameworks. Mark Mallinger, Ph.D. has spent a career studying and teaching behavioral science to graduate students in the U.S. and in Germany. His works have been published many times over in the *Journal of Management Education* and the *Graziadio Business Report*. While Dr. Mallinger has developed a few revolutionary frameworks for organizational and corporate behavior, many of his principles apply on the personal and family levels as well.

To process information within a framework allows a person to focus more on the substance of the information and what to do with it, and less on trying to figure out where to put the information. In other words, we are tempted to process all new information as it comes with no system or strategy. We take all of this information and improvise, processing differently each time. Not only is this highly inefficient, it's highly ineffective because we miss things. We do not properly allocate information into its proper context. It's like a football coach with no game plan. His team shows up for the game and he makes up the plays as the game progresses. Assuming he somehow keeps his job for a while, eventually he will probably get better at "winging it." And depending on his aptitude, he might actually be pretty good at improvising during each game. But he never reaches his full potential. His team will be demolished by any decent opponent.

In the athletic world, we know this coach would be terminated (along with the athletic director) after only a few games. But in our personal and professional world—the world outside of high pressure business, art, and athletics—we are bombarded with mediocrity. Specifically when most people think of financial planning or strategy, they don't think of process, procedure, or competency. Rather, they think of how they can avoid having to think about it. The average person, like a football coach, is compared to his counterparts. And even the above-average counterparts are achieving less than impressive results. It would be like the coach we just discussed going into each game without a game plan, but in this case none of the opposing coaches have a game plan either. They're all "winging it." So the successful ones are those that are simply smarter and quicker at improvisation. And this is life.

Ad libbing has become the norm. But we all have a limit to how well we can do, how much we can accomplish, when we rely purely on our wits. Enter the *Law of the Lid*,[13] John Maxwell's theory that an organization can rise no higher than the level of its lowest leader. This law is no doubt applicable to the *ad lib culture*. The football team can only perform to a certain level—they can only reach a percentage of their potential without a well prepared plan. Even if they're winning because all the other teams are also "winging it," it's not a positive. So, even if you're doing better than cousin Joe or sister Sally, that likely doesn't mean much. You're probably just a better improviser.

There must be a contextual method for decision-making. The path to reach our full potential is through processes and preparation. Our *framework* is the structure and design through which information flows. It is not meant to stifle creativity or inspirations, but rather to enhance it. The first step in my DMP is seeing the unseen.

Step 1: Seeing the Unseen

Dr. Mallinger introduced me to the *Johari Window*[14] which would become the starting point for my DMP. The *Johari Window* is a grid containing four parts: areas of life that are 1) known to self, 2) unknown to self, 3) known to others, and 4) unknown to others. The primary purpose of the grid is to help people see where their blind spots are and how others perceive them.

Emotion is the enemy of acumen. Feeling fights thought., so it is imperative to mitigate mood-based decision making. The basis of the DMP is to have an understanding of our competencies and our blind spots. This is harder than it might seem. The *Johari Window* gives us a technique to (fairly) quickly analyze our interpersonal competencies. The initial phase is to understand where blind spots are. For if we do not know, then we're bound to make overconfident and irrational decisions out of simple ignorance.

The Johari Window

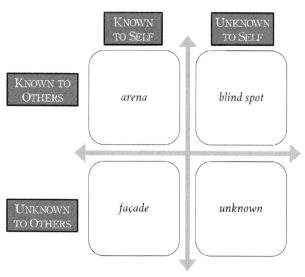

Although the *Johari Window* was developed primarily for organizational effectiveness, I think it can give us insight into many elements of financial and life effectiveness. In order to grow interpersonally, we first have to be aware of where it is that needs improvement. Most people go through life ignoring those areas and taking offense at anyone who points them out. To reach financial potential, you must move past this. In reality it is extremely valuable and important to get others' honest perception of you, even though it may sometimes be inaccurate. The *feeling* of hurt is a façade provoked by our defense and coping mechanisms—our lack of self-confidence. We subconsciously think that if we hear negative feedback, this new data will come to define us. But, in fact, it's exactly the opposite. These critiques and criticisms must not be pushed away or ignored. In certain professional and athletic environments, it is impossible to avoid criticism. And the criticized have no choice but to listen and improve. But in most of life's environments, as mentioned earlier, we (and others) simply ignore our flaws and go on acting in ways that are detrimental to our family, work, and finances. Without cognizance of our blind spots and effort to improve them, we will have no chance of reaching our full potential.

This first phase of the DMP is more of an exercise in principle than process. It is a version of the *Johari Window* that allows you to come to better *know yourself*—at least well enough to improve financial decision making. Anyone who knows you well should be a good candidate to participate in the exercise. The following are 20 statements relevant to decision making. Have at least 10 of your closest friends and family members, people you really trust, label **T** or **F** beside each of the statements.

(T = more true than false; F = more false than true)

My Window

1. *I am able to control my emotions.*

2. *I make rational decisions.*

3. *I make good financial decisions.*

4. *I have a clear vision of past events.*

5. *I am an above average communicator.*

6. *I am not usually aware of how I come across to others.*

7. *I go the extra mile to make sure I do things right.*

8. *I sometimes change an opinion to fit a preexisting belief.*

9. *I sometimes change an opinion to fit a new belief.*

10. *I am a good listener.*

11. *I often talk negatively about others.*

12. *I ignore my own flaws when pointing out the flaws of others.*

13. *I consistently make irrational comments.*

14. *I ignore evidence that does not fit my preexisting beliefs.*

15. *I speak in absolutes leaving little room for alternative opinion.*

16. *I have trouble sticking with commitments I've made.*

17. *I usually choose to make difficult decisions that need to be made rather than taking the easy way out.*

18. *I exaggerate to make myself seem smarter or more successful than I really am.*

19. *I often say things that I later regret.*

20. *I often talk too much.*

When asking close friends and family members to fill out *your window*, you must make it clear to them that you are not only open to getting their honest feedback, but that the only way for you to grow is through their honest feedback. Let them know that their politeness or biases will not help you. You need them to be brutally honest.

Before giving the assessment to others, take the test yourself and make the best attempt to judge yourself objectively. Once you've completed the assessment and you receive it back from those you asked to take it, you can adequately analyze the results. This is where your true colors show. There is nothing to rationalize. Don't try to guess who answered what and why. Just observe. Observe, as Mallinger would say, with no judgment. If the results are too positive, then start over. You need to have people that will be frank with you.

This will be the best way to get quick and likely accurate data on your decision-making skills. There is more psychology and coaching involved in truly knowing yourself and improving than I am qualified to give. But this exercise is more than sufficient for the financial DMP. Compare your scores to the scores that others give you. You will know fairly quickly, if you're honest with yourself, where the blind spots are. Use this to begin making yourself aware of potential logical and decision-making errors you (and the people with whom you come in contact) make. The primary purpose is to make you a better decision maker.

Those you would like to survey may want to keep their responses anonymous. This is better for you, too. It is most effective to observe the results without judgment or bias or knowing who answered how. Go to *TheFallofLogic.com/Window* to get an anonymous electronic version of the **My Window** exercise.

Step 2: Determine Importance

Time is of the essence for all of us. This goes without saying. The second step is to determine what to focus on and when. Steven Covey's prioritization grid from *The 7 Habits of Highly Effective People* gives us an excellent starting point. When new information comes in, the first thing to do is to run it through the Covey grid, as I call it. Section one is comprised of things that are determined to be **important** and **urgent**. Section two is made up of things that are **important** but **not urgent**. Section three, **not important** but **urgent**. And section four, **not important** and **not urgent**.

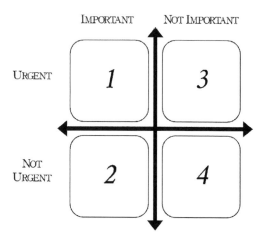

When a new task comes in—something that needs to be done—determine which section it falls into. For instance, paying the electric bill is important but not urgent—*section two*. Mastering your profession is important and urgent—*section one*. I believe that learning how to most effectively manage money is a *section one* priority.

Step 3: Your Sphere of Expertise

We should focus nearly all of our time on sections one and two, leaving a little time for section three and no time for section four. We should plan time for section one activities with great urgency, while planning time for section two activities when convenient. Financially speaking, once we have determined something to be in section one, we should then determine if this matter is in our *Sphere of Expertise* (SoE). Our SoE are those areas in which we have extreme competencies. If you are a real estate investor, then that would fall into your SoE. If a teacher, then maybe education would be a part of your SoE. Usually your profession will be within your SoE. But we certainly have the ability to make other areas a part of our SoE as well. However, be wary of thinking that you're an expert on too many things.

It is very difficult, if not impossible, to be competent on 50 plus percent of the decision-making areas that will fall into *section one or two*. You may be proficient in parenting and finance; however, it's unlikely that you're extremely knowledgeable in parenting, finance, medicine, football, baseball, soccer, school administration, international relations, human resources, and the best way to train for a marathon. A good rule of thumb: *he who knows everything is compensating for something*.

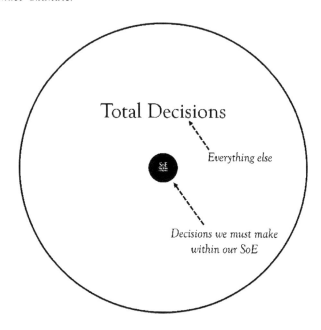

Total Decisions

SoE

Everything else

*Decisions we must make
within our SoE*

The above diagram shows the relationship between what is likely in our SoE in comparison to the total realm of *section one and two* decisions that we'll have to make. If the matter is in your SoE, you'll already know the best actions to take. If it is not in your SoE, then move to step four.

Step 4: Build a Network of Experts

We cannot know everything, and to try (or pretend to try) is a waste of precious time. A better use of time is to surround ourselves with qualified experts in various areas. Many times we will have to pay these experts for their advice, although sometimes we will not. The hard part is finding individuals who are actually experts in the matter at hand. Below is a list of questions to ask an espoused expert. Given the thinking research we've so far discussed, you will be able to make a sufficient decision as to whether or not this person is qualified.

- *What separates you from others in this field?*
- *What research have you done in this field?*
- *How many others have you helped on this topic?*
- *What were the results?*
- *What would happen if you were wrong?*
- *What do you believe that the majority does not?*
- *Why do other experts disagree with your methodology?*

You may not have to actually ask all of these questions. Some of them you may already know the answer to, and that may be the reason you sought out this person in the first place. If not, look for a person who is confined yet humble. Be wary of the "expert" who is overconfident and seems to think he knows too much. You can be certain that if no one disagrees with him, he probably doesn't have an original thought.

Step 5: Make a Decision

The final step is to act. The decision should be made based on the available data—facts, not opinions. Do not give into the temptation, especially when making family or business financial decisions, to act hastily and without going through the DMP. Many times, the process will only take a short while. Other times it may take quite a while. Either way, making a prudent decision will lead to more attractive results than jumping in and improvising, even if you're an improv comedian. As you'll see in the next chapter, most of the financial issues and problems that arise are from a lack of DMP utilization. You will find that many of the most successful individuals are those who have refined their DMP and are fully aware of what is and isn't within their SoE. Wit and intelligence can enhance success, but they are not the reason for success. Rather, the process is the foundation.

DMP Summary

#1: See the Unseen
- Ask yourself how your natural human tendencies might be distorting this matter. Mitigate blind spots and biases that may impede your ability to take in information without judgment.

#2: Determine Importance
- Use the Covey grid to determine if this issue is in section one, two, three, or four. If in one or two – make a plan to deal with the matter.

#3: Your Sphere of Expertise
- Determine if the subject at hand is within your SoE. If not, move to phase four.

If yes → Make decision supported by facts & data.

#4: Build Network of Experts
- Use relevant questioning to determine if someone is really an expert in a certain subject.

#5: Make Decision
- Make a decision based on available data. The decision should be supported by facts rather than opinions.

THINKING ABOUT MONEY

" Too many people spend money they earned...to buy things they don't want...to impress people that they don't like. "

WILL ROGERS

" Wealth is the ability to fully experience life. "

HENRY DAVID THOREAU

Money is too often the resource that controls our lives. If you think for a few moments about what money really is, it becomes clear that it is nothing more than a conduit to accomplish certain things in life. The more I think about it and the more I view the way we all treat money, the more it seems that the powerful dollar fully controls all of our lives. But why? Why do we all let money dictate nearly every move we make? It doesn't matter if you have a lot of it or if you have a little of it, nearly all of us make our decisions based on money. And, to some extent, this makes perfect sense. We have to have the resource of money to do many of the things that we want or need to do. However, in today's economy there are very few who do not have enough money to do what they need to do. Therefore, the distinction is between wants and needs.

We so badly want what we don't need in order to superficially impress those who will only be envious, and we do this so often that we almost ruin our financial lives. Then, some of us try to master our material desires and take up frugality. Below is what I call the *Frugality/Materialism Spectrum* or FMS for short.

frugality   materialism

We're all somewhere on the FMS, either far to the left or to the right. Excessive materialism leads to long-term dissatisfaction and torn relationships. It creates an environment focused on short-term perceived wants that is out of sync with what matters most.

On the contrary, the drawbacks of excessive frugality are discussed less. An overt emphasis on penny-pinching mostly leads to a lack of financial initiative and thinking small. It is essentially an admission, a belief, that you cannot do any better than your current state—that you can't add more economic value. This is a negative state indeed. I think, in many ways, those who tilt too far to the left on the FMS fall into a fear of financial success. Yet we are supposed to be as productive as possible with our God-given resources, and, in the U.S., most of our talents can be economically monetized. Frugality for the sake of frugality is a violation of the laws of productivity.

PROVERBS 10:4

Lazy people are soon poor; hard workers get rich.

This is certainly not to say that those who do not reach financial success are not productive. Some of the most productive and talented people in the world have never reached financial success. My point is that using frugality as an excuse for lack of fiscal productivity is a logical fallacy—an excuse to play small. Some will also be wary of the notion that people may think them greedy and materialistic if they are too prosperous. I can promise you that if you have that thought, then you are likely not greedy and people of maturity will not think you to be so.

This is to say that in the current economic situation, there is opportunity for financial productivity beyond any other time in history. Wealth is much more than money, and part of wealth is finding an equilibrium between the two extremes of the FMS. Frugality is, in and of itself, a noble mentality; however, it is no excuse for lack of economic productivity. On the other hand, while owning assets isn't in and of itself evil, the temptation to idolize is. Neither being on one extreme nor the other is an excuse for lack of financial education.

B. Chase Chandler

PART II

*Recognizing the Deceit of
Conventional Thinking*

7

MONETARY MADNESS

"When the government makes loans or subsidies to business, what it does is to tax successful private business in order to support unsuccessful private business."
HENRY HAZLITT

TO BEGIN PART II, LET US DISCUSS the problem of government spending. It is likely not a shock to you. You have heard politicians debate and media personalities rant about the issue. And you've likely come to some conclusions on your own. The national debt and government spending is certainly a problem. As of right now, the national debt is above $18 trillion, and certainly headed towards $19 trillion. This is going to create massive complications in the future. You see, the national debt is not just a number. It is a literal figure that our children's children will have to pay off at some point—or at least will have to keep it from escalating to the point of utter insanity. Oh wait, we're already at that point. In just a moment, we will get to how treacherous the territory we are in truly is. However, first—the problem is really more about how we *think* and how our elected public servants *think*.

In 2014 a bank analyst named Dick Bove said, "*The American government strongly believes that people should spend as much money as they get.*"[15] Why does the government want you to spend so much? Enter John Maynard Keynes. In the earlier part of the 20th century, an economist named John Maynard Keynes decided that he would write what he considered revolutionary thoughts on economics. What he was really doing was catering to the politicians need and desire to control just about anything they could get their hands on. John Maynard Keynes (and a few others) transitioned the world into an economic model of massive fiat currency. Keynesian theory gave world leaders what they desperately desired—the ability to spend as much as they wanted.

Fiat is defined as being backed by nothing. *Fiat money* is "currency that a government has declared to be legal tender, but is not backed by a physical commodity." The value of fiat money is derived from the relationship between supply and demand rather than the value of the material that the money is made of. Historically, most currencies were based on physical commodities such as gold or silver, but fiat money is based solely on faith. Fiat is the Latin word for 'it shall be'."[16] Combine the words *fiat* and *currency* and this is what we have today in the United States and all across the world. Our currency, the US dollar, is backed only by the faith and credibility of the US government. It is nothing but paper, special green paper that is. This paper is only valid because we use it on a daily basis as citizens. We pay our taxes on it, and we pay for our goods and services with it. We, as citizens, are the ones who validate or invalidate it.

Before 1971, our currency was backed by gold. From 1944 until 1971, our currency was backed 35 to 1 by gold. That is, for every $35, you could trade in one dollar of gold. This was established by the Bretton Woods, New Hampshire meeting of 1944. (To get more information on this, I highly suggest you read *The Case Against the Fed* by Murray Rothbard and *End the Fed* by Ron Paul.) Because of pressure from the French, President Richard Nixon took us off the gold standard in 1971. This entered us into an era of massive inflation in government spending. Just think about it: if all of a sudden you had a blank check to buy anything you wanted, and there were no consequences, what would you do? Well, our politicians decided to go crazy. Everyone loves Reagan. And even I am tempted to adore Reagan because he has become a conservative icon. However, most people don't realize that Ronald Reagan was the first president to double our national debt. The only reason he could do this was because of the power to print money without constraint.

People tend to think that Reagan and Clinton were simply great presidents for economic advancement. The reality is that they were the benefactors of an economic system that was allowed to print as much money as it wanted. They had a blank check for whatever they pleased. Republicans and democrats and nearly everyone else in Washington got on the spending (and money-printing) band wagon. And we didn't look back for thirty years.

Supply and demand tells us that whenever supply increases, demand will decrease. This is the story of inflation, or of rising prices. Inflation is the devaluation of our dollar by means of raising prices. As prices rise, we must earn more money to keep the same standard of living—to be able to buy the same *stuff*. The great economic boom and stock market advances of the 80's and 90's were in large part because of the massive increase of paper dollars into our economic system. (And the introduction of the 401(k) type plan, which we will discuss in a bit.) Even Keynes, the most influential economist of the 20th century, proclaimed that, *"progressive deterioration in the value of money through history is not an accident, and has had behind it two great driving forces - the impecuniosity of Governments and the superior political influence of the debtor class."* If you won't listen to me, listen to Keynes.

" By a continuing process of inflation, governments can confiscate, secretly and unobserved, an important part of the wealth of their citizens. By this method they not only confiscate, but they confiscate arbitrarily; and, while the process impoverishes many, it actually enriches some. The sight of this arbitrary rearrangement of riches strikes not only at security, but at confidence in the equity of the existing distribution of wealth. "

JOHN MAYNARD KEYNES

∞

BOOK CURRENCY

Let's look at a simple example. To set up this scenario, let's imagine that we are in a community of 100 families. Now, I know this is a bit of a stretch, but please just be imaginative with me. Let's say we, for instance, have a company and that company's stock price is ten books.[i] (We're not going to use dollars for this example because the thought of dollars has become so manipulated. It's easy to think that dollars have value when they really don't. So we're going to use books.) Let's imagine that this was a furniture manufacturer. And, in our little community, this was the only furniture manufacturer that existed. The entire company was valued at 10,000 books. Therefore, there were 1,000 shares of this company's stock. Within our community, there were only 100,000 books and we used these books as currency. 2 pints of milk cost one book. 5 pounds of grain cost one book. You get the point; we're buying things, not with dollars, but with books. That's our currency. And because there are only 100 families and 100,000 books in the entire community, prices stay constant. This is supply and demand in action. Now imagine that all of the sudden we get an influx of hundred thousand more books. So now, there are 200,000 books in the economy. However, there are still only 100 families. What happens to the price of milk and the price of grain? Well, because we have double the amount of currency that we used to have, prices double. And what happens to the price of the stock of the furniture company? It also doubles. This is exactly what happened in the 80's and 90's. It's an over simplification, of course, but it nevertheless tells the story of what occurs when you suddenly start printing money at a rapid pace.

---

[i] Think of a book, in this scenario, as a dollar. Instead of buying lunch with dollars, the people of this community buy lunch with books.

However, the US is also interesting in another aspect. We don't just print money for the sake of printing money. We print money and call it debt. Debt that will have to be paid back at some point.

As you can see in the chart on the next page, the national debt from 1980 to 1985 went up by over $1 trillion. From 1985 to the year 2000, we went from about $2 trillion of national debt to slightly less than $6 trillion. We had never seen these levels of increase before, and they are levels that should scare the living *you know what* out of all of us. As you can also see from the chart, those levels have increased dramatically to the point we are at today, where we cannot stop this train wreck. At some point, it will come to a screeching halt, but we don't necessarily know when. What we do know is that with the current political system, it is essentially impossible to stop politicians from piling it on.

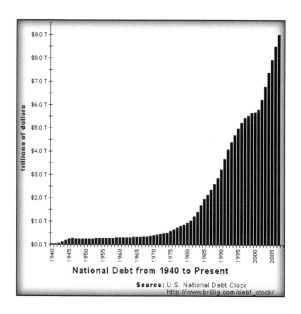

National Debt from 1940 to Present

Source: U.S. National Debt Clock
http://www.brillig.com/debt_clock/

The impact to us as citizens is greater than most people realize. (Although, because you're reading this book, I'm sure you already fully comprehend how terrible this is.) It would be reasonable to assume that at some point we couldn't even pay the interest on our national debt. As we head towards a $20 trillion (or more) in national debt, there could likely come a time in the next 5 to 10 years when the total government revenues from taxes would not cover the interest on the debt. One reason interest rates have remained so incredibly low for such an unprecedented period is because we don't have an alternative. The leaders of our country's financial matters (the Federal Reserve and the Treasury Department) know full well the brevity of this situation.

Let's talk a bit about what interest rates really are. It is easy to understand that a loaf of bread or a pack of cigarettes costs a certain amount of dollars. It is easy to understand that a home or a car costs a certain amount of dollars. Those goods cannot be utilized for free. Money is the same. Money has a cost, even though most citizens have never been taught to view money as a product. We've really only been taught to view money as a resource or a means of buying goods and services. However, money has a cost, just like any other good or service. The cost of money is the interest rate tied to that money. For instance, if you wanted to borrow $1,000, and I told you that you would have to pay a 5% interest rate per year, then the cost of that $1,000 would be $50 for that year. In other words, you would have to pay me $50 to use the $1,000. Interest rates should function as just that. That is to say, interest rates should delineate the cost of money. When someone comes in and begins to manipulate prices, it will usually result in economic devastation. Imagine that a US senator in your district demanded that all of the cupcake shops cut their prices by 70%. What might happen to these cupcake shops? Well of course, they would go out of business. The senator has no business telling the cupcake shops how much they should be charging their customers. That price is determined by the supply and demand of cupcakes in that area. There are many factors that go into this, such as how many people are in the area, the cost of real estate and supplies to make cupcakes, and the cost of employment. The senator's fiat declaration that the shops must cut their prices has no bearing on what the real price should be. It just messes everything up for the business owners, the employees, and the customers. This is what is occurring today with interest rates.

It seems we have so quickly forgotten the issues that brought along the great crash of 2008. Just recently, the government announced an operation to begin loaning money to people with lower credit scores. When are we going to learn? Affordable housing initiatives, as we know them today, were originally started by President Jimmy Carter. They sat there for a number of years after Carter's departure, until President Clinton picked them back up. Then President George W. Bush famously said in 2003[17], "*The rate of homeownership amongst minorities is below 50 percent. And that's not right, and this country needs to do something about it. We need to close the minority homeownership gap in America so more citizens get the satisfaction and mobility that comes from owning your own home, from owning a piece of the future of America...we need to make the home buying process more affordable. Some of the biggest upfront costs in a home purchase are the closing costs. Sometimes they catch you by surprise. [Laughter] Many homebuyers do not have the time to shop around looking for a better deal on closing costs. You're kind of stuck with what you're presented with. And so they end up paying more than they should. So we've proposed new rules to make it easier for buyers to shop around and to compare prices*

on closing costs, so they can get the best deal and the best service possible...The dream of homeownership should be attainable for every hardworking American. That's what we want..."

What President Bush was saying is exactly what most of the other presidents had said. He just said it more blatantly. Therefore, this is what they did. They thought it wise to push people into homes that they couldn't actually afford. The banking sector was more than willing to accommodate these government initiatives. However, alas, this was nothing but the manipulation of supply and demand. To create demand where demand should not be is to play god. Housing prices kept going up and up and up, and no one ever thought it would end. We were artificially flooding the housing market with new buyers who should have never been buyers. If the private markets had controlled the buying process exclusively, they would have been substantially more conservative in their lending practices. However, when the government got involved, it created the illusion of a backstop in case something bad happened. Moreover, something bad did happen. In response to the great crash, Congress and the Federal Reserve passed unprecedented legislation to flood the markets with currency and to keep interest rates low. As we've discussed, keeping interest rates low would give the illusion of cheap money... But it's not really cheap money. Just like the housing crash, this short-term illusion of low interest rates will end in destruction.

Many businesses are building and expanding because they have received access to this cheap money. They've been presented with the false idea that now is a good time to borrow. In reality, interest rates should be the greatest indicator of when businesses should expand. If the cost of money were truly determined by real supply and demand, then businesses would be able to recognize when money was truly cheap and when it was expensive. At the current time, it is only cheap because of manipulation.

All of this leads to one question: given these facts, how do we expect domestic and international market exchanges and economies to perform over the next ten to thirty years? Well, the reality is that we don't know. No one really knows how things are going to play out. However, we do have indicators, many of which have just been pointed out. And unless politicians learn to think and make decisions objectively overnight, the condition is not going to improve. All of the empirical evidence points to the fact that, at some time in the future, things are going to get ugly. It's simply a matter of how long the Federal Reserve (and other central banks around the world) can hold up the United States' (and the world's) monetary system.

This is not to say that you should have an extremely pessimistic attitude towards your financial situation. However, this entire equation revolves around how we think. I am not an economist, and I do not think you should take this chapter at face value. I think you should study the economic and political situation to determine how it may contribute to your financial DMP. What I do know is that many millionaires are created during economic turmoil. I think that in all likelihood, we are headed towards some sort of economic turmoil in the next 3 to 10 years. If we play our cards right, this could be a great opportunity for those that are aware of the circumstances. At the end of this chapter, I've listed a number of books on economics that I would recommend reading. It is important to remember, as Henry Hazlitt said in his book *Economics in One Lesson*, "...*either immediately or ultimately every dollar of government spending must be raised through a dollar of taxation. Once we look at the matter in this way, the supposed miracles of government spending will appear in another light.*" All of this spending and printing will be paid for by us. And the way we think about this today could very well define the next 100 years. We can take advantage of downturns in the economy, and I believe that we should. However, when the next crash does happen, it will be also be an opportunity to go back to a sound monetary and economic system.

∞

Contrary to semi-popular belief, printing money does not expand or grow our economy. As stated earlier, it simply devalues the dollar. Going back to our example before, we had 100 families in the community and they were all using books as currency. In the image below, you can see the supply and demand curve. As supply (i.e. any product or service you can think of) increases. the demand decreases. The alternate is also true. As demand increases, supply decreases.

This is the most basic, but most important, economic principle to grasp. It explains why prices go up and down. For instance, prices for real estate in Manhattan are a good bit higher than prices for real estate in Little Rock. Rental properties in Santa Monica are quite a bit higher than rental properties in San Antonio. This is all due to supply and demand. In Santa Monica and Manhattan, you have less land to work with, more regulations which keep certain players out of the market, and substantially more people looking to rent or buy condos and apartments. In Little Rock and San Antonio, you have more land and less buyers and renters—i.e. less demand.

B. Chase Chandler

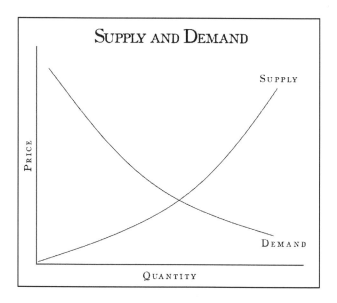

Supply and demand are also very relevant when we think about currencies. If rising prices were a function of higher demand, which they often are, then more currency coming into an economy would equal less demand for that currency. Again, let's say the grocery store owner had experienced a consistent level of demand. Then, all of the sudden, he begins to experience twice the demand (twice the amount of books, or currency, wanting to buy his goods). He would run out of food very quickly, twice as fast. Therefore, to counter that, he raises prices to offset the higher demand.

In the two upcoming graphs, you can see the effect of an influx of currency. In graph 6a, demand (in currency terms) increases when currency is pumped into the economy—but the grocery store owner does not increase prices. Therefore, he runs out of groceries (supply) in short order because people have more money-buying product. That is, instead of having two books to spend on bread and meat, a family now has four. Therefore, when the owner didn't raise prices, the family buys twice the previous amount of bread and meat. His supply runs dry and he's out of business.

All things being equal, higher demand (more people wanting to either buy or excess currency entering the economy) simply causes supply (goods and services) to be bought up more quickly.

In the second graph, 6b, the grocery store owner increases prices when demand increases and his supply stays steady. In this case, the owner notices more money being spent on his products and he sees his supply decreasing faster than usual. In order to stay in business, he cannot run out of supply. He must keep the shelves stocked. Therefore, he increases prices on his groceries out of necessity.

∞

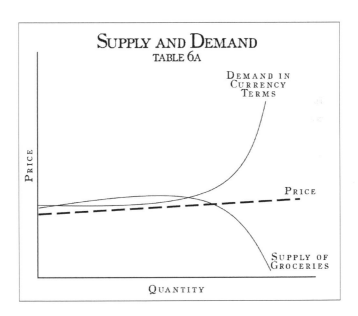

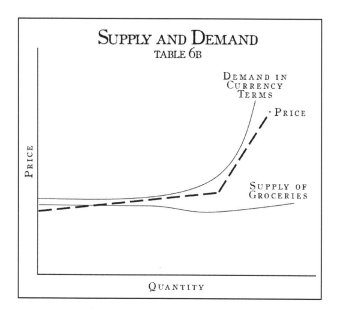

In this grocery store example, ideally, all 100 families get equal
access to the books that have been printed. Therefore, their purchasing capability rises as prices rise. However, in the real world,
this is not what happens. In the real world, elites like special interest
groups and politicians direct where the newly created currency
goes. And in 2014, it went to things like research on how monkeys
gamble, how humans would react if they met a space alien, how to
get mountain lions to walk on a treadmill, how spouses feel when
they "stab voodoo dolls," building a beer farm in New York, free
gym memberships and vacations for DHS employees, building golf
courses, overpaying for nearly everything, and buying and building
billions of dollars worth of stuff that will never be used.[18]

The overarching point here is that an influx of currency, primarily a government's manipulation and printing of currency, does
not help the citizen. It helps the special interests and the elites. It

simply raises prices for the citizen. It does not, in and of itself, grow the economy, because prices eventually adjust to account for the new currency demand. However, the special interest people get to use that newly created currency at the outset, before prices have risen. They, in essence, get to build wealth at our expense. If the currency had remained steady, then the consumer would have simply retained a consistent purchasing value. That is to say, the consumer's money would have been able to purchase the same amount of goods. The great economic fallacy is the idea that inflation causes prices to rise and incomes to rise simultaneously. However, in the U.S. we have seen quite a different story.

Economic Must Reads:

Economics In One Lesson by Henry Hazlitt

The Road To Serfdom by F. A. Hayek

America's Great Depression by Murray N. Rothbard

The Case Against The Fed by Murray Rothbard

End The Fed by Ron Paul

Human Action by Ludwig von Mises

Basic Economics by Thomas Sowell

How An Economy Grows And Why It Crashes by Peter Schiff

Meltdown by Thomas E. Woods

How Privatized Banking Really Works by L. Carlos Lara and Robert P. Murphy

The Politically Incorrect Guide To Capitalism by Robert P. Murphy

" *EVERYTHING WE GET, OUTSIDE OF THE FREE GIFTS OF NATURE, MUST IN SOME WAY BE PAID FOR. THE WORLD IS FULL OF SO-CALLED ECONOMISTS WHO IN TURN ARE FULL OF SCHEMES FOR GETTING SOMETHING FOR NOTHING. THEY TELL US THAT THE GOVERNMENT CAN SPEND AND SPEND WITHOUT TAXING AT ALL; THAT IT CAN CONTINUE TO PILE UP DEBT WITHOUT EVERY PAYING IT OFF...* "

— HENRY HAZLITT

8

THE IDEA OF RETIREMENT

" In the beginning, there was no retirement. "
MARY-LOU WEISMAN
NEW YORK TIMES, 1999

THINK FOR A MOMENT ABOUT THE concept of retirement—what the word means and where it came from. If you're not quite sure, then you're in the same boat I was when I first began pondering *retirement*. The word retire literally means to "exit" or "leave." Before the 20th century, it was used primarily in two ways: in the military, as a term for withdrawing from action or danger, and in the home, as a term for going to bed. I find it interesting to look at definitions of earlier times to see what words meant once upon a time. (By visiting www.1828.mshaffer.com you can search the meanings of various words from the 1828 Webster's dictionary.) Here are the meanings of the variations of *retire* from the 1828 dictionary:

RETI'RE, v. i. 1. To withdraw; to retreat; to go from company or from a public place into privacy; as, to retire from the world; to retire from notice. 2.

RETI'RED, a. 1. Secluded from much society or from public notice; private. He lives a retired life; he has a retired situation. 2. Secret; private.

RETI'REDLY, adv. In solitude or privacy.

RETI'REDNESS, n. A state of retirement; solitude; privacy or secrecy.

RETI'REMENT, n. 1. The act of withdrawing from company or from public notice or station. 2. The state of being withdrawn; as the retirement of the mind

The evolution of retirement from 1828 to today is less than petty. It allows us a glimpse into how and possibly why definitions have changed over many years. In the final definition from 1828, Webster's stated that retirement was *"1. The act of withdrawing from company or from public notice or station. 2. The state of being withdrawn; as the retirement of the mind."* The idea of the past was that retirement was not some glamorous occasion to look forward to. Rather, it was a forced exclusion. To retire for a period was to withdraw for rest or sleep or reflection. To retire permanently was not a choice—it was a state of being worthless. It was a state of one's inability to be productive.

The very notion of retiring and leaving productive work is a relatively modern idea. And it gives us great insight into the power of government propaganda. For most of the human existence, there was no reason to retire in the way we think of it today. A man would work from his teenage years until he could physically work no longer. A woman would do the same; some combination of working the fields (or whatever other business the family may have been involved in) and raising and teaching the children. The need to leave only came if one was physically incapable—which most often occurred at death. In 1999 Mary-Lou Weisman wrote an intriguing New York Times piece entitled "The History of Retirement, From Early Man to A.A.R.P."[19] Ms. Weisman described the birth of retirement, as we know it today:

> *"In 1883, Chancellor Otto Von Bismarck of Germany had a problem. Marxists were threatening to take control of Europe. To help his countrymen resist their blandishments, Bismarck announced that he would pay a pension to any nonworking German over age 65. Bismarck was no dummy. Hardly anyone lived to be 65 at the time, given that penicillin would not be available for another half century. Bismarck not only co-opted the Marxists, but set the arbitrary world standard for the exact year at which old age begins and established the*

> *precedent that government should pay people for growing old."*

This is where the retirement age of 65 originated. Bismark knew that the vast majority of people didn't live past age 65. And he set government funded pension plans into motion merely to retain his followers. It was by accident that pensions ever became a reality at all.

In 1919, about 15% of private employees in the United States had a pension plan through their company. There were about 300 private pension plans overall.[20] However, these plans weren't really designed for the "grow old and relax" reason. Rather, they were created to give corporations the ability to eliminate older, less fruitful employees for newer, more productive workers. This minority of U.S. companies deemed it more profitable to let certain employees go and pay them than to keep them and pay them. In 1914, many of these companies had lobbied congress and President Woodrow Wilson to give them a tax deduction for their pension savings.[21]

By the late 20's and 30's a few American influencers began to promote the idea of government pensions for everyone. In 1935 President Franklin D. Roosevelt signs the Social Security Act of 1935 into law, but not because he thinks many Americans will need it, but rather to further the progressive movement of government aid and intervention—i.e. central planning. A tax was implemented to help fund the program which was said to be "short-term."

Instead, the social security program in the U.S. has become a bedrock of political gamesmanship. Very little of what we pay in social security tax actually goes to any social security fund for our future wellbeing. It goes to the current retirees because government so poorly and senselessly manages assets. This is called a Ponzi scheme.

Over the past 40 or so years, the retirement industrial complex, as described in *Pirates of Manhattan II* by Barry James Dyke, has grown astronomically. It is now one of the most powerful and influential industries in the world. The sole reason is the amount of revenue and profit that can be generated from convincing billions of world citizens that they're better off handing their money to someone else. Governments around the world (with the help of the financial industrial complex) have convinced us, as entrepreneur Allen Darrow puts it, to "hand off the responsibility of our money to someone else. This way, when something goes wrong, it's not our fault." And so many have bought into this notion—even though it has never been proven successful.

∞

THE NEW RETIREMENT

You are likely beginning to see the holes in the concept of "retirement." When these retirement ages where set, most people weren't expected to live past them. It was a way to get the less efficient out of the workforce. The fact that these ideas have lived on to today is somewhat mind-boggling, although I think I know why. For capable people to expect to cease productivity and relax for 20 or 30 or even 40 years has never been economically sound. The entire concept is flawed. We shouldn't work for some future lazy endeavor. We should work because we want to make an impact, to build something of meaning.

I think many people have already begun to shift their mindset on retirement. However, I think we have to continue to ponder the notion of retirement, what it currently means, and what it should mean. Instead of being a time of excessive relaxation, this time in our lives should be some of the most productive and profitable years of our lives. We've worked so hard for so long and I don't think we've done *that* to do *nothing*.

Rather than using the term *retirement*, what if we called it *a season of significance*? We could continue working, but reduce the hours, focus mostly on our passions, and increase our effectiveness. There should be no set age. Whenever a person reaches the point where their professional value is high enough—whether it be age 28 or 78—they transition to this season of their lives, work in it, and improve upon it until they can work no more. The conventional notion of ceasing contribution to our society and economy is robbing us of those who can add the most value. The predecessor of that notion is one that states you should work at a mundane job for a long period of time just to someday "retire." No. We should focus on value creation, and the retirement industry is largely robbing us of those value creation opportunities. It is teaching us to ignore our fiscal responsibilities by transferring those responsibilities to another party who will never be as prudent with our capital as we could be. As we move on, you will see the damage that this industry has caused. We can change it, but we have to be diligent and financially educated.

9

THE 12% LEGEND

*"Wisdom… is often an abstraction associated not with
fact or reality but with the man who asserts it and the
manner of its assertion."*
JOHN KENNETH GALBRAITH
THE GREAT CRASH OF 1929

I WOULD IMAGINE THAT WHEN WE "tell 'em like it
is"—when we really want to *stick it to 'em!*—we better know and be
sure of the way "it" really is. That is to say, we want to know we're
telling the full truth and nothing but the truth, especially if we're
going to degrade others in the process because they can't see what
we have proclaimed to be true. However, there is a financial guru,
probably the biggest one in the world, who is utterly adamant that

the average worker can earn 12% a year in growth stock mutual funds. The main issue is the difference between an average rate of return and true rates of return, technically known as the Compound Annual Growth Rate (CAGR). In short, the distinction is that an average rate of return is simply the sum of all rates throughout all years, whereas the CAGR is the actual real rate of return you have earned over that same period. In a moment, I'll describe more extensively the difference between average rates and CAGRs. As you will see, average rates of return do not give us the full truth. They lack…. you guessed it, *context*.

I would think that this man, we'll call him DR, would want to embody truth as much as anyone—especially being that a large part of his pitch, and his market, is tied to Christianity. I wonder, in honest sincerity, if he is so stuck on certain beliefs that he would refuse to change even if it was apparent that an old belief is mistaken. In his book *How We Know What Isn't So*, author Thomas Gilovich says, "*When examining evidence relevant to a given belief, people are inclined to see what they expect to see, and conclude what they expect to conclude. Information that is consistent with our pre-existing beliefs is often accepted at face value, whereas evidence that contradicts them is critically scrutinized and discounted. Our beliefs may thus be less responsive than they should to the implications of new information.*" The recent abundance of research that has been released on how we 'cling to beliefs' suggests that we all hold tight to our own world-view, especially as we age, and that it becomes very difficult to change. As I'm going to point out, the financial "pundit" is stuck clinging to an old belief.

A few years ago, this man went off on a 10-minute tangent in which he called author and entrepreneur Peter Schiff an "*idiot*" for predicating a massive economic and housing bubble. He said that he would (the financial "guru", not Schiff), and I quote, "*try to be nice.*" He then went on to call Schiff's ideas "*absolutely ludicrous.*" He addressed the "stopgaps" of the modern stock market, attempting to make a point that there was no way Schiff could be right about a looming economic collapse. He said "*...people who predict these things are typically very uneducated...*"—and most of this was communicated as if there were no way in the world anyone could ever disagree with the financial "guru" without being completely stupid. This occurred in 2006. Not long after, Peter Schiff was proven right. The economic collapse came and came with a vengeance. *You can see that moment at:* TheFallofLogic.com/PeterWasRight.

The issue many others and I have with these actions is that, since the 2008 crash, he hasn't felt the need to address his aforementioned comments or egotistical tone. This seems to directly contradict the entire essence of humility, gentleness, and patience, which he claims to embody. Insofar as he still proclaims his faith, why wouldn't he feel the need to come out and say, "*I was wrong. I said things that were wrong. Schiff was right and I shouldn't have done that.*"

We have all said things that we shouldn't have said. It can be hard to apologize for all the things we wish we wouldn't have said. After all, this guy is super busy—as are most other super successful people. However, there is another thing—his investment advice—that seems like it negates any desire to 'come clean.' What I really mean is that, through extensive study and research, I'm certain that there are missing facts and excessively misconstrued data in his investment advice to his readers and radio show listeners. Moreover, for the life of me, I cannot figure out why he won't—as I said earlier—come clean and tell the truth. I'm baffled.

The only logical explanation is either, one, he doesn't feel that he can change his message because one key tenant of marketing is 'consistency'—and his message has been consistent for a long time.

Or, two, he hasn't been taught the difference between an average annualized rate of return (or average ROR) and a net compound annual growth rate (CAGR). I originally assumed it is the latter. And maybe, if it were a lack of understanding, that wouldn't be so bad. Financial professionals all over the country have yet to be taught the difference between average rates and net CAGRs. In fact, I believe the financial and mutual fund companies don't want people to know the difference between average RORs and CAGRs. Not until the advent and progression of the information age did the data become as available to the public—simple as it may be.

Actually, I'm sure the issue was originally a lack of fundamental understanding of average ROR vs. net CAGR, based on a 2013 interview he did with a writer from The Motley Fool.[i]

What's worse is that he says at one point in the interview that "*[he was] just trying to get people to save*," and he refers to the idea that the 12% can be "*substantiated*." After this interview, I'm sure he does somewhat understand the difference between average and CAGR, at least intellectually. However, I do not think he currently comprehends how severely his advice is damaging his followers' long-term financial strategies.

At some point in 2013, he (or someone on his staff) posted this blog article[22]:

---

[i] You can listen to that interview here: *TheFallofLogic.com/AveragevsCAGR*.

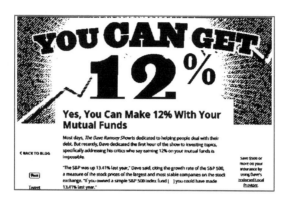

In it he is quoted as saying "*The S&P was up 13.41% [in 2012],*" and "*If you owned a simple S&P 500 index fund… you would have made 13.41% [in 2012].*" He goes on to say, "*I don't understand why those of you who are supposedly trained or purport to your readership that you actually know something about investing can't find a mutual fund with a 50-year or 70-year or 20-year track record of average returns of 12%.*" Then, the article itself states something that strikes me as extremely odd and illogical— "*it's easy to find the ones that do with online investment research tools or through a mutual fund broker.*"

In another article[23] from April of 2012, he (or his staff) stated, "*12% is not a magic number. However, based on the history of the market, it's a reasonable expectation for your long-term investments. It's simply a part of the conversation about investing.*" Just to reiterate the point (although I'm sure it's already made), this guy seems steadfast in holding to his theories by claiming that his is "*…using a real number that's based on the historical average annual return of the S&P 500*" and that "*It's not difficult to find several mutual funds that average or exceed 12% long-term growth, even in today's market.*"

I only harp on DR's "12% message" because he has gained so much influence with families all around the country. With due respect to DR, this is an issue that is, number one, causing him to lose a good amount of respect with the financially and mathematically inclined and, number two (more importantly), his followers are planning their financial future based on tremendously faulty data that you refuse to vet.

Here are some average rates of return of the S&P 500 (Source: Pinnacle Data Corp.):

1930 to 2013: 7.38%
1940 to 2013: 8.36%
1950 to 2013: 9.02%
1960 to 2013: 7.92%
1970 to 2013: 8.53%
1980 to 2013: 10.09%
1990 to 2013: 8.79%
2000 to 2013: 3.55%

All of these periods look good except for, of course, the 'lost decade' as they call it. To the untrained eye, these numbers seem to verify, to an extent, what DR is saying. Those are likely the type of numbers he and his staff used to run their illustrations.

I crunch numbers for a living. Early in my career, a very wise and humble person pointed me to 1st Corinthians 8 where it says "*[1]...knowledge puffs up while love builds up. [2]Those who think they know something do not yet know as they ought to know.*" His point to me was to always leave room to be questioned. **Always be open to correction. Never assume you're right on everything you think you know.** Now, let me analyze DR's "rightness" on this 12% topic based on real data. The rates of return I gave earlier were real data.

The rates of return DR gives are also real data. The problem is that the data is substantially out of context. And this is where he is hurting your followers—really badly.

Let's look at an example using Joe Bob. Assume Joe Bob is a 35 year old looking to save $5,000 per year for 30 years. If we used a 12% rate of return in the sense that you use it, it would look like this:

Year	Beg. Of Year Acct. Value	Earnings Rate	Annual Cash Flow	Interest Earnings	End of Year Acct. Value
1		12.00%	5,000	600	5,600
2	5,600	12.00%	5,000	1,272	11,872
3	11,872	12.00%	5,000	2,025	18,897
4	18,897	12.00%	5,000	2,868	26,764
5	26,764	12.00%	5,000	3,812	35,576
6	35,576	12.00%	5,000	4,869	45,445
7	45,445	12.00%	5,000	6,053	56,498
8	56,498	12.00%	5,000	7,380	68,878
9	68,878	12.00%	5,000	8,865	82,744
10	82,744	12.00%	5,000	10,529	98,273
11	98,273	12.00%	5,000	12,393	115,666
12	115,666	12.00%	5,000	14,480	135,146
13	135,146	12.00%	5,000	16,817	156,963
14	156,963	12.00%	5,000	19,436	181,399
15	181,399	12.00%	5,000	22,368	208,766
16	208,766	12.00%	5,000	25,652	239,418
17	239,418	12.00%	5,000	29,330	273,749
18	273,749	12.00%	5,000	33,450	312,198
19	312,198	12.00%	5,000	38,064	355,262
20	355,262	12.00%	5,000	43,231	403,494
21	403,494	12.00%	5,000	49,019	457,513
22	457,513	12.00%	5,000	55,502	518,014
23	518,014	12.00%	5,000	62,762	585,776
24	585,776	12.00%	5,000	70,893	661,669
25	661,669	12.00%	5,000	80,000	746,670
26	746,670	12.00%	5,000	90,200	841,870
27	841,870	12.00%	5,000	101,624	948,494
28	948,494	12.00%	5,000	114,419	1,067,914
29	1,067,914	12.00%	5,000	128,750	1,201,663
30	1,201,663	12.00%	5,000	144,800	1,351,463

At the end of 30 years, Joe Bob would have $1,351,463. We'll come back to this number in a bit. The issue is that 12% returns are not consistent. It's unrealistic to run 12% every year, but—to give him a bit of credit—he then says "even if you're off a little" the results will still be satisfactory.

Instead of using a 12% average rate of return, let's be conservative and use 9%. If we assume Joe Bob saves $5,000 per year for 30 years, then he would have $742,876. That's a $608,587 (or 45%) difference in the wrong direction. He may still say, "*Hey - that's still almost $750,000. I think the average American would be okay!*" Maybe. If they'd built their entire plan around the $1.3 million dollar number, though, then a 45% difference isn't going to be very fun.

Year	Beg. Of Year Acct. Value	Earnings Rate	Annual Cash Flow	Interest Earnings	End of Year Acct. Value
1		9.00%	5,000	450	5,450
2	5,450	9.00%	5,000	941	11,391
3	11,391	9.00%	5,000	1,475	17,866
4	17,866	9.00%	5,000	2,058	24,924
5	24,924	9.00%	5,000	2,693	32,617
6	32,617	9.00%	5,000	3,386	41,002
7	41,002	9.00%	5,000	4,140	50,142
8	50,142	9.00%	5,000	4,963	60,105
9	60,105	9.00%	5,000	5,859	70,965
10	70,965	9.00%	5,000	6,837	82,801
11	82,801	9.00%	5,000	7,902	95,704
12	95,704	9.00%	5,000	9,063	109,767
13	109,767	9.00%	5,000	10,329	125,096
14	125,096	9.00%	5,000	11,709	141,805
15	141,805	9.00%	5,000	13,212	160,017
16	160,017	9.00%	5,000	14,852	179,869
17	179,869	9.00%	5,000	16,638	201,507
18	201,507	9.00%	5,000	18,586	225,092
19	225,092	9.00%	5,000	20,708	250,801
20	250,801	9.00%	5,000	23,022	278,823
21	278,823	9.00%	5,000	25,544	309,367
22	309,367	9.00%	5,000	28,293	342,660
23	342,660	9.00%	5,000	31,289	378,949
24	378,949	9.00%	5,000	34,555	418,504
25	418,504	9.00%	5,000	38,115	461,620
26	461,620	9.00%	5,000	41,996	508,616
27	508,616	9.00%	5,000	46,225	559,841
28	559,841	9.00%	5,000	50,836	615,677
29	615,677	9.00%	5,000	55,861	676,538
30	676,538	9.00%	5,000	61,338	742,876

However, the reality is even much worse than this. This 9% projection is what millions of hard-working Americans have been shown. And they've been told it's conservative. Only one problem - it's bogus. Both of these projections, the 12%, and 9% calculations, are based on an average rate of return. An unsuspecting person, like yourself, looks at the average ROR and assumes it can be run as a yearly ROR. This is the key—**average rates of return lie; they tell us little, if anything, about reality.** Average ROR's are nothing but the sum of all returns divided by the number of periods (years).

Think about it this way (calculator likely needed). If you had $10,000 two years ago and earned 55% the first year then lost 37% the second year, what would your average rate of return be and how much would you have in the account at the end of two years?

**55% + (-37%) = 18% / 2 years =
9% average annualized rate of return**

Now, how much money would we have in the account?

Year 1: +55% = $15,500
Year 2: -37% = $9,765

Please answer this question: *how is it possible that we have a [positive] 9% average rate of return, but yet we lost money?*

Average rates are just that—average. They don't tell us the truth. Yes, this is an extreme example, but it makes the point, the point that the financial "guru" is not making. What matters is the true annualized rate of return—the compound annual growth rate or CAGR. The CAGR is what we have truly earned over a period of time. In the above example our CAGR is negative 1.18%, meaning we have actually earned a negative 1.18% per year. Average ROR's don't take into consideration the damage volatility does to a portfolio (read Benjamin Graham). Many times, a person doesn't learn to calculate CAGR's unless they've studied finance at an advanced level and they're working with real numbers each day. You see, the problem is that DR and most financial pundits are speaking in theory. They don't see the real consequences of their actions. However, financial professionals (financial advisors, CFO's, CPA's, etc.) do. They have to answer to the results of their real-world decisions. Oh yeah, and we haven't even begun to discuss fees and taxes yet[24].

> *" Fees pile up and ravage mutual funds like zombies, with the highest rates on actively managed funds in retirement plans. People routinely pay too much, which eats into their retirement or college kitties over time. "*
> JASON WASIK, FORBES.COM

∞

Allow me to quickly discuss the three modern market eras: 1901-1979, 1980-1999, and 2000-2013. To set the context by showing the average ROR from 1990 to 2013: 8.79%. (We looked at that number earlier.) When most people look at 8.79%, they see 8.79%. The simplest answer is the right answer, right? Wrong. They're led (or choose) to believe that this means they can earn 8.79% in mutual funds. Using Joe Bob again, if you round up to 9%—he thinks he's going to have over $740,000 in 30 years.

What you might find interesting is that the CAGR from this period, 1990 to 2013, was actually 6.51%. Take a gander at these numbers:

Year	Beg. Of Year Acct. Value	Earnings Rate	Annual Cash Flow	Interest Earnings	End of Year Acct. Value
1		6.51%	5,000	326	5,326
2	5,326	6.51%	5,000	672	10,998
3	10,998	6.51%	5,000	1,041	17,039
4	17,039	6.51%	5,000	1,435	23,474
5	23,474	6.51%	5,000	1,854	30,328
6	30,328	6.51%	5,000	2,300	37,627
7	37,627	6.51%	5,000	2,775	45,402
8	45,402	6.51%	5,000	3,281	53,684
9	53,684	6.51%	5,000	3,820	62,504
10	62,504	6.51%	5,000	4,395	71,898
11	71,898	6.51%	5,000	5,006	81,904
12	81,904	6.51%	5,000	5,657	92,562
13	92,562	6.51%	5,000	6,351	103,913
14	103,913	6.51%	5,000	7,090	116,004
15	116,004	6.51%	5,000	7,877	128,881
16	128,881	6.51%	5,000	8,716	142,596
17	142,596	6.51%	5,000	9,609	157,205
18	157,205	6.51%	5,000	10,560	172,765
19	172,765	6.51%	5,000	11,572	189,337
20	189,337	6.51%	5,000	12,651	206,988
21	206,988	6.51%	5,000	13,800	225,789
22	225,789	6.51%	5,000	15,024	245,813
23	245,813	6.51%	5,000	16,328	267,141
24	267,141	6.51%	5,000	17,716	289,857
25	289,857	6.51%	5,000	19,195	314,053
26	314,053	6.51%	5,000	20,770	339,823
27	339,823	6.51%	5,000	22,448	367,271
28	367,271	6.51%	5,000	24,235	396,506
29	396,506	6.51%	5,000	26,138	427,644
30	427,644	6.51%	5,000	28,165	460,809

Now, Joe Bob has only $460,809. That's 38% less than what he thought he'd have based on the "conservative" 9% example. It's about 65% less that the $1.3 million from the 12% example. Ouch.

Back to the three modern market eras. Let me show you the true rate, the S&P's CAGR (Source: Pinnacle Data Corp.), of these market eras.

1901 to 1979: 3.31%
1980 to 1999: 13.95%
2000 to 2013: 1.65%

Therefore, there's been one period in the 20th and 21st centuries where we saw the type of returns that DR and the financial community discuss. And equities during that period, 1980 to 1999, were primarily driven up by an expanding national debt, the introduction of the 401(k) type plan (i.e. the indoctrination of the idea that people should put all of their life savings in the stock market), the dot com boom, and out-of-wack P/E ratios.

One more thing, briefly. We haven't even discussed the impact of fees and taxes, the effect of which can reduce your long-term portfolio by 50-80%.[25] If we use a 7% CAGR (which would likely be a 9 to 11% average ROR) with a 1% fee, here's what it would look like for Joe Bob:

22	210,139	7.00%	5,000	15,060	(2,302)	227,896
23	227,896	7.00%	5,000	16,303	(2,492)	246,707
24	246,707	7.00%	5,000	17,620	(2,693)	266,633
25	266,633	7.00%	5,000	19,014	(2,906)	287,741
26	287,741	7.00%	5,000	20,492	(3,132)	310,101
27	310,101	7.00%	5,000	22,057	(3,372)	333,786
28	333,786	7.00%	5,000	23,715	(3,625)	358,876
29	358,876	7.00%	5,000	25,471	(3,893)	385,454
30	385,454	7.00%	5,000	27,332	(4,178)	413,608

Now he's got $413,608, or more than 68% less than what you told him he would have. And that's likely best case scenario. More realistically, if Joe Bob earned a 6% CAGR (likely a 7-9% average) with a 2% annual fee (closer to the average mutual funds annual fee) he would have $285,534. That is around 80% less than what Joe Bob was thinking.

Let's look at a real world example of how Joe Bob might have really done in a mutual fund. The next page shows an actual chart of an actual mutual fund's performance.

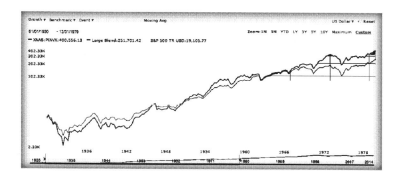

This is a chart of the Putnam Investors Fund[26], which has been around since 1925. Let's take this out 50 years. Financial "guru" DR would have us believe that we could put $10,000 in this (or a similar) fund and let it grow for 50 years at 12% per year. That would give us $2.8 million in the end. What if we only got 10% you say? Wouldn't we still be just fine? Well that would give us $1.17 million. Maybe we'd be fine, but we just miscalculated by 58%.

However, in the real world, (in the actual Putman Investors fund) if we started with $10,000 on January 1st, 1930 and let it ride to December 31st, 1979—50 years—we would have $400,556. That's a 7.66% CAGR. However, this doesn't include the upfront sales charge (5.75%) or the ongoing expense ratio (1.08%). When we include those fees, it brings our net CAGR to 6.50% before taxes. Our long-term total comes down to $219,384. Therefore, you can see a difference of only 1.16% decreases our account value by 45%. If we include taxes, it would bring our total down to the $150,000 range.

Put simply, people who use 10-12% CAGRs when projecting their investment growth in mutual funds (and the like) are looking at something like 60-80% less in their long-term accounts.

∞

There is so much data, much of which you've just seen, which shows why mutual fund fees and volatility are so detrimental. However, I'm confident that most people do not understand the brevity of the message. They do not understand why people are not reaching their financial goals—but this is one of the main reasons: the real net CAGR of their accounts is likely going to be 3-5% long-term. Maybe, just maybe, it will get up to 6% or 7%. After fees and taxes, earning a net CAGR above 6% or so is highly improbable. Many people following DR's ideas are listening to him because he has become an authority on personal finance, and he seems to be a good man. They're basing much of their financial future—mainly their wealth accumulation forecasts—on his terribly misguided figures.

In listening to and reading some of the content put out by DR and other financial pundit's over the last few years, I can't help but think of Proverbs 12:15 and Proverbs 19:20:

"THE WAY OF FOOLS SEEMS RIGHT TO THEM, BUT THE WISE LISTEN TO ADVICE."

"LISTEN TO ADVICE AND ACCEPT DISCIPLINE, AND AT THE END YOU WILL BE COUNTED AMONG THE WISE."

Many financial experts have realized this error. They've seen the shift and are open and intellectually honest about it. However, I'm afraid most are not. Whether we're talking about a traditional financial advisor, CPA, or DR—most of these folks are blind to their blindness. I'm reminded of the words from Thomas Gilovich's *How We Know What Isn't So*: "*We hold many dubious beliefs, in other words, not because they satisfy some important psychological need, but because they seem to be the most sensible conclusions consistent with the available evidence. People hold such beliefs because they seem, in the words of Robert Merton, to be the "irresistible products of their own experience." They are the products, not of irrationality, but of flawed rationality... People will always prefer black-and-white over shades of grey, and so there will always be the temptation to hold overly-simplified beliefs and to hold them with excessive confidence.*" Moreover, let's not forget Daniel Kahneman's revolutionary word in *Thinking, Fast and Slow*: "*Confidence is a feeling, which reflects the coherence of the information and the cognitive ease of processing it. It is wise to take admissions of uncertainty seriously, but declarations of high confidence mainly tell you that an individual has constructed a coherent story in his mind, not necessarily that the story is true.*"

With respect, the mainstream personal financial crowd are *confident* in a *feeling* that is dead wrong. They are "*products, not of irrationality, but of flawed rationality.*" Take heed—otherwise, your long-term results will, in all likelihood, be horrendous.

B. Chase Chandler

QUESTIONS TO CONTEMPLATE:

HAVE YOU EVER BEEN SOLD THE 10% OR
12% MYTH?

DO YOU FEEL THAT YOU UNDERSTAND
THE DIFFERENCE BETWEEN AVERAGE
RATES OF RETURN AND TRUE RATES OF
RETURN—THE CAGR?

10

THE IRRATIONALITY OF
MODERN FINANCE

"The irrationality of a thing is no argument against its existence, rather a condition of it."
FRIEDRICH NIETZSCHE

WHERE DO YOU CURRENTLY INVEST your money? The follow-up question, as you may begin to expect: Why do you put your money there? If your answer is a 401(k), 403(b), mutual fund, variable annuity, 457, or IRA, then you might have a problem. The reason that you would be putting your money in these assets is probably because someone told you to do it, and they probably used the fact that 'all of your friends are doing it' to get you to do it.

I've never met a person who truly and unequivocally understood why they funded a qualified plan. And, before you take offense, please realize that I used to set up qualified plans for a living... and I didn't know why. However, I never really wondered why. Qualified plans were the conventional wisdom—everyone knew they were the best place to save money. However, no one bothered to ask *why?* **You and I were sold on matches and 'tax-deductions'—but these espoused advantages aren't, in actuality, really advantages at all. They're smoke and mirrors.** There are many reasons why qualified plans aren't the best place to save money, and among them are these: volatility, immense fees and expenses, future taxes and the devaluation of the dollar. We'll review more details and analysis shortly.

Qualified plans are comprised mainly of 401(k) s, 403(b) s, and SEP IRAs.[i] Most of the guidelines for modern qualified plans were established in the Employee Retirement Income Security Act of 1974 (ERISA), although the 401(k) wasn't officially created until 1980.[27] It comes as a surprise to most people that the term "401(k)" isn't actually a type of financial account. It's a section of the tax code. Around 1980 a few large companies—including Johnson & Johnson, PepsiCo, JC Penney, and Honeywell—began developing the 401(k) plan based on Section 401 of the Internal Revenue Code.[28]

DB = DEFINED BENEFIT PLANS

DC = DEFINED CONTRIBUTION PLANS

Their motive in setting up a new system was to escape the binding configuration of pension plans (which are also qualified plans). Pension plans are distinguished in the fact that they are labeled as

---

[i] See the *Personal Finance Definitions* section at the end of the book for a more detailed list of qualified and non-qualified plans.

defined benefit arrangements, whereas 401(k) type plans are labeled *defined contribution* arrangements.

The difference between defined benefit and defined contribution plans is predominantly found in who is taking on the risk. In defined benefit plans, a future income payment *(benefit)* is set *(defined)*. These are what we know as pension plans—i.e. Bob works for a company for 30 years and when he retires, he's given a gold watch and a guaranteed income. Before 1980, most large companies offered DB plans as the norm—and the company was on the hook for a future retirement income stream. During the economic turmoil of the 1970's, though, these pension promises became harder and harder to reconcile. Unions and special interest groups had negotiated too much gain for employees and had not left adequate wiggle room for employers. This generated the demand for creativity—a reason to find a different strategy. The big companies wanted to mitigate the risk of massive pension liabilities[ii].

Benefits consultant Ted Benna helped mastermind and transition the companies to this different strategy.[29] In a defined contribution set up, the employee takes on the risk and the volatility of their individual portfolio. There are no guarantees provided by the employer. A DC structure gives the employee the ability to pay *(the contribution)* a certain *(defined)* amount, typically into a conglomerate of mutual funds or variable annuity sub-accounts (which are very similar to mutual funds). You'll soon see why these plans have been a complete catastrophe.

[ii] Recently, many have alleged that today's publically traded companies mistreat and underpay average employees. It is worth noting that there has been a transition from employee focus to executive focus over the last 30+ years. Unions, at least in some fashion, are to blame for this, as they have over negotiated benefits and pushed large employers to despise them. I am not defending the big companies. Executive pay has certainly risen to astronomical levels. However, I believe Henry Ford's model worked better.

Before getting into a detailed analysis of qualified plans, we need to go back to our thinking section and look at the relationship between finance and the thinking issues we've discussed.

∞

In his book *Thinking, Fast and Slow*, author Daniel Kahneman, once again, states, *"A reliable way to make people believe in falsehoods is frequent repetition, because familiarity is not easily distinguished from truth… Confidence is a feeling, which reflects the coherence of the information and the cognitive ease of processing it. It is wise to take admissions of uncertainty seriously, but declarations of high confidence mainly tell you that an individual has constructed a coherent story in his mind, not necessarily that the story is true."* Modern financial planning is more than likely getting you nowhere. The feeling of being right does not make it right. Moreover, the fact that all the "experts" are saying this or that doesn't make it right either.

Imagine for a moment that you've just visited a mechanic at a local auto shop, Chandler Tire & Auto. Your car has been making an odd noise and you think there's something wrong. You open the glass door to the small lobby area to a middle aged man, Bob the mechanic. He is standing behind the counter area and has just seen you drive up. As you walk up to the counter, you notice that Bob has some marketing material and other paperwork right beside him. You get to the counter and he begins explaining to you how their auto shop is better than every other auto shop. He shows you all of the awards Chandler Tire & Auto has won over the years. He explains, in a very in-depth fashion, that Chandler Tire & Auto's batteries, brake pads, spark plugs, alternators, fuel pumps, oil filters, tires, shocks, oils, and fluids are the best in the business. Here's your conversation with Bob:

Bob: *"How much money do you make?"*

You: *"Why does that matter?"*

Bob: *"I need to know to help fix your car."*

Reluctantly, you tell Bob how much money you make. Bob goes to the back room, runs some calculations, and comes back with a solution for your car. You're a little confused because Bob, nor any other mechanic, has looked under the hood yet. You begin to express that logical concern, but Bob assures you that everyone's problems are the same, and because you make the amount of money you make per year, he knew what needed to be done to fix your car.

Now, why would you ever in a million years take Bob's advice? He clearly hasn't investigated the problem. He cannot know what is wrong with your car. He already has a cookie cutter solution, and the only thing he needed to know about you was how much money you made. Of course, you wouldn't take this advice.

Bob took no time to figure out what was wrong. Would you not go to another auto shop to find someone who actually looked under the hood? What if a physician began prescribing medication without asking many (or any) questions? What if a judge gave a verdict without hearing testimonies from both sides? We would see that as utterly ludicrous.[iii] Yet, everyday, financial "gurus" and professionals prescribe "cookie-cutter" advice without looking under the hood. Self-proclaimed financial experts write books with advice that, they say, is the best for all. And worse, financial advisors and planners all around the country are taught to create plans that are essentially the same for every client they have.

[iii] In the non-rapper sense, of course.

In college, I had a baseball coach who taught every player to have the exact same swing. He is no longer coaching college baseball. The idea that everyone wants (and more importantly, needs) the same path to success is no more logical than the notion that we should all drive the same car or wear the same clothes. Yet, I state again, in finance (and other areas of life) we are taught to do exactly what everyone else is doing.

We've been told that there is one way to do it, with a few possible variations. If you veer from that path, be prepared to be reprimanded by the 'holier-than-thou' financial minds. This is a significant contributing factor to the denigration of the American family financial situation.

CONVENTIONAL INSANITY

" Insanity: doing the same thing over and over again and expecting different results. "
ALBERT EINSTEIN

The financial services industry has recognized for many years that most individuals crater in the face of information - in the face of having to choose between many options. So what have they done? Boiled it down to a few options from which you have to choose. And, if they are choosing the few options to have to choose from, which options do you think they're going to give—those that tilt in your favor or in theirs?

Qualified plans have become the standard savings plan for the majority of Americans. Chances are that you have a qualified plan of some sort (either a 401(k), 403(b), IRA, SEP, 457, or one of the many other qualified plans that exist). Most people have been taught (and I used to teach) that qualified plans are the most efficient places to save money. Typically, you put money away before taxes[iv], allow it to grow tax-deferred, and then pay taxes when you take the money out after age 59 ½. At that time, the logic goes; you'll be in a lower tax bracket. Only one major problem—that's not what's happening.

How does this sound for logic:

Conventional Financial Planner (CFP): *Hey, uh... Mr. Jones. Uh, I've got this good plan for you. While you're... uh... working... ya know... you should put money in this 401(k) account. You're not going to pay taxes on it now. In fact, you're not going to pay taxes on it until you retire.*

Mr. Jones: *Oh, okay. I guess that sounds good. However, what if I need the money before I retire?*

CFP: *Well, you can't touch it until you're 59 ½.*

Mr. Jones: *Hmmm. That doesn't sound so good.*

CFP: *Wait, wait, wait! There is one clause, it's kind of iffy - but you can take some money out. You just have to pay it back*

[iv] I recently heard a CPA *(of all people!)* refer to a 401(k) as tax-free. His exact words, if I recall correctly, were "Why would you not fund your 401(k)? It's tax-free." While I'm still dumbfounded by this question, it doesn't necessarily surprise me. That is the level of indoctrination that has occurred in all areas of the financial world. Now YOU know – a 401(k) is **NOT** tax-free.

into your account over a certain period of time or you're penalized harshly.

Mr. Jones: *Oh, okay. That doesn't sound very good. Therefore, there must be other benefits. I suppose there's some set tax rate in the future? Something in place so I know what I'm going to pay.*

CFP: *Well, no. There's not. We have no idea the rate of tax will be in the future.*

Mr. Jones: *So, you're saying it's like this - 20 years ago, if I were going to college, and they said, "Mr. Jones, we don't need your money now. You don't have to pay anything for college at this moment. What we're going to do is allow you to go through college with no tuition. We're going to wait 40 years and, at that time, we'll come back to you and tell you what your college costs will be based on how things go between now and then. You'll have to pay us then."*[v] *CFP, is that basically what you're saying?*

CFP: *Well, uh… you see… uh… I've never thought of it that way. It's really just a way to avoid taxes right now.*

Mr. Jones: *Yes, but you're not avoiding taxes. You're just putting them off to a later date.*

CFP: *Okay, Mr. Jones. You're clearly not getting it. So let me explain it another way. Right now, you're earning good money.*

---

[v] Now you see why the CPA's statement was so off base. Saying a 401(k) is "tax-free" is like saying this example is "free college tuition."

My plan for you is to save as much money as you can into this 401(k). When you take money someday in the future, you'll be in a lower tax bracket that you are right now.

Mr. Jones: *How do you know?*

CFP: *Mr. Jones - please make sure you hear me. I'll give you the fact that we don't know where tax rates will be and that uncertainty can be disturbing. However, you're going to keep making more and more money over the years. When you get older and start taking money out, your expenses won't be as high. Your kids will be out of the house and your mortgage will be paid off. Therefore, you won't need as much income. Therefore, you will be in a lower tax bracket.*

Mr. Jones: *So, you're assuming my expenses won't be as high. Let me think through this. I save money today. I sacrifice my lifestyle today. I reach my peak earning years right before I "retire." My kids are out of the house - so I've lost that tax-deduction. My house is paid off - so I've lost that tax deduction. My wife and I are going to be traveling more - so that will be more expensive. CFP - I don't think my expenses are going to be lower.*

CFP: (Silence)

What's interesting about this conversation is that the conventional financial planner was me. This is an actual conversation, to the best of my recollection, that I really had with a client a number of years ago. This was just one of the initial events that made me begin to think about why I was doing what I was doing, and why I believed what I believed. Later, I will address more of the detailed analysis around 401(k)s and other government-qualified plans and why we may need to rethink conventional wisdom. For now, I want you to ask yourself one question:

Do you know why you do what you do, financially?

In most cases, the answer to this question is either *"no"* or *"yes, I think so?"* (which is false). I would venture to guess that over 90% of working professionals are in one of those two categories. As you'll find out soon, not knowing—not fully understanding—your financial strategy could wind up costing you millions. More importantly, it could wind up proving a complete lack of discretion. This is the most tragic of outcomes—especially to people that pride themselves on being the best they can be. I am assuming you are one of those people.

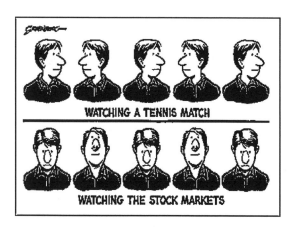

QUALIFIED PLAN ANALYSIS

Countless professional people are infatuated with 401(k) type plans. Yet the founder of these plans, Ted Benna, has called them a *"monster."*[30] Benna's disapproval stems from the fact that 401(k)s (and the like) have become overly complicated and complex.

401(k)s are usually funded with mutual funds or variable annuities. The fees in the average plan are likely north of 2%.[31] In fact, they're probably closer to 3% or 4%. Most people (and most advisors and financial "gurus") make the mistake of looking only at what's called the 'expense ratio.' Advisors and their firms are paid from this fee. However, there's more to it. A 2011 Forbes article by Ty Bernicke found, via a collection of studies, that the average mutual annual fee was 3.17%.[32] The average expense ratio in Bernicke's findings was 0.90%; while the average cost of transactions and cash drag cost, (a type of liquidity charge) totaled 2.27%—equaling 3.17%. Bernicke didn't include other costs—record keeping fees, trustee costs, 12b-1 fees, wrap fees, brokerage window fees, sales charges, early redemption fees, excessive transaction costs, and other miscellaneous administrative costs[33]— included in qualified plans.

Frankly, it doesn't matter if you don't believe me. It doesn't matter if your human resources director, your 401(k) or 403(b) administrator, or your financial advisor espouses that the fees aren't that high. They are. We have done numerous studies with real people and their real DC qualified plans.[vi] In one particular case, a 59-year-old physician had funded qualified plans and other tax-deferred accounts at about $28,000 per year (on average) from 1986 to 2013. I

[vi] You can read these studies in the Case Studies section.

was conservative with the average funding number out of a desire to make sure the analysis gave her 401(k) plan the benefit of the doubt, rather than the other way around. Her balance at the end of 2013, after nearly 28 years of annual payments, was just under $1.5 million. This physician was never taught how to calculate the net CAGR—the actual annual rate of return she was earning—which is extremely important.[vii] Her true rate of return was about 4.39%. And that was on the end. Yet, over this same period, the S&P's index performed at a 7.64% CAGR (not including dividends).

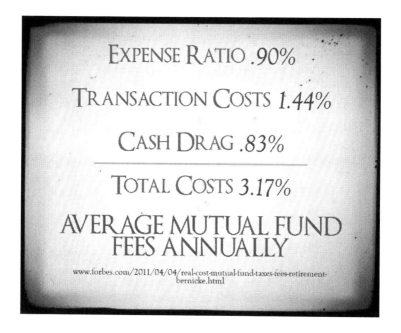

EXPENSE RATIO .90%

TRANSACTION COSTS 1.44%

CASH DRAG .83%

TOTAL COSTS 3.17%

AVERAGE MUTUAL FUND
FEES ANNUALLY

www.forbes.com/2011/04/04/real-cost-mutual-fund-taxes-fees-retirement-bernicke.html

---

[vii] See the *How To...* section to learn to calculate the CAGR and the average rate of return all by your lonesome. You can also go to TheFallofLogic.com/CAGR.

ANNUAL PMT $27,000

YEARS   27.50

ENDING VALUE 1,450,000

CAGR   4.39%

REALITY...

Based on actual case of individual who invested
from 1986 to 2013.

By reverse engineering this lady's reality, we find that she likely had a total of 3.04% yearly fees and charges. Table 8.1 details our best guess as to how her situation likely played out. Remember, this is a hypothetical recreation; but her situation—her ridiculously below average annualized rate of return—is real.

Calendar Year	S&P Returns* (without dividends)	Annual Investment	Interest Earnings	Annual Fees & Charges	End of Year Account Value
1986	25.33	$27,000	$6,839	($1,029)	$32,810
1987	4.56	$27,000	$2,727	($1,901)	$60,637
1988	6.42	$27,000	$5,626	($2,835)	$90,428
1989	31.03	$27,000	$36,438	($4,678)	$149,188
1990	(7.10)	$27,000	($12,509)	($4,976)	$158,703
1991	21.52	$27,000	$39,963	($6,860)	$218,806
1992	4.31	$27,000	$10,594	($7,795)	$248,605
1993	13.52	$27,000	$37,262	($9,511)	$303,356
1994	2.18	$27,000	$7,202	($10,262)	$327,296
1995	34.88	$27,000	$123,578	($14,527)	$463,347
1996	24.43	$27,000	$119,792	($18,548)	$591,591
1997	23.63	$27,000	$146,173	($23,249)	$741,515
1998	15.31	$27,000	$117,660	($26,940)	$859,235
1999	23.66	$27,000	$209,683	($33,316)	$1,062,602
2000	(6.26)	$27,000	($68,209)	($31,050)	$990,343
2001	(5.38)	$27,000	($54,733)	($29,263)	$933,346
2002	(14.55)	$27,000	($139,730)	($24,947)	$795,669
2003	20.94	$27,000	$172,267	($30,246)	$964,690
2004	3.07	$27,000	$30,445	($31,073)	$991,062
2005	1.10	$27,000	$11,199	($31,290)	$997,971
2006	15.00	$27,000	$153,746	($35,833)	$1,142,884
2007	4.56	$27,000	$53,347	($37,186)	$1,186,045
2008	(30.74)	$27,000	($372,890)	($25,541)	$814,614
2009	17.15	$27,000	$144,337	($29,973)	$955,978
2010	10.27	$27,000	$100,952	($32,951)	$1,050,978
2011	6.23	$27,000	$67,158	($34,812)	$1,110,324
2012	8.19	$27,000	$93,147	($37,406)	$1,193,065
2013	22.58	$27,000	$275,491	($45,465)	$1,450,090

Assuming Annual Fees & Charges of 3.04% Table 8.1

*S&P Returns from 1986-2013 without dividends (Source: Pinnacle Data Corp)

In Table 8.1, you can see the S&P returns and losses in each year, along with a 3.04% annual fee. This is a recreation of what likely happened in her qualified plans. You'll notice that her ending balance in 2013 is $1,450,090. What is thought-provoking and equally alarming is how different this is than what she thought she'd have. If she had expected a 12% annual rate of return—because that's what was shown by many up until just a few years ago—she would have thought she'd have over $5.7 million (Table 8.2). That's a delta of $4.3 million. If she'd expected $5.7 million, she would have ended up with 75% less—a stark difference. Even if she had expected that actual CAGR of the S&P from 1986 to 2013, 7.64%, she still would have ended up with 45% less. That 7.64% CAGR would've resulted in over $2.6 million. However, she had innocently been swindled. All she saw was the roughly $750,000 she'd put in and her $1.45 million account value. Her statements proclaimed that her average annualized return was 7.5% or so. On the surface, it sounded okay. However, that was a gross average rate of return, not a net CAGR. She didn't know to expect any different.

Table 8.2

Assuming 12% CAGR and No Fees

$27,000 Per Year Investment

Calendar Year	S&P Returns* (without dividends)	Interest Earnings	End of Year Account Value
1986	12.00%	$3,240	$30,240
1987	12.00%	$6,869	$64,109
1988	12.00%	$10,933	$102,042
1989	12.00%	$15,485	$144,527
1990	12.00%	$20,583	$192,110
1991	12.00%	$26,293	$245,403
1992	12.00%	$32,688	$305,092
1993	12.00%	$39,851	$371,943
1994	12.00%	$47,873	$446,816
1995	12.00%	$56,858	$530,674
1996	12.00%	$66,921	$624,595
1997	12.00%	$78,191	$729,786
1998	12.00%	$90,814	$847,600
1999	12.00%	$104,952	$979,552
2000	12.00%	$120,786	$1,127,339
2001	12.00%	$138,521	$1,292,859
2002	12.00%	$158,383	$1,478,242
2003	12.00%	$180,629	$1,685,871
2004	12.00%	$205,545	$1,918,416
2005	12.00%	$233,450	$2,178,866
2006	12.00%	$264,704	$2,470,570
2007	12.00%	$299,708	$2,797,278
2008	12.00%	$338,913	$3,163,192
2009	12.00%	$382,823	$3,573,014
2010	12.00%	$432,002	$4,032,016
2011	12.00%	$487,082	$4,546,098
2012	12.00%	$548,772	$5,121,870
2013	12.00%	$617,864	$5,766,734

*S&P Returns from 1986-2013 without dividends (Source: Pinnacle Data Corp)

Table 8.3

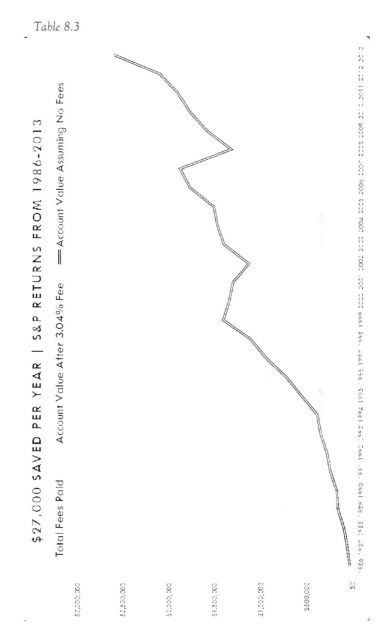

$27,000 SAVED PER YEAR | S&P RETURNS FROM 1986-2013

Total Fees Paid   Account Value After 3.04% Fee   Account Value Assuming No Fees

WAIT, THERE'S MORE...

We're not quite done yet. I mentioned at the beginning of this chapter that the match and tax breaks don't help you—that they aren't advantageous. Let me validate. Thanks to Todd Langford and Kim Butler at TruthConcepts.com, the myths of conventional qualified plans [viii] have been fully exposed. Here are the assumptions:

401(K) MATCH & TAX ANALYSIS

35 YEAR OLD—TEDDY, WE'LL CALL HIM

$100,000 CURRENT ACCOUNT VALUE—I.E. THE MUTUAL FUNDS INSIDE THE 401(K)

FUNDING $10,000 PER YEAR FOR THE NEXT 30 YEARS (TO AGE 64)

ASSUMING A 7% CAGR ON ASSETS

Table 8.4 shows the Teddy starting with $100,000 and investing $10,000 per year. In the end, he has a little over $1.7 million.

[viii] It is important to note that self-directed qualified plans allow one to invest in index funds, individual stocks and bonds, and other assets (like real estate or commodities). This has been an analysis of conventional qualified plans which are funded with mutual funds and variable annuities.

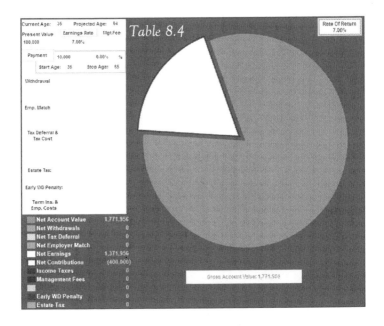

In the next table, 8.5, Teddy is receiving a match from his employer of $5,000. Therefore, he'd invested $10,000 per year, and his employer is giving him $5,000 of "free money." You'll notice that his account value jumps to almost $2.3 million, from $1.7 million in Table 8.4. His CAGR (top right corner) also jumps from 7% to 8.09%. This is because the "free money" he is getting increases his felt rate of return—meaning, he'd have to earn 8.09% on his $10,000 to equal the match his employer is providing. He's still earning the 7% CAGR on the total assets in the account, but the match, in this case, is boosting his net CAGR. This is where most people stop. They see what looks like an obvious no-brainer—conventional wisdom. However, we must take it further. We must look at the entire situation in *context*.

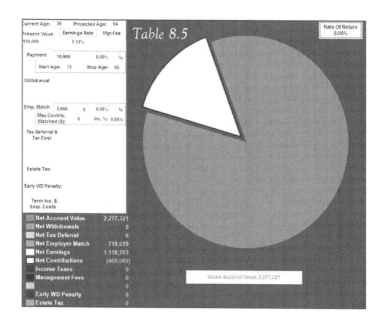

Current Age:	36	Projected Age:	64					
Present Value		Earnings Rate	Mgt.Fee					
100,000		7.00%						

Table 8.5

Rate Of Return
8.09%

Payment	10,000		0.00%	%
Start Age:	36	Stop Age:	65	

Withdrawal

Emp. Match	5,000	$	0.00%	%
Max.Contrib. Matched ($):		0	Inc. %: 0.00%	

Tax Deferral &
Tax Cost

Estate Tax:

Early WD Penalty:

Term Ins. &
Emp. Costs

Net Account Value	2,277,321
Net Withdrawals	0
Net Tax Deferral	0
Net Employer Match	718,619
Net Earnings	1,158,703
Net Contributions	(400,000)
Income Taxes	0
Management Fees	0
	0
Early WD Penalty	0
Estate Tax	0

Gross Account Value: 2,277,321

In Table 8.6, we factor in the great killer of assets—which is, of course, fees. If we use a 2% total annual fee (below the average), Teddy's account value falls to $1.43 million. His CAGR falls to 6.07%. The fee alone has reduced his account value (before taxes) by nearly half. However, *wait, there's more...*

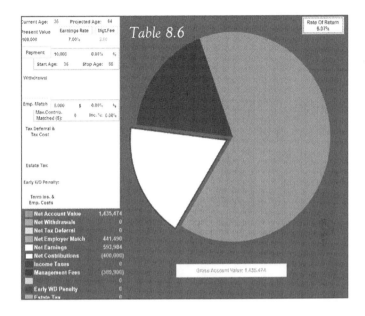

Table 8.6

Current Age: 36	Projected Age: 64	Rate Of Return 6.07%
Present Value 100,000	Earnings Rate 7.00%	Mgt.Fee 2.00
Payment 10,000	0.00% %	
Start Age: 36	Stop Age: 66	

Withdrawal

| Emp. Match 5,000 | $ | 0.00% % |
| Max.Contrib. Matched (%): 0 | Inc.%: 0.00% | |

Tax Deferral & Tax Cost

Estate Tax:

Early WD Penalty:

Term Ins. & Emp. Costs

Net Account Value	1,435,474
Net Withdrawals	0
Net Tax Deferral	0
Net Employer Match	441,490
Net Earnings	593,984
Net Contributions	(400,000)
Income Taxes	0
Management Fees	(369,900)
	0
Early WD Penalty	0
Estate Tax	0

Gross Account Value: 1,435,474

When we factor in taxes, the situation becomes even more dismal. Assuming that taxes will be the same when he's 64 as they are today, and then there is no tax advantage to the 401(k). The qualified plan is not a tax deduction, but is a tax deferral. It is simply an option to delay taxes... or maybe a pension for the government. Table 8.7 shows taxes being the same today as they are in the future. Teddy doesn't lose, but he doesn't win either. However, where do you think income taxes are headed?

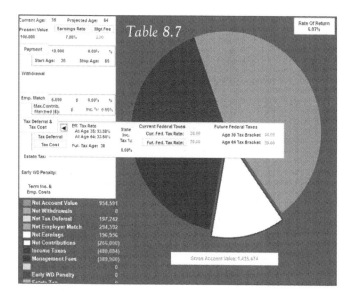

Table 8.7

Table 8.8 shows the effect of federal income taxes rising from 30% to 35%. I'm not assuming that we can know were taxes are going. The overarching point is that it won't be fun to have the majority of your life savings in 401(k)s or similar plans if they do rise. In Teddy's case, his net account value drops to $886,405 and his net CAGR to 5.81%. The point—neither the match nor the "tax break" on his contributions did any good. Additionally, he had to suffer through periods of extreme market volatility and lack of liquidity. All for a benefit that was for naught—a fairytale.

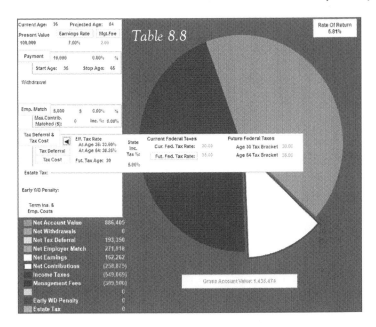

Current Age: 36	Projected Age: 64
Present Value	Earnings Rate	Mgt.Fee
100,000	7.00%	2.00

Table 8.8

Rate Of Return
6.81%

| Payment | 10,000 | 0.00% | % |
| Start Age: 36 | Stop Age: 65 |

Withdrawal

| Emp. Match | 5,000 | $ | 0.00% | % |
| Max.Contrib. Matched ($): | 0 | Inc. %: 0.00% |

Tax Deferral & Tax Cost
Eff. Tax Rate	At Age 36: 32.60%
Tax Deferral	At Age 64: 38.25%
Tax Cost	Fut. Tax Age: 39

State Inc. Tax %	Current Federal Taxes		Future Federal Taxes	
	Cur. Fed. Tax Rate:	20.00	Age 36 Tax Bracket	30.00
5.00%	Fut. Fed. Tax Rate:	35.00	Age 64 Tax Bracket	35.00

Estate Tax:

Early WD Penalty:

Term Ins. & Emp. Costs

Net Account Value	886,405
Net Withdrawals	0
Net Tax Deferral	193,350
Net Employer Match	271,918
Net Earnings	162,262
Net Contributions	(258,875)
Income Taxes	(549,669)
Management Fees	(389,980)
	0
Early WD Penalty	0
Estate Tax	0

Gross Account Value: 1,436,474

Very quickly, imagine Teddy had a (likely) more realistic fee of 3%. Then his federal income taxes rise to 40% and he experiences a CAGR similar to the one we saw from 2000-2014, 3.5% or so. Now, in our final Table 8.9, he's down to an account value of $409,334and a 2.38% net CAGR. Ouch.

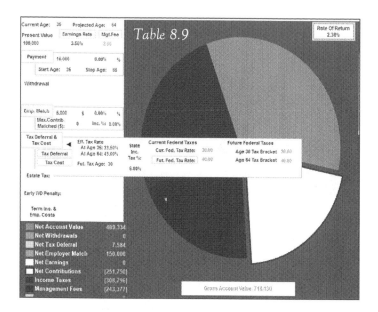

Conclusion: it doesn't matter *who* says *what* about qualified plans. The negatives heavily outweigh the positives.

∞

ALWAYS ASK "WHY?"

Hearing an explanation for why others make decisions, or why they want us to make certain decisions, is not enough. **In order to grow, we must continuously ask *why*? We must be determined to dig deeper to get to the root of the subject.** What most people are doing financially isn't working. And they are doing it because someone told them to, not because they understand it. It's nothing to take offense at. It just is what it is. What most financial advisors are advising isn't going to work either. There's much to review, but it will make you better. I promise. The process of learning and growing is ahead, even if you've already achieved great financial success. In fact, if you've already achieved great financial success, then this process of learning to ask *why?* Is even more important. And you probably already do it in many business and financial areas. If you have not yet achieved financial success, then the process of learning and asking questions is just as vital. If we want to succeed, which I'm sure we all do, we must think 'outside the box' and refuse to conform. Conformity leads to mediocrity. Don't take my word for it. Verify it.

B. Chase Chandler

QUESTIONS TO CONTEMPLATE:

IF YOU'VE EVER MET WITH A FINANCIAL PLANNER OR ADVISOR, HOW DID IT GO?

DO YOU BELIEVE YOU'RE 'FOLLOWING THE CROWD' FINANCIALLY? WHY OR WHY NOT?

IF YOU HAVE A 401(K), 403(B), SEP, TRADITIONAL IRA, OR ANY OTHER MUTUAL FUND OR VARIABLE ANNUITY—ATTEMPT TO COMPILE HOW MUCH YOU'VE FUNDED IN EACH YEAR AND WHAT YOUR CURRENT ACCOUNT VALUE IS. THEN GO TO THEFALLOFLOGIC.COM/CAGR TO CALCULATE YOUR NET CAGR.

11

THE ART OF DECEPTION

" Deceiving others. That is what the world calls a romance."
OSCAR WILDE

" The great masses of the people will more easily fall victims to a big lie than to a small one."
ADOLF HITLER

WE HAVE MORE INFORMATION AT our fingertips than any society in history. If we want to learn about something, we can simply Google it and receive every opinion that exists on any subject. So, the question is, why are American finances in the worst shape since The Great Depression? The answer is simpler than you might think.

Today, you will find most Americans don't save much and don't have a family budget. Of the families that do save, you'll find that the vast majority have money in the stock market. As of 2011, 54% of all Americans own stocks or mutual funds. This number has fluctuated between 54-% since 1999. Now consider that 28% of Americans don't save at all. That means that three-quarters of Americans who do save have money in the market. (Considering that roughly 40-50% of Americans are children or do not work, the number of working Americans investing in the stock market is probably closer to 95% or more.)

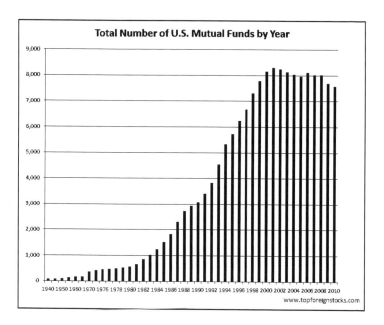

Perhaps one of the best ways to understand effective financial planning and the problems we face is to look back at history. Our country became the world's dominant nation faster than any country in history. Our ancestors came to know greater convenience and financial stability than any society before them. The "Greatest Generation," a term coined by Tom Brokaw in his book of the same title, is the one that lived through the Great Depression, which led many of them to fully appreciate the wealth we have in our country. Because of living through the catastrophe of the 1930s, many of these families gained a strong focus on frugality. Because of this focus, they built more financial security, per household, then we had ever seen before. But most of them didn't build it through the stock market.

John C. Bogle, founder of Vanguard, has been one of the greatest innovators of financial thought of our time. His experience and knowledge warrant deep study. In 2000 he gave a speech before the Town Hall of Cleveland entitled *Financial Markets and the Mutual Fund Industry*, in which he went back to his start in the financial services industry. "In 1950, stocks and bonds were barely in the public consciousness; now they seem rarely out of it. Then, past market returns had been dull and plodding; since then they have been the highest in all of US history. Then, the dividend yield on stocks was three times the bond yield; now the bond yield is nearly seven times the yield on stocks. Then, the market was dominated by individuals; now it is dominated by financial institutions ... In 1950, perhaps one million families—1 in 45—owned common stocks."

What Bogle is was saying is that in his day, people did not rely on the stock market to sustain their financial future. Depending upon on the market is a recent phenomenon. In 1950, only 2.2% of the population owned common stock!

∞

As previously established, the 401(k) plan was introduced by Congress in 1980. Previous to 1980, there was no arbitrary stock market vehicle into which Americans could blindly throw money. Most Americans kept the majority of their life savings very safe. They may have had a few stocks here and there or some money in a mutual fund, but it certainly was not the majority of their savings. In 1980, all of that changed. All of the sudden, working Americans were aggressively encouraged by Wall Street and the government to put their life savings into 401(k)s and the like. This fundamentally changed the way markets worked. From 1901 to 1979, the true rate of return in the Dow Jones Industrial Index was 3.57%. From 1980-1999 the true rate in the Dow was 14.01%! How did this happen? Let's think about that. If 2.2% of families had money in stocks or mutual funds in 1950, then it likely wasn't that much different in 1979. How many people do you know who have 401(k)s, IRAs or something similar? Pretty much everyone with a job. After the 401(k) was instituted, the markets began to roar like never before. As humans, we psychologically live in the moment or in the past – not in the future. Many of us cannot imagine what we're going to do next month, much less in 20 years. So everyone was looking at the market with the mantra "What have you done for me lately?" And it was doing a lot. As equities went up, more and more individuals and institutions put more money in. Remember supply and demand from college economics? If more people want to buy more of the same thing, what happens to the price? It goes up.

Remember this –

1. When someone buys something, it means someone else is selling.

2. In order for stocks to rise, company earnings and net profits need to rise as well.

From 1980 to 1999, we forgot those two keys to investing. People ignored the fact that every time they bought stocks or mutual funds, someone else was selling it to them. That means someone else was benefiting from their buying by selling at a profit and/or charging fees. Wall Street, Main Street, and the government also overlooked the notion that stocks should be rational. To say stocks are rational today is a blatant falsehood. Any fund manager or analyst will tell you that stocks go up and down based on what people think they're going to do in the future. This means that a company can be performing poorly, but the stock can be rising at the same time; this can happen if analysts or buyers believe the stock price could go up later. Does this make any sense? I don't think so. But as long as the market kept going up and up, no one asked questions. There was no reason to think logically or think about the future when the present was so fantastic.

Consider this tale:

In 2005, a young woman wanted to start a cupcake business. She was a finance major in college, focusing on stocks, futures and option trading, and had only graduated a few years before. She wanted to run her cupcake shop the way the publically traded companies ran theirs - by having shareholders who would buy in and own portions of the company. She started out by approaching people around town to buy shares in her cupcake shop. Once she sold 100 shares for $250 each, she was ready to open up. She used the $25,000 she had raised to get a lease on a building as well as pay herself and her new assistant a good first two months' salary.

This lady was smart and knew that her investors would want to see how their investment was doing, so she set up a website where the shareholders could check on how their stock in the company was doing. The investors loved it - each day they could see if their shares were going up or down. Then a financial analyst came to visit the shop. He told the lady that if she would value her business based on future sales, then the stock price could rise faster and she could get more investors. The analyst explained that the more investors the company got, the more money the company would have to work with and the more money she could pay herself in bonuses for her hard work. Hearing this, the young woman became very excited.

So the next day, she decided to estimate how many cupcakes she would sell the next quarter and base the stock price on that. She figured the cupcake factory could increase sales by 20% over the next three months, so she raised the stock price to $60. Seeing this increase, many of the original investors started to tell their friends, and many more investors flooded in. The more investors that wanted to buy shares, the more she would raise the price of them. (She remembered supply and demand from her economics class in college.) The process repeated itself three or four times in the first two years of the businesses opening.

She gave herself and her assistant hefty bonuses for their hard work and used the rest of the money to start a second store and buy more cupcake materials for their expected sales.

After two years, the stock price had risen to $100 a share. The shares had increased by more than 40% each year for the original investors. Unfortunately, sales began to level off. Investors started to notice, so they began calling to take their money out and invest in other lucrative opportunities. After she gave a few of the investors their money, the analyst came back and told her she had to lower her stock price. "Why?" she asked passionately. The analyst explained, "If shareholders are selling back their stock, that means it's not as valuable as it was before." Disappointed at this thought, the young lady got on her computer and changed the share price downwards to $90.

Within a few hours, the cupcake factory received calls from almost every shareholder demanding their money because of the abrupt 10% drop in price. This shocked the lady and threw her into a panic. How could she repay all of the shareholders? She couldn't sell cupcakes that fast. They had priced the shares based on the future sales, not current sales. She would have to sell some of her equipment and lay off her assistant.

Finally, when many of the shareholders had been repaid, the stock price was lowered down to $45. The following morning, the young lady woke up to a startling realization - she didn't have the help or the equipment to bake the cupcakes she had to sell. She went to the bank to get a loan, but they wouldn't give one to her because the government was tightening up on regulations and she didn't have much cash.

Within a few months, the business closed and the remaining shareholders lost their investment.

This story brings us to the conclusion that stocks cannot survive long term unless they are priced correctly. When they are not priced correctly, unknowing investors are fleeced, as depicted by the last shareholders that lost her money in the story.

In the 2000s, we all found out that the stock market was overvalued, something that sound money experts had been calling for years. We can only truly have sound money and a brighter financial future if we go back to how people managed money previous to 1980 – safely. Since the great crash of 2008, we have only exacerbated the problem. The appreciation of equities, in many ways, seems like a great comeback and seems to validate those who preached the 'buy and hold' methodology. But it's artificial. It feels good for the moment, but it will, at some point, come to a devastating end. The markets can only be manipulated for so long. No one knows exactly when the massive correction will occur—I would speculate that it will be in the next 10 years. The mutual fund and retail investment industries are desperate to keep equity prices artificially high. This is not to say that you shouldn't own stocks. But you should be more careful than the average investor.

∞

"The mutual fund industry has been built, in a sense, on witchcraft."

JOHN C. BOGLE

As we've already begun to discuss, fees can be the greatest detriment to your financial planning strategy. In this chapter we are going to look at how detrimental they really are. For some reason, the idea of "fee-based financial planning" has permeated the financial community. The overwhelming reason for this is the fact that the SEC has come out essentially in full favor of this fee-based financial planning model. There are basically three ways for financial advisors to work with their clients. On a commission basis, on fee-based terms, and on a fee-for-service basis.

The **commission basis** is typically where a large commission comes out upfront from the client's account. For instance, a person puts $100,000 in in a mutual fund with her broker, and that broker takes 5% off the top. These are typically called "A-Share mutual funds." Therefore, she now has $95,000 that will grow over time with some sort of annual fee around .20% to 1.5%. (I know that's a large range. The annual trails, transaction costs, and other fees are largely determined by how actively the fund is managed.)

The second type of planning model is the **fee-based** model. In a fee-based model, an advisor may earn 1% to 2% on average per year, depending on the client's total assets. This has become a very popular model, again, mainly because of the SEC's endorsement of it. The main reason this model has become popular, or at least the reason it initially became popular, is that it (allegedly) created a situation where the advisor could be more objective, looking at the client's needs first. In a fee-based financial planning scenario, the advisor is not actually selling a product for commission; rather, the advisor is selling a portfolio of products, and that advisor will make the same amount of money regardless of which fund or funds he puts his client into. He will receive a percentage of the overall assets each year. Theoretically, the advisor has mitigated a conflict of interest. On the surface it sounds good, but in reality it is the most costly way to invest—primarily when managed by the large firms.

These large firms (think of the common ads you see on TV) typically proclaim a fee of 1-2%. The advisor is not actually managing the money, but simply selling the services; then receiving a percentage of the percentage. Say, if the fee is 1.5% per year, a common total fee at some of the larger firms, the advisor might receive 60% of the total fee, or 0.90% of the fee. The firm then takes the rest, which pays the supervisors and company itself.

The third model is called **fee-for-service.** In this type of model, the advisor is not selling a product. Rather, she is selling her wisdom and advice for a consulting fee. There is no financial transaction taking place. Just like your attorney or your CPA doesn't actually sell you a prepackaged product, the same thing is occurring here. In this scenario, the advisor provides the client recommendations, but she is not going to make anything from that fund or portfolio management strategy. She is simply paid on an invoiced basis. As you will see, this is probably the least popular of all the models. Yet, it can be most cost effective.

As we progress, you will learn to calculate the cost effectiveness of each of these three options.

"*THE VERY FIRST PRINCIPLE THAT MUST BE UNDERSTOOD IS THAT YOU FINANCE EVERYTHING YOU BUY—YOU EITHER PAY INTEREST TO SOMEONE ELSE OR YOU GIVE UP INTEREST YOU COULD HAVE EARNED OTHERWISE.*"

R. NELSON NASH

12

CALCULATING THE TIME VALUE OF EVERYTHING

" Lost time is never found again."
BENJAMIN FRANKLIN

I VIVIDLY REMEMBER SITTING IN CLASS. It is actually one of the few things I remember from my undergraduate studies. I think it was some sort of management or strategy course, but I really don't remember. Professor Mike Emerson was a CPA and auditor by trade, but he was not your typical accountant. His mannerisms and charisma filled the room. I think it was my sophomore year—to be honest, most of college is a haze. For some reason, though, this single moment in time is glued in my memory, when Mike stated quite emphatically: *"soon, I'm going to teach you about the time value of money!"* I couldn't figure out why he was so excited about the "time value" of money. I wasn't the best of students, nor (as my teachers would tell you) the most intellectually mature. *Why would time have value and what would that have to do with money?*, I thought. Yet this is the most important concept in finance. I'd later travel to London with Mike and begin the process of actually learning about business. It was on that trip that I developed an interest, which later became a passion, in finance, financial processes, and calculations—although it would be a while before I came to fully comprehend the importance of Mike's lessons. Sometime after I graduated, he was fired for reasons of which I'm still unaware (and may like to stay unaware). Perhaps it was valid. Or perhaps he was just too unconventional for the academic world.

The importance of Time Value of Money (TVM), the concept and the principle, is widely unknown or misinterpreted by the masses. Yet, one must comprehend and learn to calculate it (in its various forms) if he or she wishes to comprehend financial circumstance and alternate solutions. I believe it has been established that *comprehension* is vital. In fact, I find it even more interesting that it's not only money that has a time value, but nearly *everything*. Let us define the relevant terms.

TVM Calculations

There are five primary variables in TVM calculations. As long as we have four of the five, we can solve for the fifth. They are:

> **Time** : measured most often in years; but also in months, weeks, or days.

Interest : the rate of interest one would earn (on an investment) or pay (on a loan) during the time represented in the calculation.

Present Value : the starting balance of an investment or the amount of the starting loan balance.

Payment : a consistent payment made into an investment or against a loan through each of the time periods.

Future Value : the ending value after all other variables are taken into consideration.

If our sample man, Joseph Dirt, wanted to calculate the payment of a new car, all we'd have to know are the other four variables. Assume he thinks the loan would be $25,000, the interest rate would be 5%, and the time period to pay the car off would be 60 months. Think for a moment about the variables—what we have and what we don't. We can use these assumptions to solve for Mr. Dirt's monthly payment in Microsoft Excel or using a financial calculator.

Dirt wants a $25,000 loan; this would be the beginning loan balance—the present value.

PV = 25,000

He believes he can get a 5% loan rate—this is the rate or i. We will enter the rate in a numerical format (i.e. .05 rather than 5%).

i = .05

He'd like to pay the loan off in a matter of 60 months (5 years). When entering this time period, it's most simple to enter it in years then divide the final number by 12. However, this will not give you the exact answer (we will discuss this further in a moment). For now, let's use 5 as the time or n (number of periods).

n = 5

So we know the present value, interest rate, and time variables. We're missing the future value and the payment. Via deductive reasoning, we can figure the future value (the ending balance). In this case it would be $0, because Dirt would be paying the loan off at the end of 5 years. Now we have four of the five. All we have to do is plug the numbers into a spreadsheet or our financial calculator. For the sake of time and ease, we'll use spreadsheets—they are the future anyway.

You can download a spreadsheet that will help you calculate (and teach you how to solve for) all five TVM variables at **TheFallofLogic.com/CAGR**. If you're interested in mastering the concept and calculations of TVM, I recommend visiting Khan Academy's TVM section. Just Google "Khan Academy Time Value of Money."

Using the spreadsheet from TheFallofLogic.com/CAGR, we can easily solve for Joseph Dirt's payment:

payment

n	5
i	0.05
pv	$25,000.00
pmt	($5,774.37)
fv	$0.00

Now let's assume that Joe, instead of wanting to take a loan for a car, had $25,000 sitting in a bank account. He wants to analyze the viability of two investment alternatives—one that pays 3% per year over 5 years, and another that pays 7% over 7 years. However, in the latter option Joe must divide the $25,000 over the period; in other words, he can't put it in all at once. In option one, we know *i*, *n*, *pv*, and *pmt* ($0 because we're not investing anything on an ongoing basis).

For option two, we know *i*, *n*, *pmt* ($25,000 divided by 7 years), and *pv* ($0 because we're starting with nothing in the investment and funding it annually). In both options, we are solving for *fv*.

But there's a catch, a distinction, when solving for savings amounts as compared to loan calculations. When we're solving for savings or investing problems, we enter the money being saved as a negative (think of it as money going away; negative = going out of our pocket; positive = coming into our pocket[i]). In this equation we'll enter *pmt* and/or *pv* as a negative.

future value

n	5
i	0.03
pv	($25,000.00)
pmt	$0.00
fv	$28,981.85

To solve for Mr. Dirt's option, we must first run the 5-year equation. Then, using the resulting *fv*, $28,981.85, we complete another calculation for 2 years. This is done because the investment we're comparing it to is 7 years. We can see that he has $30,746.84 at the end of the 7-year period.

---

[i] This seems backwards, I know. But this is how the financial authorities have set it up. However, if you ever find yourself using TruthConcepts software, contrarian Todd Langford has set it up so that negatives are for loan amounts and positives are for investment payments and present values.

future value

n	2
i	0.03
pv	($28,981.85)
pmt	$0.00
fv	. $30,746.84

In the second option, we are looking at 7% for 7 years. And the $25,000 must be invested in equal installments over the period—$3,571.43 per year. Now we enter that number as a negative and find that the future value equals $30,907.22, slightly more than the original $25,000, growing at 3% from the beginning. What we find is that, in this case, Joe would be better off going with option two. The point of this is simply to show you how TVM calculations are done. And once you get the hang of it, it's as easy as riding a Boss Hoss motorcycle with a Chevy V8 502 cubic inch engine with a semi-automatic transmission.

future value

n	7
i	0.07
pv	$0.00
pmt	($3,571.43)
fv	$30,907.22

TVM EQUATIONS

What we've just been through are the basic calculations. In many cases, that is all you'll need. As you progress it may be beneficial to learn how to calculate more complex TVM equations such as the *future value of inconsistent cash-flows* (i.e. investing or receiving varying or increasing payment amounts each period).

The following formulas use these common variables:

- PV is the value at time = 0 (present value)
- FV is the value at time = n (future value)
- A is the value of the individual payments in each compounding period
- n is the number of periods (not necessarily an integer)
- i is the discount rate, or the interest rate at which the amount will be compounded each period
- g is the growing rate of payments over each time period

PV OF A FUTURE SUM

The present value formula is the core formula for the time value of money; each of the other formulae is derived from this formula. For example, the annuity formula is the sum of a series of present value calculations.

The present value (PV) formula has four variables, each of which can be solved for:

$$PV = \frac{FV}{(1+i)^n}$$

The cumulative present value of future cash flows can be calculated by summing the contributions of FV_t, the value of cash flow at time t

$$PV \; = \; \sum_{t=1}^{n} \frac{FV_t}{(1+i)^t}$$

Note that this series can be summed for a given value of n, or when n is ∞. This is a very general formula, which leads to several important special cases given below.

FV OF A PRESENT SUM

The future value (FV) formula is similar and uses the same variables.

$$FV \; = \; PV \cdot (1+i)^n$$

PV OF ANNUITY FOR n PMT PERIODS

In this case, the cash flow values remain the same throughout the n periods. The present value of an annuity (PVA) formula has four variables, each of which can be solved for:

$$PV(A) \; = \; \frac{A}{i} \cdot \left[1 - \frac{1}{(1+i)^n} \right]$$

To get the PV of an annuity due, multiply the above equation by $(1 + i)$.

PV OF A GROWING ANNUITY

In this case, each cash flow grows by a factor of (1+g). Similar to the formula for an annuity, the present value of a growing annuity (PVGA) uses the same variables with the addition of *g* as the rate of growth of the annuity (*A* is the annuity payment in the first period). This is a calculation that is rarely provided for on financial calculators.

Where i ≠ g :

$$PV = \frac{A}{(i - g)} \left[1 - \left(\frac{1 + g}{1 + i} \right)^n \right]$$

Where i = g :

$$PV = \frac{A \times n}{1 + i}$$

To get the PV of a growing annuity due, multiply the above equation by (1 + *i*).

FV OF A GROWING ANNUITY

The future value of a growing annuity (FVA) formula has five variables, each of which can be solved for:

Where i ≠ g :

$$FV(A) = A \cdot \frac{(1 + i)^n - (1 + g)^n}{i - g}$$

Where i = g :

$$FV(A) = A \cdot n(1+i)^{n-1}$$

FORMULA TABLE

The following table summarizes the different formulas commonly used in calculating the time value of money.[8]

Find	Given	Formula
Future value (F)	Present value (P)	$F = P \cdot (1+i)^n$
Present value (P)	Future value (F)	$P = F \cdot (1+i)^{-n}$
Repeating payment (A)	Future value (F)	$A = F \cdot \dfrac{i}{(1+i)^n - 1}$
Repeating payment (A)	Present value (P)	$A = P \cdot \dfrac{i(1+i)^n}{(1+i)^n - 1}$
Future value (F)	Repeating payment (A)	$F = A \cdot \dfrac{(1+i)^n - 1}{i}$
Present value (P)	Repeating payment (A)	$P = A \cdot \dfrac{(1+i)^n - 1}{i(1+i)^n}$
Future value (F)	Gradient payment (G)	$F = G \cdot \dfrac{(1+i)^n - in - 1}{i^2}$

Present value (P)	Gradient payment (G)	$P = G \cdot \dfrac{(1+i)^n - in - 1}{i^2(1+i)^n}$
Fixed payment (A)	Gradient payment (G)	$A = G \cdot \left[\dfrac{1}{i} - \dfrac{n}{(1+i)^n - 1} \right]$
Future value (F)	Exponentially increasing payment (D) Increasing percentage (g)	$F = D \cdot \dfrac{(1+g)^n - (1+i)^n}{g - i}$ (for i ≠ g) $F = D \cdot \dfrac{n(1+i)^n}{1+g}$ (for i = g)
Present value (P)	Exponentially increasing payment (D) Increasing percentage (g)	$P = D \cdot \dfrac{\left(\frac{1+g}{1+i}\right)^n - 1}{g - i}$ (for i ≠ g) $P = D \cdot \dfrac{n}{1+g}$ (for i = g)

Notes:

A is a fixed payment amount, every period.

G is a steadily increasing payment amount that starts at *G* and increases by *G* for each subsequent period.

D is an exponentially or geometrically increasing payment amount, which starts at D and increases by a factor of (1+g) each subsequent period.

http://en.wikipedia.org/wiki/Time_value_of_money

EQUIVALENT, EFFECTIVE, AND NET CALCULATIONS

When solving for TVM variables, it is important to take it one step further and solve for (what I call) the *contextual solution*—that is, the solution that gives you the *complete* answer. When you plug the numbers in correctly, the basic formulas will give you an exact solution for the present value, future value, payment, interest rate, or time period. But there are typically other factors that need to be included to get the contextually correct result. The difference is that the contextual solution takes into account additional economic elements that the basic calculation has not yet considered. The most common contextual equations you might need are *tax-equivalent yield*, *effective rate of return*, and a few variations of *net rate calculations*.

Net Calculations

The beginning point is understanding *net rate calculations*—solving for a variable after one or more things are taken out. A net CAGR is the annualized rate of return after accounting for (subtracting) annual fees. It is easy to do this once we have had an account for a while—we would simply input our actual payments and time period, and then solve for *i* using the TVM formula. However, discovering the annual fees beforehand is a bit difficult. We'd have to dig deeper to find the expense ratios, transaction costs, and so on (think back to chapter 9). After we've found the annual total costs., then comes the mathematical component. A spreadsheet calculation can then show us the net CAGR after fees. (You can find one of these spreadsheets at **TheFallofLogic.com/CAGR**.)

Net present value (NPV), the next net calculation, is "The difference between the present value of cash inflows and the present value of cash outflows. NPV is used in capital budgeting to analyze the profitability of an investment or project."[34] NPV gives us the present value of future inconsistent cash-flows. The basic PV calculation gives us the PV of a future amount or of a consistent stream of payments. For instance, if you want to receive $50,000 per year for 20 years at a 4% rate, you can calculate the PV needed to spinoff that $50,000 each year. However, if you want to look at an increasing payment or a combination of investments and withdrawals, the NPV is needed. It's a bit more complex, but very useful. Our spreadsheets at TheFallofLogic.com/CAGR can help you calculate NPV fairly easily. But, in case you want it for your back pocket, here is the formula:[35]

$$NPV = \sum_{t=1}^{T} \frac{C_t}{(1+r)^t} - C_0$$

where:

C_t = net cash inflow during the period

C_0 = initial investment

r = discount rate, and

t = number of time periods

Effectively Speaking

An *effective rate* is generally the actual real rate when considering monthly, weekly, or daily compounding. For instance, if you had a 5% annual-percentage-rate loan compounded monthly, then the effective rate (the real rate) is not actually 5%. This can be a bit confusing, so let's calculate. The equation for such a scenario is:

$$\text{Effective Rate Of Return} = (1 + \frac{i}{n})^n - 1$$

In this formula, i stands for interest rate; n for the number of compounding periods. In that 5% loan scenario compounded monthly, the application would be:

$$(1 + \frac{.05}{12})^{12} - 1 = .051162$$

In this scenario, our monthly loan rate is .4167% (5% / 12 months). We add one to that number, then raise it to the 12th power. This gives us our effective rate of 5.1162%. This tells us that, for loans, the fewer compounding periods the better; for investments, the more compounding periods per year the better.

Tax-Equivalency

The *tax-equivalent yield*, which is somewhat self-explanatory, solves for the CAGR that would need to be earned in a taxable account to match that of a tax-free account. The equation is:

$$tax \ equivalent \ yield = \frac{Net \ CAGR}{1 - tax \ bracket}$$

If a person had a tax-free account, then **calculating the tax effective rate would produce the rate needed in a taxable account to match the rate in the nontaxable account.** If you were, for instance, earning 5% in a tax free account and were in a 30% effective tax-bracket would simply divide .05 by (1-.30):

$$\frac{.05}{(1 - .30)} = .0714$$

We see that it would take a 7.14% taxable net CAGR to match a 5% tax-free net CAGR.

On the flip side, if a person had a taxable account, you could solve for the tax-free yield you would need to earn in order to match a current taxable yield.

tax free yield = taxable yield × (1 − *tax bracket*)

If you were earning 7% in non-qualified taxable mutual funds and were in a 30% tax-bracket, the formula would be represented in this fashion:

$$.07 \times (1 - .30) = .049$$

Now we see that we would have to earn only 4.9% in a tax-free account to match our 7% in the taxable world.

The combination of each of these formulas gives one the ability to look at variables and analyze the *contextual solution* rather only the gross solution.

∞

THE REALITY OF PAYING CASH

Everything has a cost. And everything has a trade-off. In economics this is known as *opportunity cost*. This goes hand-in-hand with our aforewritten section on *contextual solutions*. The cost of buying a product is not only the amount of money you spend on that product. It is also the alternative opportunity of that amount—what you could have done with that money had you not done the thing that you did.[ii] Rarely do we think about this in the terms of our daily actions, but we should. We should frequently consider the opportunity cost of our regular purchases (and non-financially related transactions, for that matter)—but especially of our larger purchases. Most people are never taught the TVM calculations we just reviewed, yet they are so relevant to every family's effective financial management.

Wikipedia defines it this way: "The *opportunity cost* of a choice is the value of the best alternative forgone, in a situation in which a choice needs to be made between several mutually exclusive alternatives given limited resources..."[36] The more relevant definition (to you and me) might be economist and best-selling author Nelson Nash's definition: "...you either pay interest to someone else or you give up interest you could have earned otherwise." Nash gives us a bit of powerful wisdom here—insight into the most relevant integration of TVM and personal finance: *the cost of money*. This issue is often eluded to in college classroom settings, but not much in a pragmatic sense. A professor might teach about the trade-off of buying this or that; or the opportunity cost of buying a car. However, I've not heard many in the academic world discuss the relevant personal financial ramifications of *the cost of money*. Worse, it is essentially never discussed by financial "gurus."

What we need to readily understand is that 'money has a cost'—a *time value*. The best way to describe this, I think, is to imagine buying a car. We've already used car-buying as an example, so we'll stick with it. Which is a better choice: paying cash for a car or taking on debt to buy that car? Herein lies an important lesson in finance, TVM, and why conventional wisdom and the simplest answer are oft mistaken, without knowing so.

[ii] Nice wording, eh?

Unfortunately, the topic of debt has become oddly divisive. Debt is not inherently evil, but it has been advised against since biblical times. First, we must what debt is and what it is not. Debt, or at least the way it is described in the modern dictionary, is an amount of money that you owe to a person, bank, company, etc[37]. Debt has its pros and cons. You can likely state many of the negatives: lack of ability to make payments and potential bankruptcy, which leads to excessive worry in many situations. Debt is simply a promise against future income.

On the other hand, debt can be a useful and productive tool. Many of the businesses we use every day wouldn't be around if it weren't for their ability to take on (or issue) debt.

Let me give you a slightly different definition of debt than the one I spoke of earlier. Certainly debt is an amount of money that an entity[iii] legally owes to another entity. But I think we should, if we're attempting to optimize our financial position, add another element to this definition. *Real debt* **is a liability that an entity owes another entity above and beyond their liquid assets.** There is a distinction. Debt is anything that's owed. Real debt (or net debt) is the amount of debt you have that you couldn't immediately retire with your existing assets.

In the *Scenario I* graphic, you can see an example of our average Joseph Dirt. In this example, Mr. Dirt has $5,000 in cash before he takes on $20,000 of debt to buy a new car. Now he is in $20,000 of debt, $15,000 of which is real debt. (The word *real* isn't meant to imply that $5,000 of the debt isn't real or literal debt – it certainly is. But rather, that the $15,000 of net debt could not be immediately

---

[iii] By entity, I mean a bank, business, trust, or person that is loaning money to another bank, business, trust, or person.

paid off – therefore it is real or substantial.) The point here is that Mr. Dirt is taking on risk.

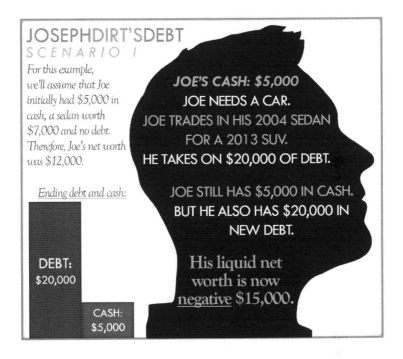

JOSEPH DIRT'S DEBT
SCENARIO I

For this example, we'll assume that Joe initially had $5,000 in cash, a sedan worth $7,000 and no debt. Therefore, Joe's net worth was $12,000.

Ending debt and cash:

DEBT: $20,000

CASH: $5,000

JOE'S CASH: $5,000
JOE NEEDS A CAR.
JOE TRADES IN HIS 2004 SEDAN FOR A 2013 SUV.
HE TAKES ON $20,000 OF DEBT.

JOE STILL HAS $5,000 IN CASH. BUT HE ALSO HAS $20,000 IN NEW DEBT.

His liquid net worth is now negative $15,000.

Now, in *Scenario II*, let's assume a couple of different variables. Joe now has $25,000 in cash and no debt. Joe heard from his parents and on the radio that it was better to pay cash for cars. So, instead of taking on debt, he decides to pay cash for his new SUV. He trades in his sedan, for which he gets a $7,000 credit, and pays $20,000 cash. His liquid net worth is now $5,000. Joe still has no debt. But what did Joe lose? He lost the $20,000. And, as we discussed earlier, he lost the *opportunity* to do something else with that money. He lost what that $20,000 could have grown to (if, of course, he had any alternative use for the capital).

JOSEPHDIRT'SDEBT
SCENARIO II

For this example, we'll assume that Joe initially had $25,000 in cash, a sedan worth $7,000 and no debt. Therefore, Joe's net worth was $32,000.

JOE'S CASH: $25,000

JOE NEEDS A CAR.

JOE TRADES IN HIS 2004 SEDAN FOR A 2013 SUV.

HE SPENDS $20,000 OF ON THIS NEW SUV.

JOE NOW HAS $5,000 IN CASH.

BUT HE HAS DEPLETED HIS CASH BY $20,000.

His liquid net worth is now $5,000.

Ending debt and cash:

DEBT: $0   CASH: $5,000

Now to *Scenario III*. This version of Joseph Dirt has the same cash and debt as *Scenario II* (that is, $25,000 of cash and no debt). Yet, this Joe decides to take a loan of $20,000 rather than use his cash. After buying the SUV, he now has $20,000 of debt, but he's still got his $25,000 of cash. The point of this is to show that there is no difference in Joe's liquid net worth between scenario II and III. In both cases, his liquid net worth is $5,000. If Joe had to pay an interest rate on his car loan (and we'll assume he did) and he wasn't earning interest on his cash, then this would be a bad deal mathematically. But, if all things were equal—if he had a 5% car loan and was earning 5% on his cash—what would the difference be? Would it be better for Joe to take a loan or to use his cash? Think about this question for a moment. Think about it in the context of everything you've read so far. Convention says that it's more expensive to take a loan. However, to repeat the imperative theme, there's more to it than that.

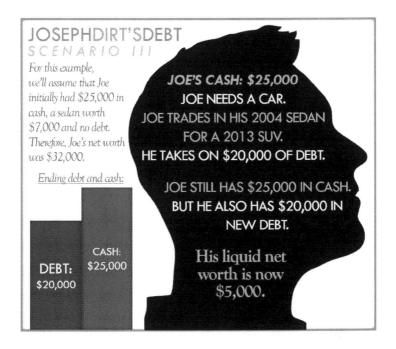

JOSEPHDIRT'SDEBT
SCENARIO III

For this example, we'll assume that Joe initially had $25,000 in cash, a sedan worth $7,000 and no debt. Therefore, Joe's net worth was $32,000.

Ending debt and cash:

DEBT: $20,000

CASH: $25,000

JOE'S CASH: $25,000
JOE NEEDS A CAR.
JOE TRADES IN HIS 2004 SEDAN
FOR A 2013 SUV.
HE TAKES ON $20,000 OF DEBT.

JOE STILL HAS $25,000 IN CASH.
BUT HE ALSO HAS $20,000 IN
NEW DEBT.

His liquid net worth is now $5,000.

The answer to the debt vs. cash question (assuming a 5% loan rate compared to a 5% growth rate and the same time period) is that they are exactly the same. There is not difference between the two. If Joe used his cash to buy the car, then he'd be giving up a (hypothetical) 5% interest rate that he could have earned on that cash. Over a 60 month period, the cash could have grown to $25,667. His opportunity cost was $5,667—that's what he lost. If he takes a loan for $20,000 at a 5% loan rate for 60 months, his monthly payment would be $375.86. So, he is losing that monthly payment each month for 60 months. The lost opportunity cost here is that he could have saved that $375.86 into the account earning 5% over the 60 month period. This would have resulted in an account value of $25,667. His lost opportunity cost of the loan payments were the exact same as if he'd paid cash—$5,667.

The point here is that, all things being equal, there is no difference between cash and debt. The "gurus" have it wrong. That's not to say that we should take out debt up to our liquid savings just for the sake of it. Any debt incurred will, of course, have an interest rate (cost) tied to it. But, if used properly, debt can be extremely productive. We will soon get to just how productive it can be.

In truth, everything has a cost. Every choice you make has some cost tied to it. To get or not to get married. To have or not to have kids. To take or not to take that job. To mow or not to mow the lawn. You have to give something up to get something else. There is no way around it. The lack of comprehension, or at least practical understanding, of economic trade-offs in everyday life leads many to misunderstand the choices they have. When you do things that you shouldn't do, they lead to adverse consequences. When you negate study for leisure, you are trading short-term pleasure for long-term struggle. The same concept that is true in economics is true in life.

> *"Winners embrace hard work. They love the discipline of it, the trade-off they're making to win. Losers, on the other hand, see it as punishment. And that's the difference."*
>
> LOU HOLTZ

QUESTIONS TO CONTEMPLATE:

ALL THINGS BEING EQUAL, WHAT IS THE DIFFERENCE
BETWEEN PAYING CASH AND USING DEBT?

WHERE DO YOU SEE THE RELEVANCE OF TVM
CALCULATIONS?

WHAT TRADE-OFFS ARE YOU MAKING (OR DO YOU
NEED TO MAKE) IN YOUR FAMILY FINANCES AND IN
OTHER AREAS OF LIFE?

13

HOME COOKED

" A lie told often enough becomes the truth. "
VLADIMIR LENIN

WHICH DO YOU THINK IS BEST: A 15-year or 30-year mortgage? It is to be expected that you have been taught a 15-year mortgage is the less costly mortgage. In this short and final chapter of
Part II, I'd like to show you why you and I have been led astray, yet
again, on the topic of mortgages. Our previous conversation of *time
value of money* principles will come in handy. For this conversation,
we're not going to discuss the various mortgage costs (like PMI).
We're going to stick with the interest rate cost and the tax ramifications.

You've likely been taught that a 15-year mortgage is cheaper
than a 30-year mortgage. Meaning, you pay less interest on a 15-

year. When looking at the analysis of any mathematical function, it is vital (if you'll allow me to reiterate) to recognize that the numbers on their face do not give the full picture. Most of the time, additional context is needed. In terms of home loans, the 'first-blush' numbers are no different.

Let's use Mr. Dirt once again—in our example he will be taking on $200,000 loan balance after the down payment. Let's assume that the 30-year rate for which he can qualify is 4.25%, and the 15-year rate for which he can qualify is 3.75%. (While historically low, these were roughly the rates at the time of writing.) On their face, these numbers seem simple. The monthly payment for the 30-year loan is $983.88; for the 15-year loan it is $1,454.44. The total payments for each loan are $354,197 and $261,800 respectively. It would seem that Dirt would have paid $154,197 of interest on the 30-year loan and just $61,800 of interest on the 15-year loan. If he were to stop here, it would be a no brainer. Of course, $61,800 is less than $154,197.

	30-Year Mortgage 4.25%	15-Year Mortgage 3.75%
Cumulative Cost of ALL Payments →	(354,197)	(261,800)
Remaining Loan Balance →	0	0
Cumulative Savings →	0	0
Net Cumulative Cost of Loan →	(354,197)	(261,800)

However, we have not yet considered the time value of that money. When Joe compounds the lost opportunity cost of the payments, we get a slightly different picture. Using a 5% interest rate, the total compounded cost of our 30 years of payments on the 30-year mortgage is $818,842. The total of our 15-year mortgage payments is $821,717. Both of these compounded costs are over a 30-year period. The only difference is that we made payments on the

30-year mortgage for the entire period, and with the 15-year mortgage, of course, our home is paid off after the 15 years. However, we're still *losing the interest we could have earned* on that money throughout the 30 years. In this example, the 15-year mortgage actually costs more (in TVM terms) than the 30-year mortgage.

	30-Year Mortgage 4.25%	15-Year Mortgage 3.75%
Compound Cost of ALL Payments →►	(818,842)	(821,717)
Remaining Loan Balance →►	0	0
Value of Savings →►	0	0
Net Compound Cost of Loan	**(818,842)**	**(821,717)**

The final step is to include the tax-deduction on interest charges. Mortgage interest at the current time can be deducted against income. Dirt would be able to deduct more interest over time from the 30-year mortgage than the 15-year mortgage (because he's paid more interest on the 30-year). This results in more compounded tax-savings ($121,001) in the 30-year scenario than the 15-year scenario ($64,648). And keep in mind, we're comparing apples to apples by running the compounded costs out for 30 years in each scenario.

	30-Year Mortgage 4.25%	15-Year Mortgage 3.75%
Compound Cost of ALL Payments →►	(818,842)	(821,717)
Remaining Loan Balance →►	0	0
Value of Savings →►	127,001	64,648
Net Compound Cost of Loan	**(691,842)**	**(757,069)**

The point of this is that, contrary to popular belief, a 15-year mortgage is *not* less costly than a 30-year mortgage. For the bank, the cost of both mortgages is about the same. They've factored in their risk on both sides and offer interest rates that align with that risk. For Dirt (and you and me) though, we get a better deal on the

30-year mortgage because of the time value of money and the tax-deduction of mortgage loan interest.

∞

One more element that must be considered: What is the value of a home that has been paid off? What is the value financially and otherwise? Sure, the value of a paid-off home could simply be that monthly payments cease to exist. There is no more requirement. This can, in essence, feel good—it can definitely provide comfort.

Nonetheless, let me state: the value of a fully paid for home is not at all financial. It is solely emotional. Or rather, let me restate. The value of a paid-for home is only financially rational so long as the CAGR that could be earned otherwise is less than the net effective interest rate on the home. Which, because of the Fed's easy money policies of the 2010-2016 period, is improbable. With a 3-5% mortgage rate (2-4% tax effective), one should be able to adequately earn a better rate with the equity of their home.

This is yet another pedagogical paradox.

The price of a home will rise or fall, regardless of if there is debt against it. The debt makes no difference there. If the money that would have been employed to pay down the home is rather deployed to other prudent savings or investing alternatives, then the homeowner (i.e. he who holds the debt) is in no more net debt than if he had not deployed the capital towards other means. Retiring debt on a home is then, often, equivalent to losing thousands of long-term dollars.

The fallacy of a paid-for home is that those dollars are tied up; locked up, really. They are buried under the tons of concrete and brick and lumber and paint. Regardless of age or mortgage status, you will soon read the manners by which you may well take back those thousands of dollars.

B. Chase Chandler

QUESTIONS TO CONTEMPLATE:

WHY WOULD A BANK OFFER A LOWER RATE FOR A 15-YEAR MORTGAGE THAN A 30-YEAR MORTGAGE?

WHAT IS THE TRUE VALUE OF A PAID-OFF HOME?

B. Chase Chandler

PART III

RISING ABOVE MEDIOCRITY

*Mastering Strategic Financial Decision Making
and Family Financial Optimization*

THEY CAME TO HIM AND SAID, "TEACHER, WE KNOW THAT YOU ARE A MAN OF INTEGRITY. YOU AREN'T SWAYED BY OTHERS, BECAUSE YOU PAY NO ATTENTION TO WHO THEY ARE; BUT YOU TEACH THE WAY OF GOD IN ACCORDANCE WITH THE TRUTH... "

Mark 12:14

INTRODUCTION TO PART III

I think it important to note that this section is less a guide on *"how to become rich"* or *"what to invest in right now"* than it is about how to think about and process financial information. There are already enough books—some good and some not—on what to do with money. And there are many different arguments and opinions on that topic.

Rather, this section (and the appendixes following) aim to help you master the financial decision-making process and optimize your family's financial situation—to think for yourself and not be swayed by one person or another. The aim is wealth creation followed by efficacy in financial management.

Of course, there are financial recommendations backed up by my experience and analysis. And I have used these strategies in my own life to good effect. This was the most difficult section of the book to write. In truth, opinion usually gets in the way of good writing. And I have made my best attempt to maintain objectivity, honesty, and intellectual intensity.

14

FINANCIAL OPTIMIZATION

"When we are planning for posterity, we ought to remember that virtue is not hereditary"
THOMAS PAINE

"While their competition is asleep, world-class leaders are up—and they're not watching the news or reading the paper. They are thinking, planning and practicing."

ROBIN S. SHARMA

ECONOMIST R. NELSON NASH ONCE stated that when things get difficult, "most people revert to whatever it is that has gotten them where they are." This is to say that the natural reaction is to revert to our previous behaviors and habits, to what we know. Financial management is, at its core, about evaluating and making decisions on *risk* and *return*. Financial optimization is about effectively analyzing them.

Viktor Frankl once stated that "Between stimulus and response there is a space. In that space lies our freedom and power to choose our response. In our response lies our growth and freedom." However, for most people, that response is usually an unconscious one. We have the ability to choose our response, to be proactive. However, most people do not realize, or are not consciously aware of, their ability (in most situations) to think and choose; rather, off-the-cuff responses are mistaken for *thinking* and *choosing*. People generally rationalize their actions to believe that they have been coherent, when, in fact, they have not actually thought through the ramifications of what they've just done. For instance, I consistently considered my wife to be in the wrong during the majority of our arguments. That was my natural response. My logic, as I worked it out in my head, could not possibly be wrong. That was my default. In reality, I wasn't intentionally *thinking* or *choosing* at all.

Stephen R. Covey expanded on Frankl's quote by stating: "Because of the space between stimulus and response, people have the power of choice; therefore, leaders are neither born nor made—meaning environmentally trained and nurtured. They are self-made through chosen responses, and if they choose based on principles and develop increasingly greater discipline, their freedom to choose increases" and "Quality of life depends on what happens in the space between stimulus and response." [38] To Nash's comment, I would add: people revert back to previous behavior patterns even when those behaviors have gotten them to an undesirable or mediocre state. What Nash was telling us is that we would rather seek (perceived) comfort in what we think we know than continue a process of reasoned thinking. Thinking logically and thinking in new ways is very strenuous. It's always easier to go back to what we've done, what our parents did, what those around us are doing, or simply to rely on our initial cataleptic reactions. When my wife and I would argue, whatever it may have been about, it was much easier to simply assume that I was right. Giving in to the enigmatic thought that she might be right (or rather, that I may be wrong) created a hefty level of discomfort. As intellectually elementary as this example may sound, it demonstrates the challenging exertion involved in taking our thinking to a higher level.

Simply put, it is extremely challenging for our comfort-seeking minds to think of and maintain thought that is distinguished from our natural mind—to think ahead about complex matters and to make decisions that may not prove beneficial for many years. In order to improve your family's financial situation, you must understand how to contemplate finance and economics and to study certain issues of the financial world.

We have examined so much to this point solely to give you the ability to guard yourself from the temptation to revert back to *what got you where you are*. You should continue to study, keep up-to-date, and vet what I've said and what anyone else says. Analogous to Plato's *Allegory of the Cave*, a great deal of your new learning will be foreign to your cave-dwelling peers. Does this make your new learning false? No more so than a colorblind man proclaiming that the sky is yellow, when in fact it is not. You have learned to, in many ways, analyze financial situations. Now it is time to put those analytical capabilities to work—to systematically manage risk and return. I call this *financial optimization*.

Phase 1: Readiness

Financial optimization is about much more than making as much money as possible or maximizing rate of return. It is about integrating life and finance. The initial phase of financial optimization is making sure that you are in a *state of readiness*—to receive information; to think, analyze and allocate that information properly; and take to action on your conclusions. Your overall mental and physical wellbeing are paramount in maintaining this state of readiness. Our feelings are not the end all be all, and I believe that we act too hastily on our feelings and intuition rather than on facts and research. Our mood often dictates our actions and pushes us to take the easy route, as has been a major subject of this book. Forgive me for the repetition, but I really do think it that imperative. The overarching point is that principle and foresight ought guide our decisions, not feeling.

However, there is a distinction between feelings of *emotion and mood* (type one) and feelings of *vigor and good condition* (type two). These two feelings are different in the sense that one drives us to choose ease, and the other substance. Decisions made in the former, type one, are primarily made for the purpose of seeking comfort in the moment. For the purpose of optimization, the latter, type two, is the state you need to adopt (not all of the time, but a good majority of the time) to effectively work through financial and life decisions. Both of these are feelings, but they consistently contradict each other. Our emotional feelings would drive us to avoid a healthy lifestyle because it's much easier and more comfortable to sit on the couch and eat junk food. Our emotional desires will regularly push us to do things that we may regret (or that we know are foolish at the time we do them). We must constantly be aware of and try to pinpoint how feelings are affecting our desires and decisions—and decide whether a current sentiment pushing us in the wrong direction, type 1, or the right direction, type two. For type one decisions, which we think will direct us to the most comfortable path, most often lead us to the path of long-term pain.

SPITZNAGEL'S CIRCUITOUS PATH

To me, there seems to be a common theme among a certain few who have reached success or have achieved something of significance. Each of these individuals, whom I have either met or read about, understands the importance and requirement of taking the difficult path rather than the easy. This is a principle of success.

I have, for a good while now, called this principle the *box of pain*, *which is the idea that* for anything worth doing, there is a period of struggle. And if there is not, then the thing is most likely not worth doing. This small box of pain is inconsequential to the enduring value derived from it. Simplistic as it may be, the power of the lesson should not go unobserved. Far too many hear the words, nod their heads, then fail to retain this knowledge in the face of the tedious.

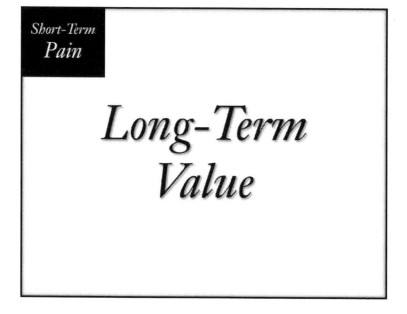

What is the quickest route from *a* to *b*? Is it a straight line? I would submit that in business and in finance, it is not. The straight line is, indeed, the most crowded path. Therefore, what looks to be the easiest way is the most difficult; and what appears to be the more arduous path, is the more rewarding. Shall we, then, enter difficulty for the sake of difficulty? Usually not. However, comparable to training the physical body, the mind and our ability to judge should also be strengthened. **The overarching deduction is that for every endeavor of worth, at least one—and many times the combination—of struggle, loss, or sacrifice is obligatory.**

This is the circuitous path: The most vital of all concepts to internalize, to engulf our mental processes. If we strive for optimal success, this is a must.

If I may recommend one book—regarding the integration of thinking and finance—it will be Mark Spitznagel's *The Dao of Capital*. In it he beautifully and philosophically[i] describes the circuitous path; what he refers to as the *roundabout* or the German *umweg*, meaning detour. Spitznagel's *roundabout* is built upon "an in-depth study of economics and human nature, the inevitable result of which is the philosophy of building a successful enterprise through the understanding of the roundabout, and learning to delay gratification to gain an advantage down the road. He does it through the study of Austrian economics and the application of the roundabout method of investing."[39] It is the process of going backward to go forward, falling in order to rise, retreating to better advance, going right to go left; delaying gratification now for a future, more advantageous result—very similar to R. Nelson Nash's *aerodynamic tailwind*, which we will discuss later in the book.

---

[i] So intensely philosophical that it seems Spitznagel is trying to deter the unmotivated reader.

It may seem, at first, an odd and even dubious notion—against our nature—and that it is. Why go backward to go forward or retreat in order to advance? Certainly it is a philosophical and logical notion, one which Spitznagel attributes primarily to ancient Chinese military methods and Austrian economic thinkers (and a few more). Herein lies the secret to financial optimization and the foundation thereof—the *state of readiness*.

The process of the circuitous path is a function of economic principle; potentially more easily understood by the previously referenced *box of pain*. It is a fight against human nature. It is "waiting and preparing now in order to gain a greater advantage later."[40]

It is important to maintain correct perspective in discussing this *box of pain-roundabout* mentality, understanding that the emotional state—the essence of who we are as humans—will tell us different. *Type one* feelings tell us that these things are pertinent; *type two* reminds us that they are not. It begins with a shift of perspective from seeing struggle as a negative to viewing it as a positive; to realizing sacrifice and loss, in this context, are intentionally entered into for a greater purpose. Because of the strain, the prerequisite for admission is mental health/stability and intellectual intensity. These are the traits that place us in the right mental state to grow, even when a circumstance is tedious.

Simultaneously, our physical health greatly contributes to feelings of vigor and good condition. We've all heard the importance of eating well and exercising. It's important to remember that mental and physical health are not necessarily separate, but combined to create our state of being. I think one of the most important components of being in the right mental and physical state is running. Research has shown that intense cardio exercise produces endorphins that attach "themselves to areas of the brain associated with emotions"[41] and trigger a positive feeling in the body, similar to the experience of morphine.[42] The science shows that if we want to feel better, which I'm guessing we're all in that boat, we can either take a few shots of whiskey or exercise. Deductive reasoning may tell you which one is the short-term solution and which one is the long-term solution.

This is a temperament and an internalization. It must become not only a part of you; it must become you. The integration of our mental and physical state and our internalizing Spitznagel's *circuitous path* creates our *level of readiness*.

Phase 2: Identifying Your SoE

The second phase of financial optimization is to recognize what is and isn't within your *sphere of expertise*. As earlier discussed, your *sphere of expertise* are those fields in which you are extremely competent. This might be real estate, education, medicine, the law, politics, online marketing, or anything else that you understand well. In chapter six, we discussed the fact that your SoE, sophisticated as it may be, cannot be too large. We cannot individually be experts on everything. When I think of some of my more intelligent (or educated) friends, I'm consistently reminded that most of them are fully aware of their competencies. One may be an expert in small business financial management and foreign luxury cars. Another an expert in pediatric cancer research and American history. These individuals may dabble and enjoy discussing and studying other topics, whatever they may be. But they have not invested near the amount of time or energy in those other topics as they have in the two or three areas that are within their SoE.

We can, of course, increase our sphere of expertise, but there are only so many things on which we can be experts—some financially profitable, some not. Some areas of SoE overlap (i.e. business financial management and personal financial management). It would often be wise to enhance our expertise in those areas that overlap, specifically if they could be profitable. Another great falsehood of our time is that you should *always* follow your passion. I would submit that it doesn't make much sense to follow your passion with no plan of financial sustainability, or if you are simply not good at it. If you love art or acting or singing, but your parents are the only ones who have sung your metaphorical praises, this may be an indicator that you need to find something else. I would also submit that even if you are gifted in an unprofitable passion, you will want to find something that you are (or can become) competent in that also produces income. As will be further delineated, it is vital for your family's income to rise over time—this is a tenant of becoming a '10 talent person.'

Phase 3: Preparation of DMP

As I outlined in chapter six, your decision making process, or DMP, must be rooted in objectivity. Not that intuition is irrelevant—it can certainly play a role—but facts and research should be relied upon much more than opinion and previous perception. Clairvoyance is a subconscious trait of the unsuccessful. They make decisions because they just *"have a feeling."* I am sure you've heard this stated by many, and have perchance, like I, stated it yourself. When that decision plays out in their favor, their magical ability to go with their gut is confirmed. When the decision produces a less than desirable outcome, the typical person ignores the process of making that decision or, better yet, blames the outcome on someone or something else. You can see the limitations of this default DMP of the masses. You certainly don't have to use my DMP (a summary of which is shown below); however, it would be wise to spend time in deep thought to create your own DMP.

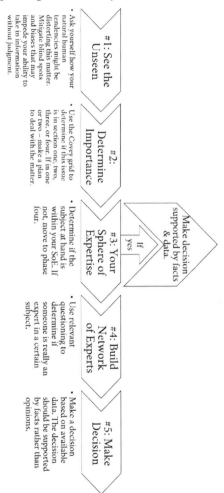

#1: See the Unseen
- Ask yourself how your natural human tendencies might be distorting this matter. Mitigate blind spots and biases that may impede your ability to take in information without judgment.

#2: Determine Importance
- Use the Covey grid to determine if this issue is in section one, two, three, or four. If in one or two – make a plan to deal with the matter.

#3: Your Sphere of Expertise
- Determine if the subject at hand is within your SoE. If not, move to phase four.

If yes → Make decision supported by facts & data.

#4: Build Network of Experts
- Use relevant questioning to determine if someone is really an expert in a certain subject.

#5: Make Decision
- Make a decision based on available data. The decision should be supported by facts rather than opinions.

Phase 4: The Planning Process

To begin the process of rising above financial mediocrity, let's lay the groundwork; the process by which you integrate your readiness, your SoE, and your DMP—this is the *planning process*. The *planning process* involves multiple steps to determine where you are financially, where you want to be, and the most efficient manner to get there. Contrary to the typical financial advisor's "planning process," here, while the steps may be cookie-cutter, the process and the complexity is certainly not. The *planning process* steps are as follows:

Step 1: Discovery—your current financial position

Step 2: Goals—where you want to be; short-term and long-term

Step 3: Potential Solutions—various paths to reach goals

Step 4: Evaluation—analyzing the various potential solutions

Step 5: Implementation—deciding which direction to go and moving forward

Step 6: Monitoring and Studying—observing the strategies over time and studying what impacts the strategies

In just a moment we will discuss how to progress through each of these steps. First, let me introduce the *Financial Hierarchy of Needs* (FHN).

FINANCIAL HIERARCHY OF NEEDS

The FHN is a pyramid of priorities of which every family should be aware. From a planning perspective, the base areas are the greatest risk. As we mitigate those risks, we move up the hierarchy.

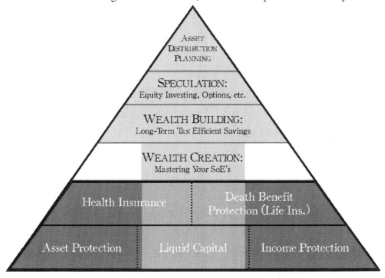

The base of every plan should be the areas you can see in grey. These are: *asset protection, liquid capital, income protection, health insurance,* and *death benefit protection* (term life insurance). These are the greatest risks that you have. And, from a planning and financial perspective, they are vital to take care of. For most people, they are quite easy to check off the planning list. It's simply a matter of knowing what to do. We will have *why, how,* and *what to do* in the next chapter.

As you move up the FHN, past the base of the plan comes *wealth creation.* This is where SoE comes in to play, as it is the arena from which you already (or will) derive income. It's not often discussed in the media or in financial planning circles, but your greatest and most profitable investment is the time and money you put into developing a profitable SoE. This is what creates your ability to earn an income, so everything hinges on this ability. This is also why the base is so integral. It protects your ability to create, add value, and earn income. Next comes *wealth building*, which is primarily safe, consistent, and tax-advantaged savings. This is not investing or speculation—rather, this is the storing place for capital earned via your SoE. Following *wealth building* is *speculation*—equity investing, options trading, etc. Speculation are those areas where you take on much risk, but the return could be significant. The final planning area is an *asset distribution plan*. This, along with the *base*, are the most neglected areas of planning; and the ones that, when unprepared for, devastate wealth.

All of these components of planning—the four phases which culminate with the financial hierarchy of needs—make up the financial optimization process. In the coming chapters you will see how correctly analyzing and implementing prudent (and sometimes unheard of) strategies will revolutionize your family's financial situation. This is the process of *rising above mediocrity*.

15

COVERING THE BASICS

" Human beings, who are almost unique in having the ability to learn from the experience of others, are also remarkable for their apparent disinclination to do so. "

" The major difference between a thing that might go wrong and a thing that cannot possibly go wrong is that when a thing that cannot possibly go wrong goes wrong it usually turns out to be impossible to get at or repair "

DOUGLASS ADAMS

AN IMPORTANT BUT OFTEN OVERLOOKED component of financial optimization is that of personal risk management. As tedious and boring as this portion may seem, I would encourage you to take it seriously. This aspect of planning is what protects the aggregate of your wealth creation and building efforts. Neglect to protect these areas, and everything could be gone in a flash. We all know of a family (or families) that have been experienced financial devastation. Many times this desolation can be avoided.

You might call these areas the "fundamentals" or the "basics." I call them *the base* of the entire plan. They are not the most fun to discuss; they lack almost any exciting facet. They require the pondering of some of the worst case financial and life scenarios. And that being the case, most people would rather avoid the conversation at all costs. I call this *Thought Prevention Syndrome*—a coping mechanism by which a person avoids the slightest hint of undesirable thought, necessary though it may be. The base of the plan, as shown in the image below, are those areas of greatest financial risk:

- The potential loss of income from an illness or death
- Needs for immediate emergency cash
- Lawsuits and other legal costs
- Hospital and other health related costs

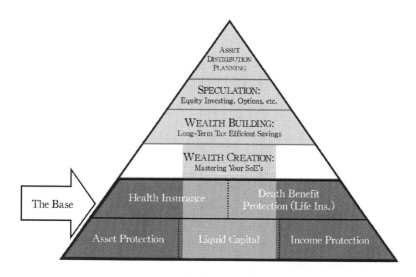

The reality is that the base, tedious as it may be, is the easiest area to take care of. For the sake of brevity I won't discuss much about the importance of health insurance. If Obama's pajama man hasn't convinced you to check out the exchanges yet, then I probably can't help you. So we'll start with the aspect to the right of health insurance—the need for death benefit coverage.

In reading the remainder of this chapter (and book for that matter), I ask you that approach it with no judgment. Rather, just observe and take in the message and the words. Once you feel you fully understand the message, which would occur when you've gotten the context of the entire book by reading it completely, then you're free to judge.

DEATH BENEFIT COVERAGE

I mentioned a moment ago the fact that many people would rather not have the conversation about some of the risk management areas. The term *death benefit* doesn't exactly add to the number of those who do. To *benefit* from *death* is, by the definition of the words, an oxymoron. However, for most families, one of the most severe financial situations would occur if either spouse were to pass away. The path to protection is life insurance.

A couple of important notes. First, when I say life insurance, I mean death benefit. For this conversation, it doesn't matter what type of life insurance we're discussing—the focus is primarily the amount of coverage. For the sake of simplicity, it may be beneficial to imagine utilizing term insurance. Term life insurance is similar to health, fire, or auto insurance; if you don't use it you lose it. The typical person can get $1 million of death benefit for $40 to $80 per month, depending on age. Secondly, it is typical for the average family to assume they need to get some life insurance on the bread-winner. But they'll often assume that they don't need any on a spouse who stays at home with the kids. I'm inclined to believe they are suffering from *Thought Prevention Syndrome*, or TPS. If you suffer from TPS, it's okay. It's nothing to be ashamed of. But, for a moment, let's imagine what might occur if a stay-at-home spouse were to pass away. Say the family had three kids. Perhaps the family wouldn't need any additional capital. Perhaps they'd be just fine. But let's consider the alternative—what may be more likely to occur. The working spouse is now left as a single parent. He or she could continue to work at the same pace, but they'd likely have to hire someone to watch the kids (either full or part-time). They'd have to eat out regularly or hire someone to cook. All of these equal rising expenses. Alternatively, the working spouse could cut their hours back and spend more time with the kids. Still, they may need a nanny to watch the kids during the day. Either scenario results in rising expenses or less work hours for the surviving spouse.

It is vital, from a death benefit perspective, to make sure that enough capital comes into the family simply to make sure that they are okay. The acronym D.I.M.E. will help you remember the areas that need to be covered.

$D = Debt$
$I = Income$
$M = Mortgage$
$E = Education$

Debt & Mortgage

From a planning perspective, these are the expenses you'll want to cover if something unfortunate were to happen to either spouse, or to a single parent. Coming up with your total debt (mortgage and other wise) is fairly easy. You simply add your debt numbers together; for instance $250,000 mortgage plus $50,000 of student loans plus $30,000 car loan equals $330,000 in total debt. To calculate the other two (future education cost for children and income needed) we will utilize our *time value of money* calculators.

Education Costs

In my experience, there are a group of parents who want their kids to pay for their own college, a group who want to pay for every dime of their children's education, and a group who are somewhere in between. But, the majority of parents (if they really stop and think about it) would like to have something set aside to help fund education in case they aren't around. I think most people would like to be remembered as having the maturity to set something aside—regardless of what they might say during an episode of TPS. (We'll discuss education in much more depth in a later chapter.) To calculate the probable cost of college for our children, we need to determine which TVM calculation is relevant. For those of you whom are new to TVM calculations, take a moment to think about what variables we have and what we need.

If you guessed FV, you were right. We're solving for the future value of college cost at our children's college age. We can find the cost of education today (our PV) and we know how long our child has until college (n). We can also make an estimate on how much college costs will increase by the time our kid(s) go to college (i). At the current time, college costs are rising 5-8% per year. We'll use 7%. Let's imagine we have two children, one age 8 and one age 5. So, we have 10 and 13 years respectively. We'll use $50,000 as the current total cost of college. We are going to perform two TVM calculations. For the 8-year-old child, we'll input present value as -$50,000. We're solving for the amount that $50,000 would grow to after 10 years at 7%. 10 years is *n* and .07 is *i*. Our payment will be input as $0. We'll do the same thing for our 5-year-old child, except we'll make n = 13. Below are the results. The 8-year-old is on the left; the 5-year-old on the right.

future value

n	10
i	0.07
pv	($50,000.00)
pmt	$0.00
fv	$98,357.57

future value

n	13
i	0.07
pv	($50,000.00)
pmt	$0.00
fv	$120,492.25

We can see that the cost of college, combined for both, is about $220,000. This is the amount we would want to have set aside if the worst occurred. So far, we have got the D, the M, and the E covered:

$$Debt \quad = \$80,000$$
$$Income \quad = \ ?$$
$$M \quad = \$250,000$$
$$E \quad = \$220,000$$

Income

The final component is survivor living income; meaning, **if you and/or your spouse passed, how much monthly income would the family need just to make it—to be okay?** This is without question the most important aspect of death benefit planning. Assuming the debt, mortgage, and education costs are gone, how much would the family need (per month) to make ends meet? For some it may be $3,000 per month. For others, $8,000 or $12,000. The answer to this question is specific to you. Whatever the answer, the next question is: how much capital is needed to spin-off that monthly amount. There will be two separate answers—one for each spouse. Then we're going to solve for the *present value* necessary to generate the correct amount each month.

For our example, let's say the answer is $6,000 per month if the "breadwinning" spouse passes away and $2,000 per month if the "non-breadwinning" spouse passes away. We must choose an interest rate that we think a lump sum of capital could earn, conservatively, to spin-off the monthly income. Remember, this capital would be invested for income, not for growth. Its only purpose is to provide the desired income. We are actually not going to use the present value calculation we learned; we are simply going to divide the annual income need (i.e. 6,000 x 12) by the interest rate, 3%. $72,000 / .03 equals $1.8 million. 3% of $1.8 million is $72,000. If our conservative investment earns 3% per year, then we will only live (mostly) off of the interest in the first few years.

Over time, however, inflation will begin to erode our principle. A good advisor will help you to determine the amount of capital needed to spinoff the income and protect against inflation. For simplicity, I'll just say you may want to be more conservative with the interest rate used. Instead of using 3%, use 2%. $72,000 / .02 = $3.6 million. Therefore, $3.6 million at a 2% interest rate would likely produce the needed income increases over time for inflation.

We would then repeat the income calculation process for the spouse; we'll use $24,000 per year as the needed income. The amounts will be a few million dollars, depending on the income needed. This may seem like a lot (and it is), but it's vital to remember that one, this is what it will take to simply provide the income. If one of the spouses passes away, you've lost their total future income. And two, for the healthy, this is quite easy to take care of. Term insurance is very cost effective for the short-term and makes sure, for a period of time, that the need is covered.

> ## SPOUSE 1
> Debt   = $80,000
> Income = $3,600,000
> Mortgage   = $250,000
> Education   = $220,000
> ### TOTAL DEATH BENEFIT NEEDED:
> = $4,150,000
>
> ## SPOUSE 2
> Debt   = $80,000
> Income = $1,200,000

Mortgage   = *$250,000*
Education   = *$220,000*
TOTAL DEATH BENEFIT NEEDED :
          = *$1,750,000*

But I'm Single...

There seems to be a good amount of conjecture floating around that assumes single people don't need life insurance. Quite a few of the financial "gurus" say that single people *never* need life insurance. In reality, if you are single and you think you're ever going to get married or have children, there is still a definite need for life insurance. The reason brings us to your greatest risk, the single largest statistical risk you have. It's not death or severe illness. Obviously, if those things occurred they would be terrible—that's why we have to protect against them, financially. But they're not the greatest risk. The greatest risk is that something happens that prevents you from getting this stuff when you know you need it—when you've got kids and a spouse and a mortgage. It is wise to get, at least, as much term as you can. The cost is almost nothing. The protection it will provide, though, is paramount to your future family.

CASH & INCOME PROTECTION

This brings us to our next protection area, income. Again, I realize that this is not the most exciting of topics to discuss. But it is utterly vital. so bear with me. Private long-term disability insurance is the most important type of insurance to own. Asset protection, cash reserves, and income protection are the *base of the base*—the greatest financial risks your family faces.

Your greatest risk is something happening that would prevent you from working—from bringing in an income. Actually, philosophically (as I mentioned earlier), your greatest risk is something happening that prevents you from obtaining insurance when you know you need it. Meaning, statistically, the chances of a health issue arising are quite a bit more likely than death or disability. This may be something that doesn't affect your work, but it would affect your ability to protect your income. As we'll discuss in a few chapters, it is most beneficial to have disability with a mutual company.

The final components are cash reserves and asset protection. I assume you know the risks and benefits of having cash on hand for emergencies. We will soon discuss the importance of keeping liquid capital on hand to take advantage of business opportunities. For simplicity, I refer you to JJ Childers book, *Asset Protection 101*, as I cannot do the topic justice without boring you to sleep.

16

THE PSYCHOLOGY OF INVESTING

" If you 're prepared to invest in a company, then you ought to be able to explain why in simple language that a fifth grader could understand, and quickly enough so the fifth grader won 't get bored."

PETER LYNCH

" Buy not on optimism, but on arithmetic."

BENJAMIN GRAHAM

FOR MANY YEARS, PROFESSED URBANE investors have subscribed to a market philosophy that proclaims assets to be priced correctly at all times. They call this *modern portfolio theory*. The theory proclaims that no investor had an advantage over any other investor because all information about a certain company was already publically available. The theory is based on the *efficient-market hypothesis*, which states that markets are *"informationally efficient"* and *"one cannot consistently achieve returns in excess of average market returns on a risk-adjusted basis, given the information available at the time the investment is made."*[43] The idea is that markets are rational, which would mean humans who are making those markets are also rational.

Upon my entering the investment world, I was taught *modern portfolio theory* (MPT) as if it were unadulterated truth. The glaring problem, though, was the lack of sensibility. How could markets always be priced correctly—that is, stocks were never over or undervalued—when stocks moved so darn much on a daily and weekly basis?

In his 2000 book *Irrational Exuberance*, Robert Shiller warned of the housing bubble. Almost no one listened. Others warned as well, mainly Peter Schiff. The financial and economic "authorities" laughed.[i] They proclaimed the science of MPT and how markets were always efficient. These MPT, and largely Keynesian, theorists were essentially engaging in a syllogistic approach. Their premise: *Markets are efficient and housing prices are rising. Therefore, the conclusion is that housing prices are priced correctly even at such high levels.* Little did they ponder the fact that, as was established in chapter seven, the government had found its way into housing, creating legislation sanctioning (and sometimes forcing) banks to loan to those who could likely not pay back. For a moment this did give us sky-rocketing home prices. Alas, it all came tumbling down.

The lesson: when government involves itself in markets of any kind, it creates distortion. It removes the potential of efficient markets. We do not really know what prices should be. In hindsight, it

---

[i] As mentioned in Part II, search YouTube for "Peter Schiff was Right."

is easy to infer the cause of the housing bubble. Shiller was one of the few mainstream academics to tout the issue. Austrians were calling it from the mountain tops, but no one was listening. Think back to each industry in which government has intervened in some way. After careful research in each topic you think of, attempt to find one where it has made the industry better than it was before. You'll find that it hasn't because it cannot. Government intervention produces only distortion and cronyism, false demand and great benefits to those who cozy up to Washington elites.

∞

The Economics of Human Action

Beyond the sober lessons of government intrusion, behavioral economics may tell us even more about short-term asset prices. Differentiated from MPT, behavioral economics is the "study of the effects of psychological, social, cognitive, and emotional factors on the economic decisions of individuals and institutions and the consequences for market prices, returns, and the resource allocation."[44] In other words, market prices are determined not by their proper value, but by individual's perception of their value. People are making the choice to buy and sell assets, and that buying and selling makes up supply and demand. People are not rational. Therefore, markets are not rational.

> *"It amazes me how people are often more willing to act based on little or no data than to use data that is a challenge to assemble."*

> *" Irrational exuberance is the psychological basis of a speculative bubble. I define a speculative bubble as a situation in which news of price increases spurs investor enthusiasm, which spreads by psychological contagion from person to person, in the process amplifying stories that might justify the price increases and bringing in a larger and larger class of investors, who, despite doubts about the real value of an investment, are drawn to it partly through envy of others' successes and partly through a gambler's excitement. "*
>
> — ROBERT SHILLER

Ironically, the origin of behavioral economics research is largely attributed to the work of Daniel Kahneman and the late Amos Tversky.[45] Their revolutionary research, the basis for part one of this book, demonstrates the fallibility of human decision-making processes. It's not just the uneducated or "lower class" that has this problem, it's all of us. Let us go back to what we learned from Kahneman. In a 2011 New York Times article he wrote, "The confidence we experience as we make a judgment is not a reasoned evaluation of the probability that it is right. Confidence is a feeling, one determined mostly by the coherence of the story and by the ease with which it comes to mind, even when the evidence for the story is sparse and unreliable. The bias toward coherence favors overconfidence. An individual who expresses high confidence probably has a good story, which may or may not be true."[46] The importance of recognizing the role that feelings play in an individual's economic decision-making is vital to understanding the psychology of investing. However, I would submit that it was Ludwig von Mises who

originally explained the modern framework for behavioral economic thought. Mises explained that value was the sum of all human
action:

> *Value is not intrinsic, it is not in things. It is within
> us; it is the way in which man reacts to the conditions
> of his environment. Neither is value in words and doc-
> trines, it is reflected in human conduct. It is not what
> a man or groups of men say about value that counts,
> but how they act.*
>
> — LUDWIG VON MISES
> *HUMAN ACTION: A TREATISE ON ECONOMICS* (1949)

Our knowledge that humans, and therefore markets, are irrational gives insight into how markets work. Markets themselves are
mainly a product of herd mentality and conformity. If the prevailing
wisdom is at any given time x, then we are inclined to believe x;
even if there is an absence of coherent data. All of these combined
actions make markets. The primary issue of which we must be cog-
nizant is that every major country, following America's lead, is engaged in utter manipulation of markets and currencies. When we
think things are *good* or *back to normal*, we must wonder if it is really
so. We must ask ourselves what *normal* really is.

If market prices are determined by human action, and if we agree
that humans are in some part creatures of feeling, then market
prices are also largely determined by human emotion. The below
image portrays the cycle of market emotions.[47] As the market rises,
people tilt towards optimism, then excitement, followed by thrill
and euphoria—a feeling that things are *great* and the market will

never go down. We experienced this during the stock market boom of the 90's. But even recently it has been quite noticeable.

The cycle of market emotions

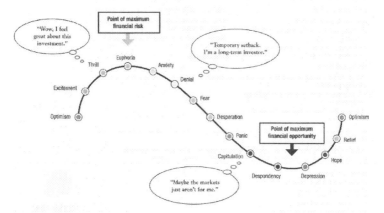

Near the end of 2013, there was a notion that things had "gotten better, back to normal." In reality, the Federal Reserve had simply printed trillions of dollars to pump into the economy. This better wasn't a *real* better—it was a *perceived* better. Market indices were up roughly 30%. I remember having a conversation with a 60ish-year-old business owner, in which he stated that he "couldn't take his money out of the market because it kept going up so much." At the time of this writing, we have just concluded that in the year 2014 the markets, while somewhat volatile, have continued to rise. We will likely see more volatility into 2015 and beyond. And no one knows when a correction will occur, but only that it will most definitely occur. If we have learned anything from history, it is that it repeats itself. The feeling that things are good does not make them good—it only confirms our bias, our perceived belief, that they are. When things turn "bad," we cannot believe we didn't see it coming.

We're taken aback by our misconception, and we attempt to rationalize.

A better methodology would be to pragmatically realize that market cycles occur; that they are fundamentally effected by human behavior and that government and Federal Reserve intermingling has influenced that behavior. To attempt to predict what's going to occur at a specific time, however, is impossible. We cannot predict what is going to occur next week or next year. No one truly knows what is going to happen or when, with the exception of God. But we can see macro trends based on history and data. And we must, in order to move forward, make assumptions based on that data.

FORECASTING

On May 9, 2002 Peter Schiff predicted that the "market was still extremely overvalued," and that housing prices would crash. He said that the "bear market would last for a long time."[48] It didn't. From October 2002 to October 2007, the S&P rose by a CAGR of more than 12%.[49] It would be five years before Schiff's proclamation proved true and, in the meantime, he'd be scoffed at by the predictably mainstream talking heads. Bottom line: we may not know the timeline, but we can see economic trends.

The following chart shows the price of the S&P from January 1, 1995, to December 31, 2014. It's easy to see highs and lows when looking at markets from this macro-perspective. As of the end of 2014 it seems we're not only at an all-time high, but that we're at a *noticeably high* all-time high. This is a fairly rudimentary analysis and conclusion, but I believe it tells us a story—a story of market cycles. As hedge fund manager Mark Spitznagel pointed out in late 2013, this looks like *"all the other major [market] tops we've seen over the past 100 years."*[50] Spitznagel also happened to predict the crash, returning over 100% in 2008.[51] I recommend visiting **The-FallofLogic.com/Bears** to view his October 2013 CNBC interview. He suggests 'mom and pop' investors have an advantage over institutional investors because they don't have to be in the market. They can step aside during, what looks to be, "market tops." This lesson should not be taken lightly by the reader. In the same month, October 2013, I spoke at a conference in Branson, Missouri. I presented a chart similar to this one, but of course, it concluded at that point in time. After mentioning some of the same points concerning market tops, I asked the group what they thought would happen next. Many of them inferred a correction, as was my intent.

S&P Index 1/1/1995 to 12/31/2014[ii]

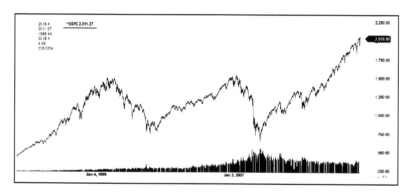

As some in the audience declared that the market was in for a correction, a subtle line on the PowerPoint slide slowly showed the market going up—hypothetically extending the market gain. *"It might go up…"* I told the crowd. *"I don't know. No one knows what's going to happen. But we all know that this looks like a pretty hefty top."*

[ii] Source: finance.yahoo.com

Then I hypothetically displayed when a dip could occur, sometime in 2014 or 2015.

"*What do you think the statistical chance of the market rising is during periods 1 and 2?*" I asked.

"*What do you think the chance of a drop is during period 3?*"

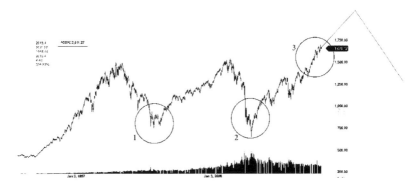

My point was not that I (or anyone else) knew when a correction might occur—only that the statistical chance of a considerable drop was more probable to occur, historically, at these highest of highs (period 3). On the flip side, the chance of the market rising considerably was more likely to occur at the lowest of lows (period 1 and 2). This is not to say that we can know when the *highest of highs* or the *lows of lows* is precisely occurring. But we must make a general macro assumption. It is (and was) a question of risk vs. reward. The risk at the top is too significant; say a 30% chance the market will rise over the next year by another 5-15% and a 70% chance it will fall 15-40%. On the other hand, there is a reward at the bottom: a 70% chance it will rise 15-40% and a 30% chance it will fall 5-15%.

The individual investor that heeded Spitznagel's advice in October 2013 (or mine, although I cannot compare my investing

knowledge or results to his) would have lost out on a 13.44% annualized return (in an S&P 500 index) from November 1, 2013
through the end of 2014.[iii] Does this make his warning any less le-
gitimate? Absolutely not. The risk/reward equation did not make
sense. It's not about stock picking or market timing. It's about a
general understanding of market cycles. As Mark Spitznagel
pointed out, individual investors can be more agile than institutional investors. This is a part of our *cognoso*; our *prudentis*.

∞

THE PRICE OF CONFORMITY

A disconcerting problem that families (and investment advisers)
face today is a regulatory environment which largely operates on
conventional wisdom—on conformity. We'll shortly return to why
regulators seem to have things upside-down.

One of the conforming notions is 'buy-and-hold' investing, even
though the results of convention haven't been so good. DALBAR
reports the average investor to have earned a 2.1% CAGR from
1992 to 2011.[52] This has been used to critique the behaviors of individual investors. But I've not heard anyone compare it to what an
investor would have earned if they'd invested exclusively in an S&P
500 index fund, the cheapest way to invest in the market. A few
commentaries have mentioned that they'd have earned 7-8% annualized.[53] Back to Occam's Razor—the simplest answer would be to
assume that individual investors are just stupid and move on. But
alas, it seems the financial "gurus", journalists, and regulators have

---

[iii] The S&P index increased from 1,762.64 (11/1/2013) to 2,058.90 (12/31/2014)

missed something. In a way they are right, and in a more relevant way they are wrong.

What if our sample man Joe had invested $5,000 per year into the S&P from 1992 to 2011? **What if he'd subscribed to the buy-and-hold methodology? Would he have earned 7-8%? The answer is no.** Assuming a 0.30% annual fee on his index fund, Joe would have earned around 5.59%. This is significant in at least two ways. One, the gurus ran (or ran with) the CAGR with a lack of context. If Joe had $5,000 in 1992 and let it ride, then yes, he would have earned 7.50%. But that's not what the average investor does. The average investor saves over a period of time. Joe's CAGR, after saving $5,000 per year, would have been 5.59%.[iv] Two, a 7.80% CAGR in the S&P index fund[v] would have produced $241,260 at the end of 20 years. In reality, his account would have been at $185,770—a difference of $55,490. If we calculate the same numbers using a 3.17% fee per year (the average annual mutual fee we looked at in chapter 10) we get a 2.31% CAGR. Maybe this sheds some light as to why the average investor has really experienced such low returns. In reality, this is confirmation of many of the points Spitznagel was raising.

[iv] Assuming a 0.30% fee and no taxes in both equations.
[v] As is noted here: http://www.thestreet.com/story/11621555/1/average-investor-20-year-return-astoundingly-awful.html

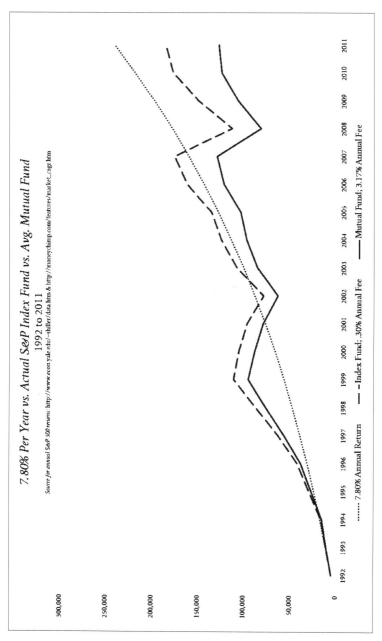

7.80% Per Year vs. Actual S&P Index Fund vs. Avg. Mutual Fund
1992 to 2011

Source for annual S&P 500 returns: http://www.econ.yale.edu/~shiller/data.htm & http://moneychimp.com/features/market_cagr.htm

········ 7.80% Annual Return   — – Index Fund: .30% Annual Fee   —— Mutual Fund: 3.17% Annual Fee

Amazingly, regulators view 'buy-and-hold' as the safest and most effective way to invest. Likely because they've taken the analysis out of context. For some reason they turn a blind eye to fees and volatility, the things that destroy a portfolio; yet they consider options and short selling[vi] too risky.

> *"Conforming one's actions to be in accordance with conventional wisdom rather than one's own judgments is not only a natural thing to do; for fiduciaries it is also required by law."*

ROBERT SCHILLER

This is certainly not an endorsement of excessive trading or attempting to regularly time the market (although, if you've got the time, you may find Tom Sosnoff, founder or *thinkorswim*, and his online shows at tastytrade.com to be quite fascinating). Rather, it is an appeal to reason. It's an appeal to think freely and analytically. It's an appeal to know why you're making decisions rather than listening to the (often uninformed) advice of others.

[vi] See Appendix B for more educational resources.

MONKEYS AND STOCKS

November 28, 2011

Time magazine: *What about experts? Shouldn't we trust their instincts?*

Daniel Kahneman: *There are domains in which expertise is not possible. Stock picking is a good example. And in long-term political strategic forecasting, it's been shown that experts are just not better than a dice-throwing monkey.*

From the TIME article "10 Questions for Daniel Kahneman"[54]

Can a monkey be a better portfolio manager than a human? A 2014 Economist article detailed just that: "In a study Robert Arnott and his co-authors picked 100 portfolios, each with 30 equally-weighted stocks from the 1,000 largest American stocks by market capitalization. 94 of the 100 'dartboard portfolios' did better than a market cap-weighted portfolio of all the 1,000 stocks."[55] Another study from the Cass Business School in London found that randomly generated portfolios (i.e. picking random stocks from each asset class) out performed managers the majority of the time.[56] Legendary investors (i.e. Benjamin Graham, Peter Lynch, and the often over-quoted Warren Buffet) have consistently warned to invest only in companies you understand—that investing should be solely focused on safety of principal and generating a return. Anything else is not investing, but speculation.[vii]

The buy and hold investors (and their advisors) of the 1990's, likely many readers of this book, were not inherently right in their

---

[vii] My own paraphrasing of Benjamin Graham's famous quote from *The Intelligent Investor*.

decision to invest in mutual funds and the like; even though $10,000 would have grown to $45,000. No moreso than they were wrong from 2000 to 2009; when their $45,000 would have shrunk to $35,000. [viii] Confirmation bias, however, leads one to believe that he has made an adequate decision when things are going well; and someone else has misled him when things aren't going so well. But, in fact, the result is largely random and uncontrollable. Or, as Nassim Taleb tells us, "When things go our way we reject the lack of certainty." [57] We need certainty. We need to think we know. But the reality is that we do not know. Again, Taleb: "We favor the visible, the embedded, the personal, the narrated, and the tangible; we scorn the abstract." [58]

The overarching point is that we cannot expect to know the future result of today's equity investing market. When the market is headed up, everyone looks good. When it reverses course, everyone looks bad. In fact, this is not really an investing market at all—rather, speculation. And it's not that speculation is all bad all of the time. But it shouldn't be the foundation of an entity's financial strategy. To assume that we can do the same thing that worked in the anomaly of the 80's and 90's will likely prove detrimental. However, we can see things more clearly when we look at the macro data.

Let me also say that certain people will have an expertise in certain industries. Whether it be oil and gas, commodities, tech, media, pharma, or any other specific field—a deep expertise may lend itself a higher chance of success. Of course this seems obvious to you and me. However, it serves to point out that one, excessive risk should only be taken when a person fully understands that risk, and therefore has extensive knowledge in the corresponding field; and

---

[viii] Based on S&P 500 with dividends; including 1.50% annual fee.

two, that we should not own volatile and speculative assets about which we know nothing, which the majority are doing. Financial wealth is created not by blindly and arbitrarily tossing money at risky assets. A coach does not thoughtlessly select his pitching rotation. A physician does not haphazardly choose the procedure. A chef does not unsystematically pick ingredients. Consistent success in any endeavor, while involving luck, is not the byproduct of a random assortment of decisions. It is the result of understanding the psychology of one's personal wealth creation and management function. Meaning, the next step of *optimization* is to fully know your own economic value for creating wealth, followed by the management of that creation.

" First there is the *seen*, visible and immediate, that which is most easily grasped. Then there is the yet *unseen*, what comes next as the consequence of the former, realized in the latter—which can, indeed, become the *foreseen*. "

MARK SPITZNAGEL
The Dao of Capital
First Edition (pg 75)

17

THE CREATION AND
SUPERVISION OF WEALTH

" The majority of men meet with failure because of their lack of persistence in creating new plans to take the place of those which fail. "

NAPOLEON HILL

" During my service in the United States Congress, I took the initiative in creating the Internet. "

AL GORE

AS THE LAST CHAPTER CONCLUDED I mentioned the importance of knowing your economic value. What I mean is your SoE and the parlaying value it can bring to your local or to the national economy—that which you can make money from. In order to build real long-term wealth, you must provide some product or service that people either want or need. Your ability to add value economically (combined with your ability to manage expenses and assets) is what will determine your long-term financial health.

There is a difference between wealth *creation* and wealth *management* (supervision). One is your method of creating value and (eventually) profit. The other is the process of prudently preserving and supervising the assets you have built. The former is a process in which you are actively engaged, and the latter is passive in that you are not monitoring the accounts on a daily or weekly basis.

WEALTH CREATION

The only way to *create* financial wealth is through success in some sort of business. The only way to build *lasting* success in business is through failure. This is another paradox of life. We can only learn through struggle.

Society has evolved over time to espouse that, to a great extent, salaries are important. I ask you: Where does this notion come from? Is a salary not someone else simply telling you what you're worth? Granted, in certain situations, a salary is warranted. Maybe for a person wanting to work under little pressure. Maybe the physician or attorney who is better off working with a large group to manage costs. But in general, these are still performance-based pay conditions. The idea of a salary has largely given us the façade that work equals pay. If fact, work does not equal pay, and that is why so many muddle along through the murky waters of weekly paychecks. Results and value, these alone equal pay. And learning to provide value and generate effective results only comes through some sort of pain or struggle; in business, in medicine, in law.

The physician endured at least eight years of it. The attorney, four in law school and at least four as a lowly associate. The business owner, often five to fifteen years of hard and tedious labor, during which all others are paid first, before the real fruits are seen.

Hence the teachings of, say, Dave Ramsey—where he attempts to help people avoid failure and pain and struggle—are many times the very teachings that lead to a life of mediocrity. He failed, went bankrupt, and learned some lessons; but failed to learn the most valuable—that wealth cannot be created by playing it safe.

Maybe you're in sales. Or possibly an executive. Maybe you're a business owner or commodities trader. Or perchance, you're in the medical, engineering, or some other professional field. Whatever the case, this is your *active* wealth building arena. This field, whatever it may be, is your expertise. And the greater the expert you become and the better you market your services, the more value you can give. The foundation of your family's wealth comes from this.

You might get lucky on this deal or that stock. But in the long run the vast majority of your wealth is created via your sphere of expertise. Neither I, nor anyone else, can tell you what your wealth creation arena is (or should be). Many of you are already aware of it... for those who are not, I recommend James Altucher's *Choose Yourself!*

Income Generating Assets

Another part of your active arena is made up of the assets and investments in which you develop some specialty. I know a few commercial and residential real estate investors who invest to create income from those assets. I know a few others who trade options (not the same as stock-picking), a slightly more active daily endeavor.

Once you've identified your value and begin to make money from it, it is time to move to the supervision of that wealth. I use the term *supervision* because I find it more fitting for the process. It is more a procedure of controlling and enhancing than one of simply maintaining. Again, creation is active. Supervision is passive.

WEALTH SUPERVISION

The supervision of wealth, or financial management, is the focus of this third section. Contrary to conventional financial wisdom, wealth is not created by passive savings and investing. Rather, it is managed by the passive. The *passive* can (and often should be) a manner of financing the *active*. The primary focus is security of principle and inflation protection.

This is one reason the stock market is often so ill-suited for savings dollars. The volatility and lack of understanding of its investors creates substantive misunderstanding. When the market goes up, the investor thinks he or his advisors have done something right. When the market goes down he thinks his advisors have done something wrong, or, if he doesn't have advisors, it is the fault of the economy. The reality is that the 'buy and hold' investor is more often buying at the top and riding a little up; then selling near the bottom and forgoing slightly more to lose.

Wealth supervision is much more than hoping for a good return. It is the essence of financial prudence. It is the capital holding place, the current asset to be deployed later. Managed well, capital may sit for long periods of time to wait for the right opportunities. It may grow at a conservative and tax-efficient pace, which is just fine and much better than rushing into something that would be better off not rushed into. In truth, wealth supervision is focused on managing risk and analyzing assets—our aforementioned concentration on risk and return.

Managing Risk

"We have no future because our present is too volatile.
We have only risk management."
WILLIAM GIBSON

Risk should be defined as much more than volatility. It should be well understood and constantly monitored. We have already covered (in chapter 16) the strategies of personal catastrophe risk management. Now, we delve into the arena of business and investment risk management.

There are seven types of financial and economic risk of which to be keenly aware.

1. Economic Risk
2. Market Risk
3. Inflation Risk
4. Interest Rate Risk
5. Income Risk
6. Personal Risk
7. Liquidity Risk

Each of these should be mitigated to the greatest extent, although it is impossible to diminish all risk. Some risks can be managed and others are outside our control. This is okay and must be accepted. Understanding which ones we can effectively manage and how we can do so—this is the game.

18

ANALYZING ASSETS

"*The ultimate authority must always rest with the individual's own reason and critical analysis.*"
DALAI LAMA

"*The price of light is less than the cost of darkness.*"
ARTHUR C. NIELSEN

"*In God we trust, all others must bring data.*"
W. EDWARDS DEMING

IN THE COURSE OF BEING FINANCIALLY prudent, one must learn to properly analyze assets. As you already know, it is vital that they (and we) analyze options as opposed to leaning on the opinions of others, whoever they may be. To reach financial success, we must learn to scrutinize the data. This does not mean that we do not ask others for their interpretation of the data. It does indeed mean that we should be able to point out potential errors in judgment or lack of knowledge from those to whom we may have previously blindly listened.

In this chapter, I'll analyze the properties of passive savings and investing assets. Most of these assets you'll recognize because of their common use among the masses. Some, however, you may scoff at, or at least the masses would do so. I would encourage you to be nonjudgmental—realize that any scoffing you may do would most assuredly not be by means of analysis or scrutiny of the financial data. Remember, ~~judge~~ observe first, and then judge.

THE PERFECT ASSET

If you were to write down on a sheet of paper the ideal characteristics you would want in a savings or investing asset, what would they be? What would you want out of your account? If you may, indulge me for just a moment. What benefits would you desire if you could choose with no limitations? You should imagine the perfect asset. It might entail the aggregate of the following:

- Safety
- Some sort of guaranteed return
- A no-loss provision (meaning, you can't lose money)
- A competitive net CAGR
- Tax-deductible contributions
- Tax-deferred growth
- Tax-free withdrawals
- Full control; ability to use when needed (liquidity)

Again, this is not an exercise in reality, but one of imagination. (You may notice that I didn't include *"outstanding CAGR"* or *"20% per year"* because that is not the point of passive savings, but active SoE. Also, *"20% per year"* would not be an exercise in imagination. It would be an exercise in futility.) The reality is that your wealth, once you've built it, must reside somewhere. And it is quite logical to find the most effective residing place.

Common Assets

These are the most common of the financial assets, in my experience, owned and utilized by families:

Qualified:
- 401(k), 403(b), 457
- IRA's: Traditional, SEP, SIMPLE
- Roth IRA

Non-Qualified:
- CD, Money Market
- Mutual Funds, Brokerage & Fee-Based Accounts
- Home Equity
- Cash-Value Life Insurance

These are the seven most common assets I see. We have already discussed the value, or lack-thereof, of qualified plans. The only exception to our earlier discussion would be the potential value of Roth IRA's (if they are invested properly, which we will discuss in a bit). Oddly, the order of American investing in these vehicles, from top to bottom, is backwards. We are taught, via propaganda and absurd complexity, to invest in the vehicles that are the least beneficial. The following chart details the benefits we detailed just a moment ago as they relate to the corresponding assets above. While simple, I urge you not to take it lightly.

	401(k) 403(b) 457	I R A	Roth IRA	Cash Value Life Ins.	Mutual Funds	Home Equity	CD, Money Mkt
Safety				X			X
Guaranteed Return				X			X
No-loss Provision				X			X
Competitive CAGR	X	X	X	X	X		
Tax-Ded Cont.	X	X					
Tax- Free Withdrawal			X	X	X	X	X
Full Control and Liquidity				X	X		X

You may notice that, of the aforementioned benefits, cash-value life insurance wins the prize. And it's also the least popular among the public. Families have been warned of the perils and expenses of it and the greed of insurance agents by the "gurus" for quite a few years now. But little-to-no warnings have been directed towards those savings and investing vehicles of lesser benefit. The question is: *why?*

The answer is, undeniably, convention—the kind which has plagued mankind for ages. ***"Life insurance as an asset?"*** You might ask. The irrational desires to conform and the preconceived notion of "insurance" can make it quite easy to brush any mention of it aside. Diverging from the prevailing wisdom, I submit to you that life insurance, when structured properly, is one of the most effective passive assets. Don't take my word for it. Let the attestable facts speak for themselves.

19

A SLIGHT MISUNDERSTANDING

"The single biggest problem in communication is the illusion that it has taken place."
GEORGE BERNARD SHAW

IF YOU'VE BEEN AROUND THE FINANCIAL community, much you fully realize the current perception of life insurance as an asset. It seems that every financial "guru" shouts from the mountain tops to *"buy term and invest the rest."* But where did this come from? Where did this notion of buying term and investing the difference originate, and what exactly is "the rest?" I do think it vitally important to know the history and relevance of life insurance as an asset.

The history of life insurance is vast, being that it is one of the eldest products in American history. The first policies in America were bought around the late 1760s.[59] The origins of life insurance, however, go back to 100 B.C., when Roman military officer Caius Marius founded a "burial club" to insure the cost of laying to rest his troops.[60] The idea caught and expanded throughout the Roman Empire. Over time the concept grew to include ministers and, eventually, regular citizens.

If you think about it, the concept is a very rational one. There was a cost of dying and, as abysmal as it might have been to think about, it was very real. Instead of taking this risk on yourself, you could have spread the risk over a large group of people. Originally it was a group of men that agreed to each pay a portion of the aggregate cost of burial and a stipend, for a time, to the deceased's family.

By the late 1800's in the U.S., life insurance had become very popular with only one problem: clients were unhappy that their families would only get a benefit if the insured passed away. Until this time, term insurance was the only option. Clients would pay a certain premium for a certain death benefit, but that premium would increase each year with the statistical chance of death. This only made sense. Insurance is not a gamble, it is a dispersal of risk. As a person gets older the risk of death increases, therefore the premium goes up. Eventually that premium gets so high that it becomes unaffordable.

Term Life Insurance

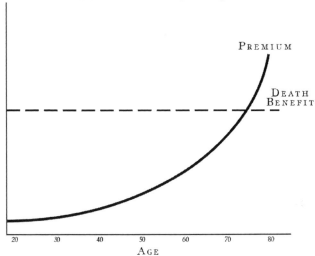

People demanded a new option, and this is where permanent life insurance got its start. It was to be called *whole life insurance* because it would be around for one's whole life, whereas term insurance was meant to be around for a certain *term* of time. In the original whole life insurance set-up, the insured (the client) paid an agreed-upon premium from their current age to age 100. In exchange, the life insurance company gave the client a guaranteed death benefit and a cash-value. The cash-value was actually the death benefit reserves that the company kept on hand, given the statistical chance of the client's death. It (the cash-value) had to legally grow to the death benefit amount by age 100. So the life insurance company calculated what they thought they could earn and backed into what the client would have to pay in order to get a certain amount of whole life insurance.

Whole Life Insurance

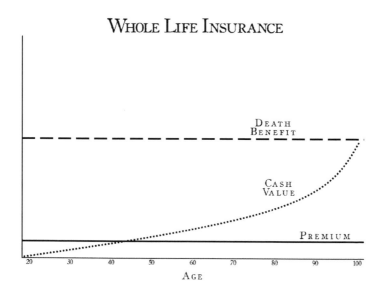

Over the years, the perception of the life insurance industry has gone from one of prestige to one of sliminess. In some ways this is warranted. In some ways it is not. Either way, the perception is not the reality, and those who go solely on their perception lack objectivity.

Buy Term and Invest the Rest

As we have discussed, the late 70's and 80's were filled with massive market upswings and interest rate manipulations. From the early 1900's to the late 1970's, Americans saved large amounts of their money in and trusted certain life insurance companies. That began to change in the mid-1980's when Charles Givens, one of the first financial "gurus," wrote that a person should never buy whole life insurance because term life was so much cheaper. Since that time many financial authors and espoused experts have followed suit—including, but not limited to, Dave Ramsey and Suze Orman. They have said that people should always *buy term and invest the difference*—claiming that one could earn a higher overall rate of return. The difference he referred to was the delta between a supposed term premium and a whole life premium.

One of the reasons for the rise of the *buy term and invest the difference* mantra was the fact that interest rates and market returns were catapulting to astronomical levels. As a response, the life insurance industry created universal life and variable universal life—a type of plan where the death benefit is not truly permanent, and the cash value is invested in some sort of outside asset (like a CD or a mutual fund). Near the end of this chapter, I will analyze the universal life system. For now, though, let's look at the practical application of *buying term and investing the difference.*

In the chart below you can see an example of a 30-year term insurance policy on a 35-year-old male, one that is often promoted by the "gurus." The death benefit is by the black line, and the premium is by the gray line. For 30 years the premium is consistent at $2,000 per year. This is very low considering the $1 million dollar death benefit. This is all well and good, except for the fact that there is a reason the life insurance company can charge such a low rate to this 35 year old healthy man: the statistical chance of his death before the 30 year period is up is next to nil. The insurance company is charging what it needs to protect against the small percentage of middle 30-year-olds it knows will pass away during this 30-year stretch, which is the vast minority. After the 30-year stretch, the premium jumps dramatically to levels that the man will almost certainly not pay. This is on purpose. The insurance company doesn't want to (and doesn't need to) take on the risk of a person who has paid in so little. And they do not know how his health has progressed. The term has served its purpose, and now it's gone. The premium has been a pure cost (just like you think of nearly every type of insurance), and if one hasn't used it then they have nothing to show for it at the end of the period.

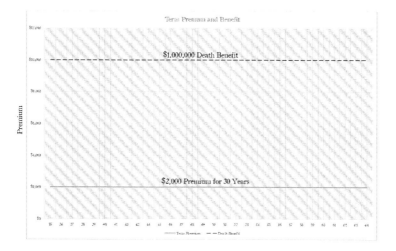

On the other hand, the often misunderstood whole life policy, is simply the counter to term. As will be further established, it is not a "rip-off," nor is it expensive. It is an actuarial calculation of how much one would need to invest on a level basis to guarantee a death benefit for his entire life. In the next two chapters I will examine the different types of life insurance companies and permanent life insurance policies. This is an example of the most basic type of whole life that has been around for 150 plus years.

In the chart below, the higher black line represents the death benefit, which starts at $1 million. The lower black line represents the cash value and the grey line represents the total premium paid.

The annual premium in this example is $12,228. So, this 35-year-old male pays that $12,228 each year for 30 years. At the end of the 30-year period, he has funded a total of $366,840. He has $742,625 of cash value and a death benefit of $1,600,467.

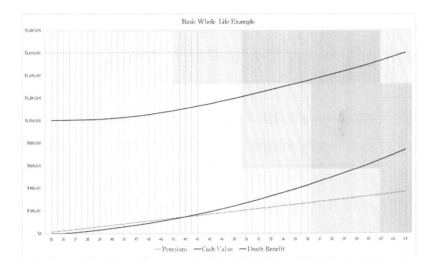

Now, let's compare the two scenarios. In scenario one, the term plan, the gentleman would invest the difference of the term and whole life premium. That difference would be $10,228 ($12,228 minus $2,000). Assuming the cash value reaches $742,625 at age 64, a projection based on the interest rate environment of 2015 or so—we need to run a time value calculation to see what interest rate (CAGR) we would have to earn on our "difference" to match that long-term cash value.

In order to properly analyze the situation, we must know where we might invest the difference. Let's go with the prevailing wisdom: mutual funds. To compare apples to apples, we need to assume some annual fee and annual tax for the mutual funds. For this example, I assume a 1.50% annual fee and a 20% annual tax on earnings. **The resulting CAGR that this person would have to earn is 8.15%.** That is, on his "difference" he'd have to likely earn a 10-12% average on his assets. Maybe this is possible. But given the market data we've examined so far, it's unlikely.

Year	Earnings Rate	Annual Cash Flow	Interest Earnings	Tax Payment	Misc. Fees	End of Year Acct. Value
35	8.15%	$ 10,228	$ 833	$ (133)	$ (166)	$ 10,762
36	8.15%	$ 10,228	$ 1,710	$ (274)	$ (341)	$ 22,086
37	8.15%	$ 10,228	$ 2,633	$ (422)	$ (524)	$ 34,000
38	8.15%	$ 10,228	$ 3,603	$ (577)	$ (717)	$ 46,537
39	8.15%	$ 10,228	$ 4,625	$ (741)	$ (921)	$ 59,728
40	8.15%	$ 10,228	$ 5,700	$ (913)	$ (1,135)	$ 73,608
41	8.15%	$ 10,228	$ 6,830	$ (1,094)	$ (1,360)	$ 88,212
42	8.15%	$ 10,228	$ 8,020	$ (1,285)	$ (1,597)	$ 103,579
43	8.15%	$ 10,228	$ 9,272	$ (1,485)	$ (1,846)	$ 119,748
44	8.15%	$ 10,228	$ 10,589	$ (1,696)	$ (2,108)	$ 136,761
45	8.15%	$ 10,228	$ 11,976	$ (1,918)	$ (2,384)	$ 154,661
46	8.15%	$ 10,228	$ 13,434	$ (2,152)	$ (2,675)	$ 173,497
47	8.15%	$ 10,228	$ 14,969	$ (2,398)	$ (2,980)	$ 193,315
48	8.15%	$ 10,228	$ 16,583	$ (2,656)	$ (3,302)	$ 214,168
49	8.15%	$ 10,228	$ 18,282	$ (2,928)	$ (3,640)	$ 236,110
50	8.15%	$ 10,228	$ 20,070	$ (3,215)	$ (3,996)	$ 259,197
51	8.15%	$ 10,228	$ 21,951	$ (3,516)	$ (4,371)	$ 283,489
52	8.15%	$ 10,228	$ 23,930	$ (3,833)	$ (4,765)	$ 309,049
53	8.15%	$ 10,228	$ 26,012	$ (4,167)	$ (5,179)	$ 335,944
54	8.15%	$ 10,228	$ 28,204	$ (4,518)	$ (5,616)	$ 364,242
55	8.15%	$ 10,228	$ 30,509	$ (4,887)	$ (6,075)	$ 394,018
56	8.15%	$ 10,228	$ 32,935	$ (5,275)	$ (6,558)	$ 425,348
57	8.15%	$ 10,228	$ 35,488	$ (5,684)	$ (7,066)	$ 458,313
58	8.15%	$ 10,228	$ 38,173	$ (6,115)	$ (7,601)	$ 492,999
59	8.15%	$ 10,228	$ 40,999	$ (6,567)	$ (8,163)	$ 529,496
60	8.15%	$ 10,228	$ 43,973	$ (7,043)	$ (8,755)	$ 567,898
61	8.15%	$ 10,228	$ 47,101	$ (7,545)	$ (9,378)	$ 608,304
62	8.15%	$ 10,228	$ 50,394	$ (8,072)	$(10,034)	$ 650,820
63	8.15%	$ 10,228	$ 53,857	$ (8,627)	$(10,724)	$ 695,555
64	8.15%	$ 10,228	$ 57,502	$ (9,211)	$(11,449)	$ 742,625

Additionally, at the end of the 30 year period, the man has no life insurance, and he likely has a very volatile asset. The point of this analysis is not to say that one should or shouldn't buy whole life insurance. It is only to say, so far, that the reasons for not doing so are blatantly erroneous—specifically when we look at the real data. To the Givens' (and others') credit, they began stating that the *buy term and invest the difference* model was effective about the time that interest rates on CD's were near 10%. Well, in that case, sure, *buy term and invest the difference* looks pretty solid. But that's a false context. Then the more recent "gurus" compared it to the stock market of the 80's and 90's. Once again, a false context.

Furthermore, corporations, banks, and special interest groups put billions of dollars each year into properly structured life insurance. Google "Walt Disney life insurance," "JC Penny life insurance," and "John McCain life insurance." You will find that these are just a few of the more public examples of how (relatively) modern business and political leaders have used life insurance as a financial asset.

OPTIMIZING CASH VALUE

As just mentioned, banks, corporations, special interest groups, and many of the nation's wealthiest individuals have and continue to shift large amounts of capital into properly structured mutual PLI policies. However, they do it differently than the typical person. The average person is sold by an average insurance agent or financial advisor. Most of the time these agents and advisors are taught by their firms to sell the most commission-heavy policy possible. However, there is a better way to do it. The Internal Revenue Service dictates how efficient a policy can be via *section 7702* of the tax code. This delineates the *Modified Endowment Contract* (MEC) rules.

The MEC rules and *IRC section 7702* came from the *Technical Corrections Act of 1988* (H.R 4333, S. 2238). The TCA was created because the super wealthy of the time were stashing millions of dollars into short-pay life insurance contracts. Previous to the TCA of 1988, if a person wanted to put $1 million into a life insurance contract, they could likely get about 95% directly into cash value. Meaning, only about 5% would go to the base premium. The US. Department of Treasury noticed that millions of dollars were foregoing treasuries (a type of fixed income investment offered by the government) for mutual company permanent life insurance policies (MCPLI). Many of these massive funders of MCPLI were politicians and special interest groups. The majority of these people didn't want to change the rules, but they compromised (I suppose) and created IRC section 7702—which dictates what percentage of a premium can go directly to cash value.

Most working citizens are not at all aware that money can go directly to cash value. In fact, most advisors aren't really aware of this either. If they have any knowledge of MCPLI, it is mainly of the type we looked at earlier. In the coming chart you will see two examples. The left side is the same policy that we viewed graphically a moment ago. Yet, in this case we see the numbers. The "Total Premium" column represents that total amount of money we've put in overtime—$12,228 per year multiplied by the number of years. The cash value column shows our accessible cash value. And the death benefit column shows the insurance amount. It is not until year twelve that our cash value exceeds our total funding. Thinking in context—this is not necessarily a bad thing. But it could be better.

You can see a slightly different scenario on the right. In this case, instead of the entire $12,228 going to the whole life premium, we are putting as much of it as the MEC guidelines will allow directly in to the cash-value. In this case we have about as much money in our cash value account as we have funded by year nine. You can also see that the long-term result (a cash value of $742,325 and a death benefit of $1,600,467 on the left; a cash value of $809,427 and a death benefit of $1,625,136 on the right) is not all that staggering. This is because the expenses of the policy mainly come in the first two or so years—and they come mostly from the base premium rather than the amount that is going directly to cash value. This is a topic we will discuss in more depth in the next chapter.

The primary benefit of structuring a policy in this manner is the early access to cash. Again, the cash value is safe, tax-advantaged, and grows well overtime. The more capital we can get into a plan, the better it is for our long-term financial situation. In the coming chapters we will go into more depth on why MCPLI is bar none one of the most effective assets in the U.S. today and why you should make it the foundation of your aggregate plan. Throughout the analytical process you must remember— it is not about opinion or pontification. It is about data. Just because you've heard from a person whom you trust that life insurance is a bad investment does not mean that it is true. No more than your trusted ancestors believed that the earth was flat, that cars would never travel faster than stagecoaches, and there would never be a market for personal computers.

B. Chase Chandler

		All Base Policy					Max-Non MEC Policy		
Year	Age	Total Premium	Cash Value	Death Benefit	Year	Age	Total Premium	Cash Value	Death Benefit
1	35	$12,228	$160	$1,000,756	1	35	$12,228	$5,446	$574,597
2	36	$24,456	$489	$1,002,231	2	36	$24,456	$11,311	$600,457
3	37	$36,684	$8,067	$1,004,347	3	37	$36,684	$21,494	$626,434
4	38	$48,912	$19,114	$1,007,117	4	38	$48,912	$33,954	$652,551
5	39	$61,140	$30,709	$1,010,509	5	39	$61,140	$47,087	$678,793
6	40	$73,368	$43,525	$1,017,034	6	40	$73,368	$61,291	$706,568
7	41	$85,596	$57,539	$1,026,392	7	41	$85,596	$76,570	$735,716
8	42	$97,824	$72,728	$1,038,264	8	42	$97,824	$92,927	$766,090
9	43	$110,052	$89,118	$1,052,397	9	43	$110,052	$110,399	$797,567
10	44	$122,280	$106,696	$1,068,552	10	44	$122,280	$128,994	$830,033
11	45	$134,508	$126,155	$1,086,509	11	45	$134,508	$149,111	$863,387
12	46	$146,736	$146,861	$1,106,067	12	46	$146,736	$170,436	$897,563
13	47	$158,964	$168,809	$1,127,003	13	47	$158,964	$192,985	$932,440
14	48	$171,192	$192,132	$1,149,170	14	48	$171,192	$216,892	$967,986
15	49	$183,420	$216,842	$1,172,391	15	49	$183,420	$242,193	$1,004,119
16	50	$195,648	$242,914	$1,196,498	16	50	$195,648	$268,915	$1,040,823
17	51	$207,876	$270,342	$1,221,405	17	51	$207,876	$297,083	$1,078,052
18	52	$220,104	$299,077	$1,246,980	18	52	$220,104	$326,692	$1,115,773
19	53	$232,332	$329,125	$1,273,127	19	53	$232,332	$357,791	$1,154,004
20	54	$244,560	$360,442	$1,299,782	20	54	$244,560	$390,385	$1,192,748
21	55	$256,788	$392,943	$1,326,865	21	55	$256,788	$424,433	$1,232,004
22	56	$269,016	$426,701	$1,354,332	22	56	$269,016	$460,055	$1,271,822
23	57	$281,244	$461,695	$1,382,114	23	57	$281,244	$497,275	$1,312,199
24	58	$293,472	$498,089	$1,410,172	24	58	$293,472	$536,290	$1,353,176
25	59	$305,700	$535,877	$1,438,469	25	59	$305,700	$577,160	$1,394,797
26	60	$317,928	$573,615	$1,467,903	26	60	$317,928	$619,250	$1,437,876
27	61	$330,156	$613,180	$1,498,790	27	61	$330,156	$663,516	$1,482,395
28	62	$342,384	$654,513	$1,531,180	28	62	$342,384	$709,930	$1,528,420
29	63	$354,612	$697,626	$1,565,063	29	63	$354,612	$758,530	$1,575,993
30	64	$366,840	$742,625	$1,600,467	30	64	$366,840	$809,427	$1,625,136

MEC References:

http://en.wikipedia.org/wiki/Endowment_policy

http://www.law.cornell.edu/uscode/text/26/7702A

http://www.law.cornell.edu/uscode/text/26/7702

The Rise and Fall of Universal Life

Before moving on, let me address the general concept of universal life. Universal life became, for a short while, the primary type of permanent life insurance sold—even thought is wasn't categorically permanent. This was largely a response to the high interest rate period of the 1970's and 1980's. The Life Insurance Company of California (later became E.F. Hutton) first introduced UL in 1979.[61] It was created primarily as a means of competing with the high interest rate environment of the time. But it has now become a means of reducing risk for the insurance company.

Earlier we went through how term insurance works. Universal life is nothing more than term insurance with a cash fund, which will eventually be eaten up either by volatility (if it is variable universal life) or rising term costs. Universal life comes in a few shapes and sizes: universal life (UL), variable universal life (VUL), and equity indexed universal life (EIUL; also known as fixed indexed universal life or FIUL).

The black line in the chart entitled "Universal Life" shows a state premium in a hypothetical universal life policy. The grey line represents the term cost within the policy—the cost of the death benefit coverage. In the early years, the difference between the 'stated premium' and the 'term cost' goes to some side fund. This side fund is invested in either money market funds (UL), mutual fund type investments (VUL), or a concoction similar to the fixed indexed annuity asset that we discussed in the previous chapter (EIUL).

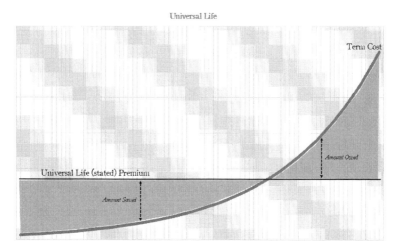

Throughout the first few years, the stated premium is higher than the term cost. But at some point the term cost surpasses the stated premium. At this point, the excess term cost is subsidized by the cash value. As my team and I (with the help of very kind actuaries) have performed much analysis, it is clear that UL really only works for the family in a consistently high interest rate environment. In the following example you will see that, in almost any long-term scenario, UL or any variation results in less than impressive results.

The below diagram will serve for our example. The term cost starts at $700 and rises from there. The stated UL premium is $4,000. By year 21 the term cost exceeds the stated UL premium and the difference begins to eat up the cash value.

Universal Life Simulation

Year	Age	Term Cost	UL Premium	Difference	Year	Age	Term Cost	UL Premium	Difference
1	35	$700	$4,000	$3,300	21	55	$4,299	$4,000	-$299
2	36	$767	$4,000	$3,234	22	56	$4,708	$4,000	-$708
3	37	$839	$4,000	$3,161	23	57	$5,155	$4,000	-$1,155
4	38	$919	$4,000	$3,081	24	58	$5,644	$4,000	-$1,644
5	39	$1,006	$4,000	$2,994	25	59	$6,181	$4,000	-$2,181
6	40	$1,102	$4,000	$2,898	26	60	$6,768	$4,000	-$2,768
7	41	$1,207	$4,000	$2,793	27	61	$7,411	$4,000	-$3,411
8	42	$1,321	$4,000	$2,679	28	62	$8,115	$4,000	-$4,115
9	43	$1,447	$4,000	$2,553	29	63	$8,886	$4,000	-$4,886
10	44	$1,584	$4,000	$2,416	30	64	$9,730	$4,000	-$5,730
11	45	$1,735	$4,000	$2,265	31	65	$10,654	$4,000	-$6,654
12	46	$1,900	$4,000	$2,100	32	66	$11,666	$4,000	-$7,666
13	47	$2,080	$4,000	$1,920	33	67	$12,775	$4,000	-$8,775
14	48	$2,278	$4,000	$1,722	34	68	$13,988	$4,000	-$9,988
15	49	$2,494	$4,000	$1,506	35	69	$15,317	$4,000	-$11,317
16	50	$2,731	$4,000	$1,269	36	70	$16,772	$4,000	-$12,772
17	51	$2,990	$4,000	$1,010	37	71	$18,366	$4,000	-$14,366
18	52	$3,274	$4,000	$726	38	72	$20,110	$4,000	-$16,110
19	53	$3,586	$4,000	$414	39	73	$22,021	$4,000	-$18,021
20	54	$3,926	$4,000	$74	40	74	$24,113	$4,000	-$20,113

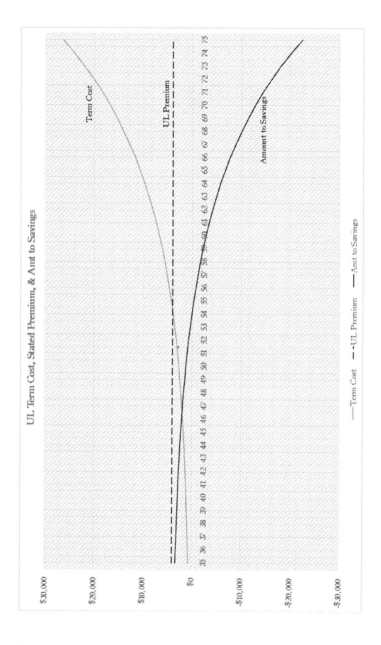

UL Term Cost, Stated Premium, & Amt to Savings

Term Cost

UL Premium

Amount to Savings

—— Term Cost   – –UL Premium   —— Amt to Savings

In this case we have a positive delta going towards savings until age 55, at which point our cash value would begin to deteriorate to the term cost that is above our stated premium. Of course, all of this is dependent on our continuing to pay the UL premium, which many people are taught they do not have to do.

When UL was invented, we were looking at 8-10% CD rates. Assuming an 8% CAGR on the saved amount, we would have over $300,000 at age 75. But if we assume only a 5.30% CAGR, we're out of money at age 75.

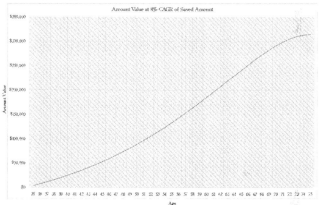

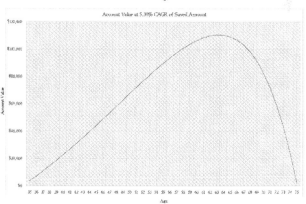

With a 5.30% CAGR on the saved money, our UL policy blows up on us at age 75... and this assumes that we save that $4,000 every year. It gets worse. When we assume a lesser CAGR, say something like 4% (which is closer to what has actually occurred), our UL policy runs out of cash at age 72. If we'd had a variable universal life plan (VUL), which would have been invested in some combination of mutual funds, the results wouldn't have been much better. The below chart assumes the savings dollars are invested in a Dow Jones Index fund as the side account. The dotted line is the account value. The solid black line is the total amount of premium paid. You can see that it appears fairly attractive when the market is booming in the mid-90's. However, after a return to normal, by the end of year 2013 we end up with just over $114,000 and we've experienced a -1.78% CAGR.

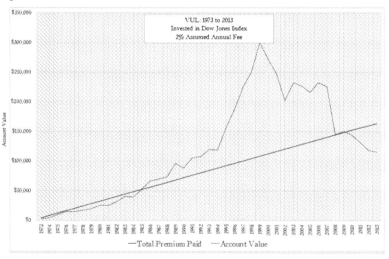

In summation, UL plans are not effective because the rising cost of term. Additionally, the cash value is tied to some asset in which you could have invested outside of life insurance. Because of the rising term cost and the unknown future return of the asset, the consistent effect of UL (and its various forms) is the worst of both worlds. On one hand you have a low early cost of insurance. But, on the other, you have a policy that will often end with little to no cash value or death benefit.

There is, however, a type of permanent life insurance that is exceptionally prudent when structured properly. This is the type that I referred to in the section describing the MEC rules. Allow me to introduce the concept of the mutual company.

20

MUTUAL UNDERSTANDING

"There are seven sins in the world: Wealth without work, Pleasure without conscience, Knowledge without character, Commerce without morality, Science without humanity, Worship without sacrifice and politics without principle."

MAHATMA GANDHI

FOR SIMPLICITY, WE DID NOT ENTER into how life insurance companies differ in the last chapter. In truth, the topic is strikingly simple, yet full of interesting complexity. (At least that's what I tell myself.) There are two types of life insurance companies: *mutually held* and *publically traded*. You're likely familiar with how publically traded companies work. They are bought and sold on a stock market exchange each day. Their owners are the stockholders. They must answer to and satisfy two parties: their customers and their stockholders. Mutually held companies, on the contrary, are owned by their policyholders. They do not have two masters to serve.

The public company must answer to shareholders, analysts, and the board of directors for its quarterly performance. Each quarter, analysts publish an EPS[i] number along with many other business metrics that the company should meet. If the company meets most of these metrics for the quarter, then all is well. If not, somebody's in trouble. The executives, and the board for that matter, have a significantly vested interest in keeping the company profitable each quarter. On one hand, it's how they keep their job. On the other, much of their compensation is in the form of stock, stock options, and bonuses tied to EPS and other performance business metrics. This isn't in-and-of-itself bad—it's what it has become that is so dangerous. **In this era of speculation, the majority of publically traded companies have been forced to put short-term interests over the company's long-term interests.**

PUBLICALLY TRADED COMPANY

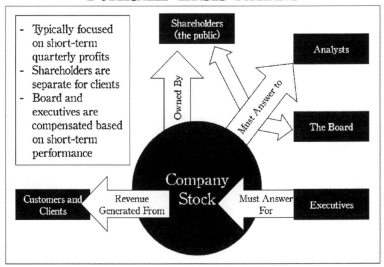

---

[i] Earnings Per Share

Mutual companies maintain a more attractive arrangement —mainly in the fact that they hold aligned interests. The mutually held company is owned by its clients. Therefore, what is in the best interest of the shareholder is most often in the best interest of the client. The company is privately held, doesn't have to answer to quarterly analyst demands, and is singularly focused on the long-term financial health of the enterprise. In short, the mutual company does not have to serve two masters. Its clients are its owners, and its owners are its clients.

This may seem like only a slight difference. It's not. This difference in structures breeds a massive difference in long-term safety and performance.

MUTUAL COMPANY

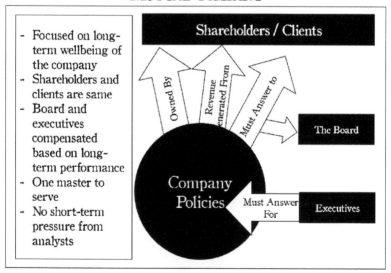

Gandhi once said that there were seven sins in the world: "Wealth without work, Pleasure without conscience, Knowledge without character, Commerce without morality, Science without humanity, Worship without sacrifice, and Politics without principle." I find each of these relevant to the discussion of mutual vs. publically traded life insurance companies and their relationship to your financial situation. Of course, publically traded companies are not evil. Most of what you buy, use, watch, and eat each day is provided by a company traded on either the NYSE or NASDAQ. But in the case of publically traded life insurance companies, I believe most of them went public in the first place for the wrong reasons.

You're already fully aware that the 80's and 90's were the largest 20-year bull run in modern stock market history. It seemed that all you had to do was throw your money at stocks, and you'd be on your way to a healthy retirement. Internet moguls were going public daily—and being paid handsomely. A few insurance companies wanted to tag along for the ride.

When a corporation goes public, the owners are selling shares to the public, or at least offering ownership to the general public. When a person like you or me buys those shares, we now assume partial ownership and risk for how that company performs. This is called an *initial public offering*, or IPO. The process boosts the company's balance sheet in the short-term because modern finance has taught that public companies should be traded at a higher multiple than private ones. So, an IPO might warrant a valuation of 15 or 20 times the companies EBITDA. The rationale for this, Wall Street promoters proclaim, is that financial records are now more publically available and the ownership is more liquid (meaning it's easier to buy and sell ownership shares). On that basis, neither the valuation nor the IPO sound all that bad. The problem enters when we look at the potentially devious incentives.

The 1990's through the early 2000's became somewhat of a popular time for mutual life insurance companies to demutualize.

Meaning, they would hold an IPO to transition from their mutual status to a publically traded status. The reasoning for this was callous at best. They claimed that it was to raise capital (companies would often IPO to raise capital for expansion purposes). They claimed they wanted to go into new international markets, and that this process would expand profit margins and diversification for current policyholders/owners. Even though these companies were doing quite well and were considered some of the safest in the world, they claimed they could boost revenues, profits, and current assets (cash). Specifically, it was the higher level executives and the board arguing for this change. They pulled out their spreadsheets and Ivy League pedigrees to validate their motivation. And this is where it got fishy.

Not long ago I was speaking with one of the top executives for one of the largest insurance companies in the world. This person explained to me how and why so many insurance companies demutualized in the simplest of manners, and I quote: *"to give the board and C-level executives a massive payday."* These IPO events would (and did) create massive short-term revenue and profit increases because of the new capital generated from selling shares to the public. These C-level types structured their compensation packages to pay out large amounts at the time all this new money came in. This person, who understandably wants to remain anonymous, was a mid-level executive at the time, but claims that *"everyone knew what was going on."*

Bottom line: really smart people can make really dumb decisions look really rationale, because they're that smart. We've seen this across the board, but especially on Wall Street and in Washington, where bending arguments produces enormous money and power.

The life insurance companies that remained mutual have seen great benefits. And they're likely the strongest companies in the world today. *Mutual Company Permanent Life Insurance* (MCPLI) is probably the least understood asset, especially by financial "gurus" and the general public. When I spoke of the *max-non MEC* type of optimization in the last chapter, I was specifically speaking of MCPLI. The illustration shown of an *all base policy* as compared to a *max-non MEC policy* was an example of MCPLI. The benefits here—which we'll discuss in more depth in the next chapter—are tax-advantaged growth and distribution, safety, a competitive tax-equivalent CAGR, liquidity, a guaranteed loan provision against the cash value, and the (often underestimated) value of a permanent death benefit. And one more thing. MCPLI, when structured properly, is the farthest from "expensive."

Overhead Expenses

To espouse that MCPLI is expensive is to lack context or to lack any understanding of what MCPLI is. At its core, MCPLI cannot be "expensive" because the policyholders are also the shareholders. Therefore the only expense there is, overtime, is the cost of doing business. The existence of the mutual company is solely for the benefit of the policyholder. The policyholder's primary desire should be for the company to remain solvent and profitable for many years to come. Decisions made within a mutual company are with that in mind. Over a period of time, what is best for the company is best for the policyholder. The profits are distributed to the owners (which are, again, the policyholders). Therefore, MCPLI is the essence of efficiency for the family's long-term finances; who gets to take part in one of the safest and most competent businesses of modern history.

We are, however, trained to think short-term. The truth is that MCPLI only appears expensive to the untrained eye—when a person is looking at it from a conventional vantage point. Remember the circuitous path, the box of pain. Upfront costs are indeed high, relative to other assets. But this leads to a much lower long-term cost. Imagine for a moment that you had a choice between two assets:

In the first you paid 1.50% per year of the account balance. This is known as a fee-based portfolio, today's most common conventional investing recommendation.

On the other asset, imagine you paid 50% the first year, 10% in years two through ten, then 4% per year after that—but these percentages are paid on the contributions, rather than the balance. This is a more aggressive version of MCPLI—meaning it's actually less. The numbers above are used for the sake of simplicity.

In this analysis we will look at funding $24,000 per year for 25 years. We'll assume that we earn 6% per year on both assets. I encourage you to judge the results for yourself on the next page.

At this point, it would be wise to take into consideration Spitznagel's roundabout mentality. MCPLI, though it is unknown to most, is the essence of 'going backwards in order to go forwards.' We retreat for the purpose of gaining a long-term asset that becomes our most valued, safer asset. In the coming chapter I will explain the value of the liquidity for financing purposes.

Fee-Based Portfolio (1.50% annual fee)

Year	Beg. Of Year Acct. Value	Earnings Rate	Annual Cash Flow	Interest Earnings	Misc. Fees	End of Year Acct. Value
1		6.00%	24,000	1,440	(382)	25,058
2	25,058	6.00%	24,000	2,944	(780)	51,222
3	51,222	6.00%	24,000	4,513	(1,196)	78,539
4	78,539	6.00%	24,000	6,152	(1,630)	107,061
5	107,061	6.00%	24,000	7,864	(2,084)	136,841
6	136,841	6.00%	24,000	9,650	(2,557)	167,934
7	167,934	6.00%	24,000	11,516	(3,052)	200,398
8	200,398	6.00%	24,000	13,464	(3,568)	234,294
9	234,294	6.00%	24,000	15,498	(4,107)	269,685
10	269,685	6.00%	24,000	17,621	(4,670)	306,637
11	306,637	6.00%	24,000	19,838	(5,257)	345,218
12	345,218	6.00%	24,000	22,153	(5,871)	385,500
13	385,500	6.00%	24,000	24,570	(6,511)	427,559
14	427,559	6.00%	24,000	27,094	(7,180)	471,473
15	471,473	6.00%	24,000	29,728	(7,878)	517,323
16	517,323	6.00%	24,000	32,479	(8,607)	565,196
17	565,196	6.00%	24,000	35,352	(9,368)	615,179
18	615,179	6.00%	24,000	38,351	(10,163)	667,367
19	667,367	6.00%	24,000	41,482	(10,993)	721,856
20	721,856	6.00%	24,000	44,751	(11,859)	778,748
21	778,748	6.00%	24,000	48,165	(12,764)	838,150
22	838,150	6.00%	24,000	51,729	(13,708)	900,170
23	900,170	6.00%	24,000	55,450	(14,694)	964,926
24	964,926	6.00%	24,000	59,336	(15,724)	1,032,538
25	1,032,538	6.00%	24,000	63,392	(16,799)	1,103,131
Totals	1,032,538	6.00%	600,000	684,532	(181,401)	1,103,131

MCPLI Type Account

Year	Beg. Of Year Acct. Value	Earnings Rate	Annual Cash Flow	Interest Earnings	Misc. Fees	End of Year Acct. Value
1		6.00%	24,000	1,440	(12,000)	13,440
2	13,440	6.00%	24,000	2,246	(2,400)	37,286
3	37,286	6.00%	24,000	3,677	(2,400)	62,564
4	62,564	6.00%	24,000	5,194	(2,400)	89,357
5	89,357	6.00%	24,000	6,801	(2,400)	117,759
6	117,759	6.00%	24,000	8,506	(2,400)	147,864
7	147,864	6.00%	24,000	10,312	(2,400)	179,776
8	179,776	6.00%	24,000	12,227	(2,400)	213,603
9	213,603	6.00%	24,000	14,256	(2,400)	249,459
10	249,459	6.00%	24,000	16,408	(2,400)	287,467
11	287,467	6.00%	24,000	18,688	(960)	329,195
12	329,195	6.00%	24,000	21,192	(960)	373,426
13	373,426	6.00%	24,000	23,846	(960)	420,312
14	420,312	6.00%	24,000	26,659	(960)	470,010
15	470,010	6.00%	24,000	29,641	(960)	522,691
16	522,691	6.00%	24,000	32,801	(960)	578,533
17	578,533	6.00%	24,000	36,152	(960)	637,724
18	637,724	6.00%	24,000	39,703	(960)	700,468
19	700,468	6.00%	24,000	43,468	(960)	766,976
20	766,976	6.00%	24,000	47,459	(960)	837,475
21	837,475	6.00%	24,000	51,688	(960)	912,203
22	912,203	6.00%	24,000	56,172	(960)	991,415
23	991,415	6.00%	24,000	60,925	(960)	1,075,380
24	1,075,380	6.00%	24,000	65,963	(960)	1,164,383
25	1,164,383	6.00%	24,000	71,303	(960)	1,258,726
Totals	1,164,383	6.00%	600,000	706,726	(48,000)	1,258,726

THE STREET LOCKDOWN

Wall Street has quite the lockdown on the marketing, advertising, and general promotion of financial products. In fact, certain financial publications and websites will not even allow advertisements specifically for MCPLI. Because of the significant revenues generated from traditional financial products (mainly mutual funds and fee-based portfolios), *the Street* has a vested interest in keeping things the way they are. If word were to get out about the cost of their strategies contrasted with the cost of other more valuable strategies, they'd be in a world of hurt.

As you analyzed on the previous page, the fees coming from MCPLI are little compared to that of the popular fee-based account. On the other hand, mutual companies (for good reason) do not frivolously spend advertising dollars to influence the public.

COMPLEXITY

MCPLI is far from complex, yet its foreignness makes it seem just that. If complexity exists, it is mainly because of the government's intervention via section 7702. Adding to the misconception are insurance companies' lack of focus on getting the message out; mainly by a lack of advertising, public relations, and lobbying dollars (plus the inert failure to attract modern marketing minds who would obviously rather go to Silicon Valley or MSNBC/CNBC/Fox News/CNN/Bloomberg).

The reality is simple. MCPLI is, in my opinion, the most prudent foundational asset. You place savings dollars in an MCPLI policy overtime and:

-   you let it grow without worry
-   you earn a competitive, safe long-term CAGR

- you have a permanent death benefit
- you have liquidity for emergencies or opportunities
    - via collateralized loans or withdrawals
- if managed correctly, you receive a tax-free income

The combination of these benefits cannot be found in any other asset. And the reality is, there is no other arrangement like this mutual company structure in the financial world. With other passive savings and investing assets, the company's aim is to profit off of you. In this set up *you* are receiving that profit as *you* are an owner of the company.

An Aside on Convention

If, by chance, you are much like me when I begin to realize the vast misconceptions of traditional financial planning methods, you may be wondering: why are so many people so adamantly for fee-based and other securities based strategies?

I think the answer is quite simple. On one hand, it is much easier to go with convention than against it. On the other, their livelihood, or at least their perception thereof, is based on these traditional methods. Imagine the family financial planning shop that vigorously sells their money management strategies at 1.5% per year. Assuming they manage somewhere between $50 and $200 million, you can begin to grasp their revenue.

However, for the consumer, it is analogous to buying a car where, in one location it is selling for $40,000. Thirty miles down the road the same car is selling for $25,000. Would one be so naïve as to claim the salesman's knowledge or expertise as a reason to buy the first location's car? Of course not. Yet, this is exactly what is occurring in the financial planning world. Consumers are buying a product they, money management, that they could get far cheaper; through our MCPLI PES strategy, followed by, if they want to be in the market, index funds.

" A false but clear and precise idea always has more power in the world than one which is true but complex. "

ALEXIS DE TOCQUEVILLE

21

" If you want something new, you have to stop doing something old."

PETER F. DRUCKER

ONE OF THE MORE IMPACTFUL BOOKS I have read in the past few years is Peter Thiel's *Zero to One*. In it he beautifully describes the process of how things are created. He says making something that already exists better is going from 1 to *n*. However, for anything to go from 1 to *n*, it must have first been created; some entrepreneur, inventor, or thinker must have taken that thing from 0 to 1.

The epiphany here is in the pondering of the importance of the creation of new things—new information, new products, and new services. The enhancement of existing things is certainly important. But Thiel shows us why the future has always been defined by the new. It is difficult to think of what new things can and will be created. It's easy to think of how already existing technology will be improved. But to ponder the things we don't yet know about and to ponder the value created by those who have created the new is mind boggling. Imagine not having Facebook or PayPal or text messaging. Better yet, imagine not having personal computers or cell phones. It's hard to ponder not having these things; but there was once a time where we couldn't. We couldn't imagine there existence.

Because of our *status quo biases*, we often downplay truly new ideas. We're quick to jump on new improvements to old products, but the completely new scares us. Or, as in the early days of automobiles and computers, we don't see the practical need for their existence.

In the financial world there have been few constructive innovators. There have been many innovators (think 401ks, credit default swaps, and credit cards), most of whom have had a negative impact on families. A few of the more positively impactful innovators were these:

Benjamin Graham, a Columbia University finance professor, wrote a book called *The Intelligent Investor* (as well as many others) in which he encouraged thorough analysis, rather than speculation. Graham would go on to teach Warren Buffet the art and science of value investing.

John Bogle noticed the long-term effect of mutual fund fees. He founded The Vanguard Group in 1974 and became the father of low cost investing and index funds.

Bill Gross saw an opportunity for a fixed income bond market to coincide with the rapidly growing stock market, so he created the Pacific Investment Management Corporation (PIMCO). Although he's had his fair share of recent issues, Mr. Gross is credited with revolutionizing the bond market.

Each of these individuals took us from 0 to 1 in some area of finance. But there is one who, arguably, did the most for personal finance. Only his findings, while utilized by some of the largest corporations and wealthiest families, have yet to be accepted by the mainstream. They largely defy convention because they use the aforementioned *MCPLI*, and it has been difficult for the masses to accept. The person I'm speaking of is Nelson Nash. Much of this chapter would not have been written if not for his discoveries.

THE NASH PRINCIPLES

In the last chapter, I mentioned that MCPLI was the most effective foundational tool for a family's finances. Nash was the first modern professional to point this out. Many others have attempted to improve upon it, to take it from 1 to n, but it was Nash that, in this arena, took us from 0 to 1.[i]

The principle he brought to the forefront was that controlling the financing process—*the "banking" process*—was most important to controlling the wealth building process. Let me explain.

For every dollar spent, we lose not only that dollar, but we also lose what it could have done for us—what it could have grown to. Paying cash, as we earlier analyzed, does not in-and-of-itself save us money. This is Nash's essential principle: *we finance everything we buy*. We either pay interest for debt that is taken out or we give up the interest we could have earned.

---

[i] I would submit that, while others have pointed out some of the benefits of mutual company policies, Nash was the first one to point out the advantages in the context of *financial optimization*. Others viewed MCPLI as a potential diversification tool, rather than as the foundational asset of a family's finances.

Therefore, the contemporary emphasis on earning a higher *'rate of return'* is somewhat of the wrong focus, considering it would make more sense to focus on keeping more of the *opportunity cost* of our capital.

MCPLI gives us access to capital; it creates long-term cash and death benefit liquidity and becomes our own *financing* system.

Nash called this a financial tailwind: "It is like building an environment in the airplane world where you have a perpetual tailwind instead of a perpetual headwind."[62] This *aerodynamic tailwind* creates opportunity far surpassing conventional methods.

THE PRIVATE ECONOMIC SYSTEM

In truth, when you follow Nash's principles, you are effectively creating your owned privatized financial and economic strategy. You are choosing to maintain full control over assets, rather than hand control to the government (either through unknown tax implications or potential socialization). You are creating your own *private economic system* (PES). Assuming you agree that your financial wealth comes from some specialty, the next conclusion would be that your wealth has to reside somewhere; at least during the periods when it is not being deployed in your SoE. The purpose of PES and Nash's principles are to maximize the productivity of this capital residence.

The following chart will serve to set the stage for our discussion of MCPLI as the foundation of the family's financial strategy. It is an example of a 35 year old funding $24,000 per year from age 35 to age 65.

MCPLI

Age	Premium	Cash Value	Death Benefit	Age	Premium	Cash Value	Death Benefit
35	$ (24,000)	$ 16,052	$ 766,551		Age 56 - 75		
36	$ (24,000)	$ 35,948	$ 840,071	56	$ (24,000)	$ 884,083	$ 2,391,646
37	$ (24,000)	$ 62,606	$ 912,829	57	$ (24,000)	$ 951,166	$ 2,473,618
38	$ (24,000)	$ 90,647	$ 985,037	58	$ (24,000)	$ 1,021,443	$ 2,556,457
39	$ (24,000)	$ 120,164	$ 1,056,728	59	$ (24,000)	$ 1,095,039	$ 2,640,053
40	$ (24,000)	$ 149,715	$ 1,142,032	60	$ (24,000)	$ 1,171,887	$ 2,724,570
41	$ (24,000)	$ 180,798	$ 1,221,384	61	$ (24,000)	$ 1,252,118	$ 2,810,368
42	$ (24,000)	$ 213,494	$ 1,300,242	62	$ (24,000)	$ 1,335,818	$ 2,897,986
43	$ (24,000)	$ 247,874	$ 1,378,690	63	$ (24,000)	$ 1,423,075	$ 2,987,659
44	$ (24,000)	$ 283,996	$ 1,457,023	64	$ (24,000)	$ 1,514,012	$ 3,082,954
45	$ (24,000)	$ 321,787	$ 1,534,792	65		$ 1,585,717	$ 3,009,630
46	$ (24,000)	$ 361,495	$ 1,612,455	66		$ 1,660,815	$ 3,037,151
47	$ (24,000)	$ 403,219	$ 1,690,303	67		$ 1,739,000	$ 3,091,655
48	$ (24,000)	$ 447,026	$ 1,767,781	68		$ 1,820,387	$ 3,148,159
49	$ (24,000)	$ 493,046	$ 1,844,893	69		$ 1,905,049	$ 3,206,375
50	$ (24,000)	$ 541,292	$ 1,921,818	70		$ 1,993,080	$ 3,266,684
51	$ (24,000)	$ 591,912	$ 1,998,632	71		$ 2,084,704	$ 3,329,365
52	$ (24,000)	$ 645,001	$ 2,075,794	72		$ 2,180,009	$ 3,395,583
53	$ (24,000)	$ 700,664	$ 2,153,261	73		$ 2,279,175	$ 3,465,131
54	$ (24,000)	$ 758,981	$ 2,231,672	74		$ 2,382,283	$ 3,537,805
55	$ (24,000)	$ 820,063	$ 2,311,078	75		$ 2,489,083	$ 3,613,176

Liquidity & Utilization

In the 'cash value' column, you can see the amount of capital that is available to use from year to year. One can use this capital for any purpose (car purchases, real estate, vacations, etc.), or they can simply let it sit and grow.

There are two ways to utilize the cash value, either through a withdrawal or a policy loan. A withdrawal is quite simple in that it is simply taking money out. **A policy loan, on the other hand, is different in that it is a loan *against* the cash value.** It is not a withdrawal. The policy loan is coming from the insurance company's general loan portfolio, not from your cash value. This is money that they would have invested (or loaned out), but as a policyholder we have the right to take a loan *against* the cash value we've built up. We can use it to buy a car, fund education, go on vacation, invest in ventures within our SoE, or anything else we deem necessary.

The benefit here is that, when we take a policy loan, we are not interrupting the compounding of our cash value. Of course, as we earlier learned, money has a cost and that cost is the interest rate. So when we take a policy loan we must pay it back to the insurance company at the going interest rate (often tied to the Moody's Corporate Bond Index). The advantage is the flexibility we have in taking the loan and paying it back on our time line. We are allowed to pay the loan back on our own schedule. The insurance company does not give us time period. This can be a disadvantage if not properly managed. It is important to set up an amortization payback schedule (or to have an idea of how an investment may produce income or a return to pay off the loan).

At the end of this chapter, I have included a case study written by my firm's research team. It describes the reason a business might use PES as a current asset, but is relevant to the family as well.

Safety

Another benefit of MCPLI is safety. We have a guaranteed rate of return and cannot lose money over the long-term. This is the key tenant of any foundational asset. Mutual life insurance companies have been around for over 150 years and have been some of the most consistent in the U.S.

The guaranteed return gives a baseline. The addition of dividends (the profit of the company being returned to us as owners) creates the overall long-term CAGR. Once dividends are credited to a policyholder's cash value, they are there for good—they cannot be taken away or lose value.

Fee & Tax-Equivalent CAGR

The *fee and tax-equivalent CAGR* is the rate we would have to earn in another asset to simply match the long-term annualized rate of return of the cash value, assuming different fee and/or tax variables. Our net CAGR on the policy is 4.51% at age 75. But we can't assume that because another asset might earn a 7% or 8% average, it beats the 4.51% CAGR on the MCPLI cash value. As a reference point, the shaded rate *5.83%* indicates what we would have to earn if we were in a 15% tax bracket and had a 0.5% fee per year on another account. Maybe this would be an index fund type asset. We'd have to earn a CAGR of 5.83% on that index fund, which would likely be a 7-8% average, just to match the long-term growth of the cash value.

Annual Fee	Tax Bracket						
	0%	15%	20%	25%	30%	35%	40%
none	4.51%	5.30%	5.64%	6.01%	6.44%	6.94%	7.51%
0.5%	5.03%	5.83%	6.17%	6.54%	6.98%	7.47%	8.05
1.0%	5.56%	6.37%	5.70%	7.08%	7.52%	8.02%	8.60%
1.5%	6.10%	6.91%	7.24%	7.63%	8.06%	8.56%	9.15%
2.0%	6.64%	7.45%	7.79%	8.17%	8.61%	9.12%	9.71%
2.5%	7.19%	8.00%	8.34%	8.73%	9.17%	9.68%	10.3%
3.0%	7.74%	8.56%	8.90%	9.29%	9.73%	10.2%	10.8%

On the other hand, assume we are in a mutual fund, but it is in a Roth IRA so there is no tax effect. If we had a 2.5% annual fee on that fund, we can see that we would have to earn a 7.19% CAGR to match the long-term growth of the cash value. Meaning, if we earned 7.19% each year in our mutual fund, we would have the exact same amount of money as we would in the MCPLI (shown earlier) at age 75. **Unknown though it may be, the significance of this discovery should not go unnoticed. A 7.19% CAGR in a Roth IRA would likely be a 9% average rate of return. And that would likely contain a good amount of volatility in the form of market swings. Whereas MCPLI takes us to the same place without the volatility, but with liquidity.**

Tax-Efficiency

MCPLI, when structured to maximize efficiency without exceeding the MEC limits, is quite tax-efficient. You put money in after-taxes, it grows tax-deferred, then can be accessed to generate tax-free income. It could be compared to a Roth IRA in this respect, although there are a few differences. For instance, Roth IRA's have contribution limits, whereas MCPLI does not. More about the differences and uses of tax-efficiency will be discussed in the next chapter.

Unlimited Contributions

Finally, it should not go unnoted that MCPLI gives the ability to contribute at much higher amounts than nearly any other tax-advantaged plan. There are no regulations on contributions. However, a person can only purchase about 20 to 25x her annual income in death benefit. In one respect this creates a "limit" of sorts. For instance, a 45-year old female (in good health) with an annual of $200,000 could get $4 million in death benefit. This could parlay into roughly $130-150,000 in funding per year. Meaning, if she funded a new PES policy at $150,000 per year, it would produce roughly $4 million of death benefit. Provided she doesn't have a couple million bucks in the bank, she will not have the capacity to do $150,000 per year with a $200,000 pre-tax income. So, for all intents and purposes, she has no limits because she can do as much as she wants to do.

Uses

I have personally used the system to invest in commercial and residential real estate, pay taxes, travel, and pay bonuses to employees. My wife and I have found it to be quite a refreshing strategy, and my firm has worked with families and businesses to implement PES. Overall, and as cliché as it might sound, I do believe the process of coming to understand *Nash's Principles* and PES are life-changing. In the next chapter we will take a deeper look at how to use the system to create wealth.

The PES model is designed to maximize wealth-building and management. It is not a static model, but a fluid cycle of productivity. The foundation, MCPLI, is the definitive cash management tool. If we need to, we can let it sit and grow and never utilize the policy loan feature. However, to optimize the creation of wealth, we deploy capital into our SoE. This could be any number of endeavors, and it will be different for each person. The goal is to generate cash-flow. As this cash-flow is produced, it goes to pay off policy loans and increase our policy system. As more discretionary income enters, it is most wise to implement new policies—therefore, increasing the preferential liquid capital to utilize in the future.

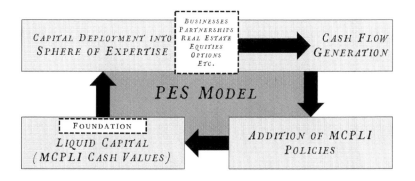

CLOSED-MINDEDNESS

I'm still amazed at the complete lack of openness from academic and other corporate communities. In 2013 I sponsored leading Austrian economist, Dr. Robert Murphy, to speak at my alma mater, Harding University.

I'm fairly confident that one of them wrote an amusingly negative Amazon review of my more succinct first book, *The Wealthy Physician*. The apparent reader transcribed:

"*This book purports to be informative and exciting, along with making complex financial decisions easy for physicians to understand. We've all heard about how physicians are so horrible at financial planning, so who wouldn't want to read a book that promised all that? Plus, no one likes to think that they're being led astray by conventional financial planning wisdom as this author claims.*

Unfortunately, I found the book to be none of the above. After reading it, I understand that the author is a supporter of independent mutual funds as opposed to large financial planning companies, and he also advocates some kind of life insurance deal whereby you can loan yourself money and still get paid interest on the principle. It sounds totally too good to be true, which gets to my personal principle that if it sounds too good to be true, it probably is..."

Believe me when I say that I am very open to discussion and disagreement. I pray that I remain that way, assuming that I am currently open-minded to people's varying opinions. What I find odd is that the reader stated that one of the reasons they read the book was that "*...no one likes to think that they're being led astray by conventional financial planning wisdom.*" Of course they could have gotten that from the title or the chapter headings. He or she goes on to state: "*It sounds totally too good to be true, which gets to my personal principle that if it sounds too good to be true, it probably is.*" Via deductive reasoning, it was easy for me to recognize that "Indoctrinated" (this person's Amazon name) hadn't actually read the book because, in the latter half of the book, I address this and mention Todd Langford's ideas of things being 'too good to be true.' Langford, co-founder of TruthConcepts.com, has done much for the financial analysis community in the past few years. He has stated on many occasions that the idea of *"if it sounds too good to be true then it probably is"* is likely based on a false premise. If it were true, then we wouldn't have running water, electricity, automobiles, airplanes, personal computers, or any other modern convenience. It is a logical fallacy. It's essentially saying that *"if the masses can't understand it, or don't want to take the time to understand it, then it's probably not true."*[ii] Langford would say, and I would agree, that rather than assuming it's too good to be true, investigate it fully. Learn to analyze the evidence and resist the temptation to jump to assumptions.

In the first chapter I retold the story from David Saucer's *The Cash Residence*—the story of the pink ambulance. The reality of MCPLI is that it is simply the most efficient savings asset in the U.S. This is our *pink ambulance*, financially. It gets us from point *a* to point *b* more efficiently than any other savings asset. Life insurance happens to be the tool. **The medics didn't buy the *pink ambulance* because it was a *pink ambulance*. They bought it because of what it could achieve. In the same manner, we don't buy MCPLI because it's MCPLI, but because of what it can accomplish.** The structure of the mutual company is an ignored gem in the financial services industry. It's rare to find something so properly aligned in retail financial services. But for a person to overcome his preconceived notions is even rarer.

Let us continue to develop our objectivity.

[ii] Again, I am open to disagreement and dialogue. But it must be in context and founded in facts—not ignorant and hateful conjecture.

Financial Strategy in the 21ˢᵗ Century

A CASE STUDY
THE CHANDLER ADVISORS RESEARCH TEAM

In early 2013 Chandler Advisors, LLC was hired by a mid-size private company to analyze their financial position and recommend potential strategies to enhance long-term capital efficiency.

At Chandler Advisors, we take an unconventional approach regarding capital structure, financial ratios, and cash management. By utilizing Economic Value Added™ (EVA) principles (originally developed by Stern Stewart & Co. in New York, NY) – primarily analyzing the 'cost of capital' – and somewhat complex insurance strategies, we believe a company can more efficiently manage capital over the long-term. We call it *Financial Strategy of the 21ˢᵗ Century*.

Times have changed. Uncertainty has swept through the real economy and is likely here to stay. The Federal Reserve is pumping fiat currency into the markets and buying assets that no one wants in an attempt to keep interest rates down. In truth, the last 30-plus years have been significantly unsustainable. We saw a stock market boom from about 1980 to the late 90's fueled by speculation and impractical thinking. P/E ratios soared to levels never before seen (Appendix 1). The fact is that if interest rates were to rise too quickly, or potentially at all, the U.S. government would have trouble paying the interest of its debt.[63] If and when (*if* being the key word) interest rates do rise, it will very likely heave the U.S. into a tail spin of having to take on even more debt to pay the debt interest which will, of course, simply compound the national debt at a more rapid rate.

These issues are already causing massive turmoil around the globe and even in the U.S., although 'quantitative easing' is acting as the short-term band aid for the American economy. For every action, there is an equal and opposite reaction, and there will be consequences for the immense spending and printing of money in which the U.S. has engaged. We feel confident that these consequences will have a negative effect on American businesses unless they have properly planned. In the next few pages, we outline an actual client situation and the solutions we implemented in order to help protect and prepare the company financially.

Client Background

Summit Engineering[iii] is a mid-size software engineering firm that provides consulting services to companies nationwide. They have 12 offices in seven states and eight shareholders (the partners). In 2012 their revenues were just north of $80 million with an operating income of about $4.14 million, an increase of 128% from the previous year. The company's cash and cash equivalent assets exceeded $8 million, with a rise of about $4.1 million from 2011 to 2012. Summit's industry tends to do well during perceived good economic times and fall off during poor economic conditions.

During our initial conversations, Summit seemed to believe that 2013 was going to be another strong year, but they were a bit worried about another financial crisis. 2008 and 2009 had been difficult years for the company. As the economy began to slide downward, so did their customer's perceived need for Summit's services and products. At year-end 2009, revenue had dropped by a net amount 37% from 2007. This created a loss for the year and a significant

---

[iii] (For confidentiality the client's name and industry have been changed.)

strain on cash. Their founder was adamant about being a zero debt company, but during the crisis they were forced to collateralize some of their non-current assets on unfavorable terms. They were able to pay the debt off by mid-2012.

We first discussed extensively Summit's financial position and future goals. With no debt and strong revenues, the company leadership believed it was an excellent time to reevaluate the prudence of their financial structure and long-term strategy.

Preliminary Findings

After a few in-depth conversations with the CEO and CFO of Summit, we uncovered the company's primary five year goals. The first was to be the one leading mid-size software engineering firms in the country by attracting top talent from prestigious universities. They felt that hiring three to five top level engineers or analysts per year would increase capacity to take on new clients and grow the company. With 89 employees, the company had a profit-per-employee of about $46,500. The board and executive leadership were very focused on maintaining or enhancing profit-per-employee even with company growth. The partners felt that they had enough momentum to bring in clients to meet these revenue goals, but wanted to be sure that they had the human capacity to adequately serve new clients and preserve their reputation in the industry.

The second primary goal was to reach $120 million of revenue with an operating profit margin of 8% within five years. This would mean revenue growth of an 8.45% CAGR and an increase in the operating profit margin of 2.83%.

Company leadership seemed to have a good grasp on how to reach these five-year goals, but one question remained: *How do we avoid another situation like 2008-09?*

Key Issues

The executives already knew that they wanted to position the company with greater financial strength – but the question was *how* – there were a few different directions the firm thought it could take.

We identified three critical issues and opportunities that needed to be addressed with the financial strategy/structure solution:

1. Summit survived and thrived because of the business procurement skills of the partners and a few key non-partner sales people. These individuals brought in about 95% of the revenue.

2. Of the 89 employees, most of the 'procedural work' was completed by about 20 engineers and analysts that were deemed difficult to replace because of their specialized knowledge and relationships with company clients.

3. Summit's cash on hand was around $8 million EOY 2012 and by mid-2013, the time we presented our recommendations, cash and cash equivalent assets had increased to $11.5 million. Most of the capital was sitting in low interest money market bank accounts waiting to be deployed for hiring, marketing, bonuses, and infrastructure enhancements. The company wanted to continue increased liquid capital for the purpose of investing and acquiring other companies during the next economic recession – but they also wanted this safe capital to be earning more than 0.

Recommendations

From the three critical issues, our team constructed three recommendations for Summit Engineering. Summit traditionally operated on a cash basis, financing new projects and enhancements through capital on hand.

However, company leadership had never fully appreciated the cost of capital when making budgeting decisions. We believed that Summit leadership's ability to understand and practice Economic Value Added (EVA) would be a critical component to making prudent growth and budgeting decisions. EVA takes into consideration the 'cost of capital' and is a relatively simple calculation, but is not readily practiced by most mid-size companies and, until the early 90's, was not typically considered by some of the most sophisticated companies in the world.

$$EVA = \textit{Net Operating Profit After Taxes (NOPAT)} - \textit{(Capital x Cost of Capital)}$$

EVA was developed, as mentioned earlier, by Stern Stewart & Co. and is meant to capture the "true economic profit of a company."[64] The 'cost of capital' can be found by determining the cost of either, one, borrowing (getting a loan from the bank), two, the CAGR that could be earned in an alternate safe asset, or a combination of the two. In Summit's case, EVA is vital because it would measure the efficiency of their capital investment. Because they had no debt, we would not be looking at the cost of borrowing, but rather the CAGR opportunity cost (the interest they could have earned on their cash) of an alternative safe asset. For instance, let's assume the company needed to invest $5 million to increase NOPAT by $7 million over five years. We'll use a 4% earnings rate on capital.

$$\$7,000,000 - (\$5,000,000 \times (1 + .04)^5) = \$916,735$$

In this scenario, the true economic profit of this project (the EVA) would be $916,735 – meaning, yes the company gained $2 million over the five year period, but the net benefit was $916,735 after considering the 'cost of capital.' This 'cost of capital' was

$6.083 million. The question then becomes, is the risk worth the reward? Maybe. But many companies are beginning to see the colossal value of *recapturing* this cost of capital. For instance, if Summit spent an average of $2 million per year over the next 20 years on capital projects, their cost of capital at 4% would be $21.938 million – meaning, they would have invested $40 million over the 20 years, and those investments could have alternatively grown to $61.938 million. We first pointed out [to Summit] that money had a cost, which was a relatively simple fact. The more involved notion was what to do about it.

We recommended that Summit set up their own *internal financing system*. A place where they would hold capital, use it for capital projects, and then literally pay themselves interest based on the going market rate; they would set up an amortization schedule to payback over a period of time. This would accomplish two objectives. First, it would force prudence when looking at expansion and new projects. The company would have to forecast positive cash flows that would be sufficient to make the amortized payments (although, since they were their own debtors, the company would have significant payment flexibility if needed). The second objective was that this would ensure that cash on hand continued to grow over time. This strategy would enhance the probability that Summit would have plenty of capital on hand to survive the next economic meltdown and even acquire assets or companies that would become significantly undervalued during an economic downturn.

There were a few ways to accomplish this *internal financial system*. Of course, the money needed to be fairly liquid. For the first option, we used an example of a bank CD earning 2%. If the company needed to invest $1 million, then they would pull the capital from the CD and create an amortization table to pay back at, for example, 5%. As you can see on the right, their monthly payment would be $18,792.93 on a 60-month amortization schedule. Then we looked at the five-year effect of that payment on the company's current assets. If Summit was able to make the payments back into the 2% CD, they would end up with $1.186 million, as seen on the right.

The next option we presented to Summit was somewhat unconventional, or at least unknown by most small and mid-size businesses in America. However, Fortune 500 companies and special interest groups have been using this strategy since the early 1980's. The second option involved utilizing the same strategy delineated above with one slight change: recognizing, as Albert Einstein stated, that "compounding interest is the eighth wonder of the world." Interest works best over time and uninterrupted. We explained to Summit that the most effective way to never interrupt compounding interest and accomplish the *internal financing system* was through a very uniquely designed, maximum-funded mutual company permanent life insurance contract. Many people have somewhat negative connotations towards permanent life insurance – but, then again, most people have never seen a maximum-funded contract before.

A permanent policy has three main financial components – the premium (funding amount), the cash-value (the accessible capital while the insured is alive), and the death benefit (the amount that goes to the beneficiary when the insured dies). A policy will have three technical components – an insured, a beneficiary, and an owner. (In this case, the company would be the owner and beneficiary, while the key executives would be the insureds. For an individual – the breadwinner may be the owner and the insured, while the spouse and family would be the beneficiary.)

Most life insurance agents sell a type of insurance policy that has little to no cash-value for the first few years. This is because the majority or all of the premium (the funding) is going to what is called base life insurance premium. So if an entity puts a certain amount of money into a life insurance policy, nearly every dollar would go to buying life insurance coverage for the first two or three years. However, there is a little known provision in section 770 of the Internal Revenue Code, which allows the majority of funding, with some limitations, to go directly to accessible cash-value. These policies are considered some of the safest assets in the U.S., and, when structured correctly, present significant early liquidity for a company or an individual. When structured in this fashion, these polices have generated consistent 5% CAGR's for over 100 years. Our recommendation was that Summit begin transferring liquid capital at a relatively steady pace into these policies. We will look at the actual recommendation in just a moment.

Killing Multiple Birds with One Stone:
The Power of Mutual Company Contracts

When most firms think of financial products, they think of them in singular terms—Summit was no different. Large corporations have been using this insurance system for internal financing and key executive protection for many years. These highly sophisticated entities use mutual company insurance contracts because of the multitude of uses – the functional leverage a policy provides.

We explained to Summit that they too could 'kill multiple birds with one stone.' We had already discussed with them the fact that they had 20-30 key employees and partners who generated and/or serviced most of the business. They acknowledged that if any one of these key people were to pass away, it would be a major hit for that division and possibly for the entire company. Our recommendation was that Summit acquire max-funded mutual company policies on these key employees. These policies could also

Mutual Insurance Company
Collectively owned by the policyholders
$80 billion portfolio
$10 billion loan portfolio

be used for the financing purpose. In short, the policy cash-values would act as short-term emergency capital and long-term investment capital, and the death benefit would act as protection against the loss of key revenue generator.

Collateralizing Cash-Value

Earlier we discussed what the financing strategy would look like if Summit used CD's to hold and access capital. But what if they used cash-value? We explained to Summit that they could use the life insurance cash-value in one of two ways – they could either take it out as a withdrawal, or they could take a policy loan. When a mutual company policyholder takes a policy loan, the money doesn't actually come from his or her cash value – it comes from the insurance company's general loan portfolio. Policyholders can take a loan based on the amount of cash-value in their policy. If Summit had $500,000 in cash-value, then they could typically take about 95% of that number in the form of a collateralized loan, which would come from the insurance company – not their policy. This is money that the insurance company would be loaning out in one way or another – so, if we take a policy loan *against* our cash-value, then we must pay interest back to the insurance company. We explained to Summit that this would actually be very beneficial to [Summit] in the long-run. Using the same example from the CD financing strategy, let's say Summit needed $1 million for a capital project. If they had $1 million in their cash-value growing at a 4.5% long-term CAGR, then they could take a collateralized loan at a 5% loan rate. (For comparison purposes, we are going to assume that Summit could collateralize the entire $1 million cash-value.)

As seen above, the policy loan would come from the insurance company's loan portfolio, and Summit would pay interest back to the insurance company. This is beneficial because Summit would not interrupt the compounding interest within their cash-value.

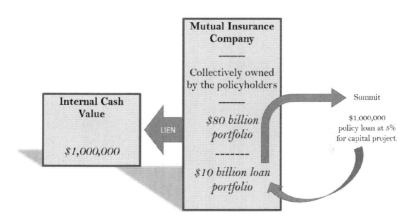

Then we analyzed for Summit the difference between earning 4.5% compounding on the cash-value side vs. paying a 5% amortized payment over a five-year (60-month) period. Summit would simply pay back the same $18,792.93 per month that they did on the CD financing example, except here they would be paying this money back to the insurance company – but their cash value would continue to grow.

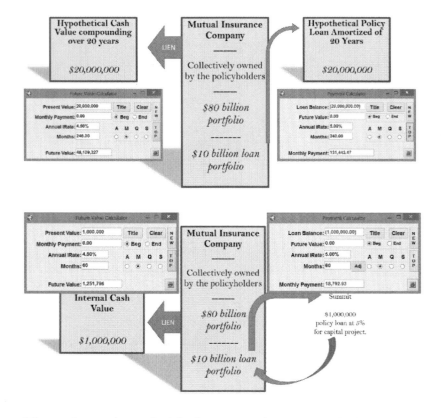

The total cost of capital of the $18,792.93 that they paid back to the insurance company is $1.186 million (what we would have earned pre-tax had we made the payment back into the CD mentioned earlier). The five year capital difference between the cash-value option and the CD option is $64,977. This may not seem like a lot, but consider the fact that Summit will be investing multiple millions of dollars over the next 20 to 50 years. If we run the example over a much longer period of time, the numbers begin to stick out even more.

In the above example we use $20 million over 20 years. The long-term cash-value is over $49 million, and the payback schedule amortized over 20 years equals $131,433.47 per month. To be fair, we must calculate the interest we could have earned in the CD if we had taken money out of the CD and paid it back at the same level over 240 months. As you can see to the right, the monthly payment into a CD at 2% would have resulted in a $38.8 million balance – Over $10 million shy of the cash-value in the insurance policy.

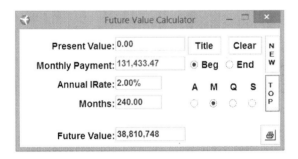

By using the *internal financing system* and optimizing it with properly structured mutual company policies, we projected that Summit could increase their capital on hand by at least 20-30% over the next 20 years. We suggested that Summit began transitioning about $750,000 per year that was either already sitting in cash or new cash-flow that would be going to cash. The $750,000 of total funding would be split up in the form of key person policies among the various key employees and partners of the firm. We aggregated all policies in the illustration below to show the long-term impact. One major aspect that has not yet been described in this case study is the tax advantages of permanent life insurance. The net CAGR of the policy over 20 years would have been 4.40%, but this is not comparing apples to apples regarding the CD example. If Summit were to fund premiums on an after-tax basis, then they could take capital out in the future tax-free (this can be done either through withdrawals of basis or policy loans. Technically the cash-value grows tax-deferred and can be accessed tax-free if done correctly.) With the CD the company would be paying tax at its highest marginal bracket each year.

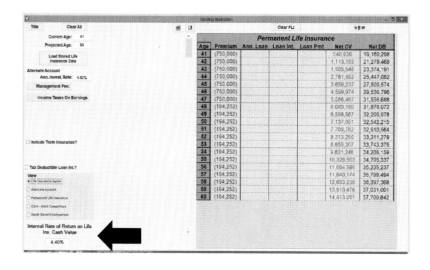

The below illustration shows the effective rate the company would have to earn in a CD simply to match the long-term growth off the cash-value – 6.28% every single year.

Funding Illustration

| Title | Clear All | | Clear PLI | NEW |

Current Age: 41
Projected Age: 60

Load Stored Life Insurance Data

Alternate Account
Ann. Invest. Rate: 0.00%
Management Fee:

Income Taxes On Earnings
Income Tax Bracket: 30.00%
C.G. Tax Bracket: 0.00%
% Earnings As C.G.: 0.00%
?Tax Credit For Losses ✓

Include Term Insurance?

Tax Deductible Loan Int.?

View
x Life Insurance Inputs
- Alternate Account
- Permanent Life Insurance
- Cash - Cash Comparison
- Death Benefit Comparison

Interest Rate on Alternate Account To Match PLI
8.28%

Permanent Life Insurance

Age	Premium	Ann. Loan	Loan Int.	Loan Pmt	Net CV	Net DB
41	(750,000)				540,938	19,160,298
42	(750,000)				1,113,155	21,279,468
43	(750,000)				1,905,546	23,374,191
44	(750,000)				2,781,592	25,447,082
45	(750,000)				3,659,237	27,500,574
46	(750,000)				4,599,574	29,536,796
47	(750,000)				5,558,467	31,558,688
48	(194,252)				6,080,190	31,878,072
49	(194,252)				6,588,867	32,205,978
50	(194,252)				7,137,051	32,542,215
51	(194,252)				7,708,782	32,910,564
52	(194,252)				8,313,260	33,311,279
53	(194,252)				8,950,307	33,743,375
54	(194,252)				9,621,240	34,208,159
55	(194,252)				10,326,503	34,705,337
56	(194,252)				11,064,986	35,235,237
57	(194,252)				11,840,174	35,799,494
58	(194,252)				12,653,238	36,397,368
59	(194,252)				13,510,476	37,031,001
60	(194,252)				14,415,061	37,700,642

Pros and Cons

The company would give up slight early liquidity in the insurance strategy scenario, but the long-term tax-advantages, growth, and insurance on key employees (*we thought*) heavily out-weighed the CD self-financing strategy. Then when we considered the cash-value collateralization aspect, it seemed that the insurance strategy was certainly the direction to choose. We also explained to Summit that they would not have to take a loan from the insurance company. If they could find more favorable terms at another financial institution, then they could still use the cash-value as collateral and retain the capital elsewhere. The policy loan provision would simply give the company easy access to the capital.

The CD would provide full liquidity from the beginning, but the price to pay would have been very sluggish long-term growth – likely costing the company at least $5 million in capital appreciation (Appendix 2).

Implementation

The company decided to begin by funding a total of about $550,000 per year divided between 17 of its key executives and partners. Certain associates of the company were deemed to be 'more' economically valuable, and death benefit calculations were constructed at a higher level for certain partners.

Chandler Advisors facilitated and procured the overfunded policies with three mutual companies. In early 2014, Summit began looking into funding additional policies on other key employees.

Appendix 1

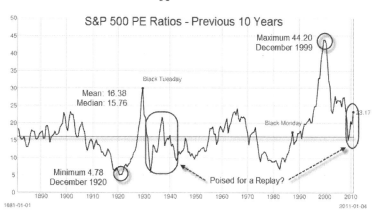

Source: http://globaleconomicanalysis.blogspot.com/2011/01/s-500-pe-ratios-well-above-mean-and.html

22

DEPLOYING PES

"You are what you do, not what you say you'll do."
C.G. JUNG

"Take time to deliberate, but when the time for action has arrived, stop thinking and go in."
NAPOLEON BONAPARTE

I WAS TEMPTED TO CALL THIS SECTION *"Retirement Planning and PES."* But, as you'll recall, I don't really like the general notion of retirement as it's widely used. Rather, let's stick with the term *"season of significance."* As you enter this period of your life (I'm assume the majority of readers are not quite there yet), you will need some sort of income. This could be in the form of SoE income—meaning, you may make money from business ownership, partnership interests, rental real estate, or consulting. It could also be in the form of asset distribution—meaning, drawing income from the total of your portfolio. The most ideal scenario is to have some combination of both.[i] It is also quite relevant to discuss how PES can be deployed in the relatively near-term, regardless of age.

I refer back to the distinction between *Wealth Creation* and *Wealth Supervision*. Deploying PES (policy loans) is a large part of the former, while letting capital sit and accumulate or taking income is part of the latter. This chapter is focused on the utilization of PES for wealth-building and future income generation purposed.

As you well know by now, PES alone and MCPLI are not investment or wealth building tools. The cash value and liquidity provided by them, however, provides the capacity to take advantage of opportunity. Still, the most important part of seizing opportunity is building your SoE so that you first know what opportunity to cease. Otherwise, the *Private Economic System* can take you only so far (although, it's probably farther than what the majority is currently doing.)

For our upcoming examples, we'll use a 40-year-old couple. For simplicity, we'll just view one PES policy showing $3,000 per month being contributed beginning at age 40. Keep in mind, these examples are hypothetical. Although I personally and many others have used policies in this manner, you should be able to note the possible risks involved.

REAL ESTATE

The following numbers show an example of the couple using PES to purchase cash-flowing real estate. In reality, there are many

---

[i] Unless you're worth $50+ million, then you're free to give your time away.

other active SoE assets that could be invested in, but real estate is one of the easiest to understand. Also, I have used my PES policies to purchase residential and resort properties for the purpose of creating cash-flow. (So far so good, for me, but before entering this arena it would be wise to google "rental property horror stories." After which, if you're still interested, go for it.) Keep in mind, the analysis is kept simple for various reasons, mainly to keep you attentive. There are many numbers on the coming pages, so hang in there.

This theoretical couple funds $36,000 per year. The first line is the end of the first year, in which they'd be 41 years old. The *Net Cash Value* is simply the *Gross Cash Value* minus any outstanding *Policy Loan* amount. These early years are the *box of pain*. As you can see, their total cash value is less than their cost basis (the total amount they've paid into the plan).

Age	Premium	Policy Loan	Loan Interest Paid	Loan Principle Pd	Net Cash Value	Gross Cash Value	Death Benefit
41	$ 36,000				$ 23,350	$ 23,350	$ 1,295,971
42	$ 36,000				$ 48,043	$ 48,043	$ 1,398,905
43	$ 36,000				$ 83,932	$ 83,932	$ 1,500,563
44	$ 36,000				$ 124,712	$ 124,712	$ 1,601,035
45	$ 36,000	$ 100,000	$ 4,400		$ 67,466	$ 167,466	$ 1,600,461
46	$ 36,000	$ 87,448	$ 3,848	$ 12,552	$ 124,826	$ 212,273	$ 1,711,513
47	$ 36,000	$ 74,895	$ 3,295	$ 12,552	$ 184,332	$ 259,228	$ 1,821,785
48	$ 36,000	$ 62,343	$ 2,743	$ 12,552	$ 246,021	$ 308,365	$ 1,931,433
49	$ 36,000	$ 49,791	$ 2,191	$ 12,552	$ 310,019	$ 359,810	$ 2,040,630
50	$ 36,000	$ 37,238	$ 1,638	$ 12,552	$ 376,436	$ 413,674	$ 2,149,550

At age 45 they take a policy loan[ii] for $100,000 to help make a down payment on a triplex, which will spin-off $4,500 per month ($1,500 per apartment) in rental income. The triplex cost a total of

---

[ii] The policy loan rate at the time of this writing was 4.40%. That will likely rise as it is tied to the Moody's Corporate Bond Index. A rising interest rate environment will also likely increase long-term dividends. This analysis views interest and dividend rates at 2015 schedules.

$380,000; they put $30,000 of cash down and took a bank loan for the other $250,000 at 5% on a 15-year note. Their bank payment is $1,977 per month.

Age 45

Triplex Purchase Price	$380,000

Cash Down Payment:	$30,000
Policy Loan:	$100,000
Bank Loan:	$250,000

Beginning Rental Income:	$4,500/mo
Annual Increase in Rental Income:	2.50%

They dedicate the entire rent payment towards the policy loan and the bank loan. They don't pay anything against the policy loan's principle in the first year except for the interest. The put the difference of the rent received minus the policy loan interest towards the bank loan.

At age 46, they begin paying (actually, their renters begin paying) the debts down. They pay the annual interest on the policy loan plus $12,552 on the principle. The rest goes towards the bank loan. By age 51, the bank loan is paid off.

Age	Premium	Gross Cash Value	Policy Loan			Rental Income Per Year	Total Policy Loan Payment	Net Cash Value	Bank Loan	
			EOY Policy Loan Balance	Loan Interest Paid	Loan Principle Pd				Payment to Bank Loan	EOY Bank Loan Balance
41	36,000							23,350		
42	36,000							48,043		
43	36,000							83,932		
44	36,000	124,712						124,712		
45	36,000	167,466	100,000	4,400		54,000	4,400	67,466	49,600	212,900
46	36,000	212,273	87,448	3,848	12,552	55,080	16,400	124,826	38,680	184,865
47	36,000	259,228	74,895	3,295	12,552	56,182	15,847	184,332	40,335	153,773
48	36,000	308,365	62,343	2,743	12,552	57,305	15,295	246,021	42,010	119,452
49	36,000	359,810	49,791	2,191	12,552	58,451	14,743	310,019	43,708	81,717
50	36,000	413,674	37,238	1,638	12,552	59,620	14,190	376,436	45,430	40,372

Then, at age 51, the couple has an opportunity to buy into an apartment complex. There buy-in will be $500,000. They use $30,000 of their own cash; $300,000 in the form of a policy loan; and $170,000 from the bank. (At age 51, they still have $40,372 left on the original loan, which the bank rolls into their new loan.) They will receive $5,500 per month of rental income with a 3.5% increase per year.

Age 45 — Triplex Purchase Price $380,000

Cash Down Payment:	$30,000
Policy Loan:	$100,000
Bank Loan:	$250,000
Beginning Rental Income:	$4,500/mo
Annual Increase in Rental Income:	2.50%

Bank Loan #1

Year	Beg. Of Year Loan Balance	Interest Rate	Annual Payment	Interest Paid	End of Year Loan Balance
45	250,000	5.00%	-99,600	12,500	212,900
46	212,900	5.00%	-38,680	10,645	184,865
47	184,865	5.00%	-40,335	9,243	153,773
48	153,773	5.00%	-42,040	7,689	119,452
49	119,452	5.00%	-43,708	5,973	81,717
50	81,717	5.00%	-45,430	4,086	40,372

Age 51 — Apartment Complex Buy-In $500,000

Cash Down Payment:	$30,000
Policy Loan:	$300,000
Bank Loan:	$170,000
Beginning Rental Income:	$5,500/mo
Annual Increase in Rental Income:	3.50%

Bank Loan #2

Year	Beg. Of Year Loan Balance	Interest Rate	Annual Payment	Interest Paid	End of Year Loan Balance
51	212,940	5.00%	-111,975	10,647	111,602
52	111,602	5.00%	-91,500	5,580	25,682
53	25,682	5.00%	-26,966	1,284	
54					
55					
56					

They repeat a similar process from their triplex; paying the policy loan interest plus $25,105 on the principle on their PES policy. The rest of the rental income goes to pay down the bank debt. In the chart below, you can view the culmination of their efforts. The bank loan is paid off at age 53. The far right column shows their net rental income from the triplex and apartment complex.

Age	Premium	Gross Cash Value	Policy Loan BOY Policy Loan Balance	Loan Interest Paid	Loan Principle Pd	Rental Income Triplex	Rental Income Apartments	Total Policy Loan Payment	Net Cash Value	Payment to Bank Loan	BOY Bank Loan Balance	Net Rental Income
41	36,000								23,350			
42	36,000								48,943			
43	36,000								83,932			
44	36,000	124,712							124,712			
45	36,000	167,466	100,000	4,400	12,552	54,000		4,400	67,466	49,600	212,900	—
46	36,000	212,273	87,448	3,848	12,552	55,080		16,400	124,826	38,680	184,865	—
47	36,000	259,228	74,895	3,295	12,552	56,182		15,847	184,332	40,335	153,773	—
48	36,000	308,365	62,343	2,743	12,552	57,305		15,295	246,021	42,010	119,452	—
49	36,000	359,810	49,791	2,191	12,552	58,451		14,743	310,019	43,708	81,717	—
50	36,000	413,674	37,238	1,638	12,552	59,620		14,190	376,436	45,430	40,372	—
51	36,000	472,090	337,238	14,838	—	60,813	66,000	14,838	134,852	111,975	212,930	—
52	36,000	534,037	312,134	13,734	25,105	62,029	68,310	38,839	221,903	91,500	111,602	—
53	36,000	599,173	287,029	12,629	25,105	63,270	70,701	37,734	312,143	26,966	25,682	69,270
54	36,000	667,737	261,925	11,525	25,105	64,335	73,175	36,630	405,812			101,080
55	36,000	739,799	236,820	10,420	25,105	65,826	75,737	35,525	502,979			106,037
56	36,000	815,485	211,715	9,315	25,105	67,142	78,387	34,420	603,769			111,110
57	36,000	894,837	186,611	8,211	25,105	68,485	81,131	33,316	708,226			116,300
58	36,000	977,974	161,506	7,106	25,105	69,855	83,970	32,211	816,467			121,614
59	36,000	1,065,021	136,402	6,002	25,105	71,252	86,909	31,107	928,620			127,054
60	36,000	1,156,156	111,297	4,897	25,105	72,677	89,951	30,002	1,044,859			132,626
61	36,000	1,253,526	86,192	3,792	25,105	74,130	93,100	28,897	1,167,333			138,333
62	36,000	1,355,995	61,088	2,688	25,105	75,613	96,358	27,793	1,294,907			144,178
63	36,000	1,463,755	35,983	1,583	25,105	77,125	99,731	26,688	1,427,772			150,168
64	36,000	1,577,141	10,879	479	25,105	78,668	103,221	25,584	1,566,262			156,305
65	36,000	1,696,374	10,879		10,879	80,241	106,834	10,879	1,696,374			176,196

At the age of 60, the couple has over $1 million in net cash value and income of $132,626 from the rental properties. By age 66, they've paid off the policy loan, have nearly $1.8 million of cash value, and rental income of over $192,000 per year. In truth, they probably enter the *season of significance* around age 54—at which point they own real estate valued near $1 million, have strong cash flow coming from that real estate, and enjoy around $500,000 in net cash value. The reality of the situation, though, is likely more attractive than this.

Age	Premium	Gross Cash Value	Policy Loan EOY Policy Loan Balance	Policy Loan Loan Interest Paid	Policy Loan Loan Principle Pd	Rental Income Rental Income Triplex	Rental Income Rental Income Apartments	Total Policy Loan Payment	Net Cash Value	Bank Loan Payment to Bank Loan	Bank Loan EOY Bank Loan Balance	Net Rental Income
66	12,004	1,798,448				81,846	110,573		1,798,448			192,419
67	12,004	1,905,634				83,483	114,443		1,905,634			197,926
68	12,004	2,018,206				85,153	118,449		2,018,206			203,601
69	12,004	2,136,270				86,856	122,594		2,136,270			209,450
70	12,004	2,260,039				88,593	126,885		2,260,039			215,478
71	12,004	2,389,638				90,365	131,326		2,389,638			221,691
72	12,004	2,525,098				92,172	135,922		2,525,098			228,094
73	12,004	2,666,449				94,015	140,680		2,666,449			234,695
74	12,004	2,813,873				95,896	145,604		2,813,873			241,499
75	12,004	2,967,611				97,814	150,700		2,967,611			248,513
76	12,004	3,127,724				99,770	155,974		3,127,724			255,744
77	12,004	3,294,446				101,765	161,433		3,294,446			263,198
78	12,004	3,467,954				103,800	167,083		3,467,954			270,884
79	12,004	3,648,476				105,877	172,931		3,648,476			278,808
80	12,004	3,836,330				107,994	178,984		3,836,330			286,978

What if the couple enhanced their PES system by implementing new policies over time? This is what it would look like if the couple purchased new policies at age 44 and 51:[iii]

[iii] This illustration shows the aggregate of starting multiple policies.

Age	Premium	Net Cash Value	Death Benefit	Age	Premium	Net Cash Value	Death Benefit
41	$ 36,000	$ 23,350	$ 1,295,971	66	$ 31,070	$ 3,533,238	$ 8,159,786
42	$ 36,000	$ 48,043	$ 1,398,905	67	$ 31,070	$ 3,750,556	$ 8,344,199
43	$ 36,000	$ 83,932	$ 1,500,563	68	$ 31,070	$ 3,978,425	$ 8,535,688
44	$ 60,000	$ 140,395	$ 2,358,896	69	$ 31,070	$ 4,216,966	$ 8,734,178
45	$ 60,000	$ 99,727	$ 2,420,619	70	$ 31,070	$ 4,466,556	$ 8,939,788
46	$ 60,000	$ 181,944	$ 2,593,234	71	$ 31,070	$ 4,728,290	$ 9,153,984
47	$ 60,000	$ 268,642	$ 2,764,420	72	$ 31,070	$ 5,001,790	$ 9,376,090
48	$ 60,000	$ 358,788	$ 2,934,425	73	$ 31,070	$ 5,287,120	$ 9,606,124
49	$ 60,000	$ 452,567	$ 3,103,524	74	$ 31,070	$ 5,584,678	$ 9,844,288
50	$ 60,000	$ 550,157	$ 3,271,994	75	$ 31,070	$ 5,894,910	$ 10,090,713
51	$ 96,000	$ 365,302	$ 3,961,646	76	$ 31,070	$ 6,217,966	$ 10,345,638
52	$ 96,000	$ 512,015	$ 4,227,101	77	$ 31,070	$ 6,554,283	$ 10,609,243
53	$ 96,000	$ 676,678	$ 4,493,076	78	$ 31,070	$ 6,904,215	$ 10,881,882
54	$ 96,000	$ 849,501	$ 4,764,247	79	$ 31,070	$ 7,268,200	$ 11,163,892
55	$ 96,000	$ 1,029,951	$ 5,038,132	80	$ 31,070	$ 7,646,911	$ 11,455,513
56	$ 96,000	$ 1,218,045	$ 5,314,110	81	$ 31,070	$ 8,040,240	$ 11,756,671
57	$ 96,000	$ 1,413,974	$ 5,592,479	82	$ 31,070	$ 8,444,791	$ 12,067,726
58	$ 96,000	$ 1,618,020	$ 5,873,354	83	$ 31,070	$ 8,859,636	$ 12,388,632
59	$ 96,000	$ 1,830,436	$ 6,156,808	84	$ 31,070	$ 9,286,762	$ 12,719,717
60	$ 96,000	$ 2,051,637	$ 6,442,861	85	$ 31,070	$ 9,725,845	$ 13,061,217
61	$ 96,000	$ 2,286,039	$ 6,740,998	86	$ 31,070	$ 10,176,036	$ 13,413,197
62	$ 96,000	$ 2,531,521	$ 7,045,067	87	$ 31,070	$ 10,642,321	$ 13,776,314
63	$ 96,000	$ 2,788,221	$ 7,354,658	88	$ 31,070	$ 11,116,131	$ 14,151,274
64	$ 96,000	$ 3,057,958	$ 7,672,417	89	$ 31,070	$ 11,598,854	$ 14,539,680
65	$ 96,000	$ 3,326,004	$ 7,982,182	90	$ 31,070	$ 12,084,454	$ 14,934,652

At age 70, they have nearly $4.5 million of cash value, plus the aforementioned rental cash-flow and real estate values… plus whatever other assets they may own (index funds, personal residence, business interests, etc.)

You may wonder why they have a continuous funding amount all the way to age 90. This couple could certainly stop funding the plan as they reach their later years. But, if they have the cash-flow to continue, why would they stop? If they've got the $31,070 to pay into the policies from age 66 on, then they'll more than likely have a desire to put it into their PES policies—being that, the cash value in the later years is extremely efficient, tax-advantaged, and safe.

For instance, the return at age 72, in that one single year, is about 5%. Remember from our TVM equations, the tax-equivalent return is the *ROR ÷ (1-Tax Bracket)*. Here, if they were in a 30% bracket, they'd have to earn 7.14% in a CD or money market account to match the earnings of the MCPLI. In truth, most people of a certain age will want to continue funding these plans as long as they possibly can. The cash value becomes their *superior* and *safer* asset. They went right in order to go left.

The Evolution of Financial Thinking

In part one we discussed a concept called the *Evolution of Thinking*. I promised you that I would further explain the financial relevance in part three. This is me keeping that promise.

In the same way that *thinking* evolves over time, our financial thought processes transform to something many people never saw coming in their earlier years. The 50-year-old thinks differently than the 30-year-old, and the 70-year-old different than the 50-year old. We can now, however, foresee this is coming. Simply put, the older you get the more you value safety, security, and certainty.

In the previous example, the couple purchased cash-flow real estate using their PES policies. You may wonder, why use the policies—*why not just save the money in cash?* The answer, I believe, requires a much higher level of thinking than we've financially been taught.

As we've discussed, MCPLI gets more and more efficient with time. While it's not a bad thing for a 75-year-old to start a plan, it's certainly better to start it sooner. MCPLI and the cash value provide us two significant advantages. One, we don't have to interrupt the compounding of our capital. We can take a policy loan against our capital. Two, even if we do not yet realize it, at some point in the future we will have a great appreciation for safer, more tax-advantaged dollars. The safest and most tax-efficient place is MCPLI. The reality is, whether you're 30 or 50 or 70, you will likely need a safe (and potentially income-producing) asset in 20 or 30 years.

During one of the seminars, Thomas (from part one) drew the following graph. The point at the bottom left is our 'current level of thinking.' The point at the top right is our 'future level of thinking.' There will be things that we will wish we would have done. But for some reason, we don't often look for what those things might be. And we can't make decisions with our *current level of thinking* that will get us to where we will want to be in our *future level of thinking*. Confused yet? The point was that we must raise our thinking to a level from which we can see the future impact and relevance of today's decisions.

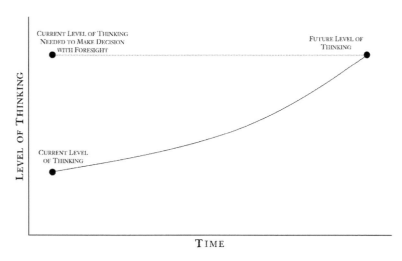

This is relevant, of course, to many areas of life, but especially finance. I've had conversations with many about personal and business financial planning. Over and over again I hear people (usually starting around the age of 30) say *"I wish I would have done…"* or *"I wish I would have known…"* or *"If only my parents had taught me…"*

I think it's psychologically easier to wish we would have done or known something than to actually take action in the present. It's certainly much easier to just brush study or action aside in the present. Mastering the *evolution of thinking* principle is a matter of raising our thinking to a level from which we can so clearly see what we're going to *wish we would have done* that we decide to make the mature decision today. And that's what it's all about—maturity.

The questions is *what can I do today to prepare for the future—to plan with foresight?* The answer: PES.

INCOME

When a person desires to take income from their PES policies, it can be accomplished tax-free. However, it must be structured and managed correctly. Tax-free income is generated by withdrawing cost-basis first. MCPLI is considered a *tax-deferred first-in-first-out* asset. Meaning, it is one of the few assets with which you can take out what you've put in first. (Most assets require the withdrawal of earnings first.) This cost-basis withdrawal is not taxed because we funded the plan with after-tax dollars.

After we've taken out our last dollar of cost-basis, we can begin to use policy loans as income. Policy loans are tax-free, but it would be wise to make sure we don't take policy loans as income until later in life. Reason being, if we take a policy loan and don't pay it back, then interest is accruing. At our death, the death benefit will pay off the policy loan. If this process is structured and managed well, it creates a tax-free income during our later years. The benefit of this cannot be overstated. A good advisor can help you be sure that you do it right.

I hope you will believe me when I say that this book is written with intellectual honesty. My goal is **not** to make you a client of my firm, Chandler Advisors. I believe there are quite a few good advisors out there who can help you with PES.

Of course, we would be honored to interview you to see if Chandler Advisors is the right fit for you, and vice versa. For the purpose of objectivity, I have compiled a list of advisors I know and trust at **TheFallofLogic.com/Advisors**. You are more than welcome to contact Chandler Advisors at **ChandlerAdv.com/Contact**

OVER-UNDER: ISSUES OF VALUATION AND INVESTING

"*Bull markets are born on pessimism, grow on skepticism, mature on optimism, and die on euphoria.*"
SIR JOHN TEMPLETON

"*The contrary investor is every human when he resigns momentarily from the herd and thinks for himself.*"
ARCHIBALD MACLEISH

So, the foundation of PES is MCPLI. Similar to our *Financial Hierarchy of Needs*, the foundation the *PES Model* is liquid capital. Now the question becomes, within our SoE, how will we know when to invest and how much? This is, indeed, far from an exact science. The simplest example may be cash-flow real estate. It is simple insofar as we understand that the real estate has a price and a value—and that these are two separate things.

whole slew of additional issues that they didn't think about because they don't think about unintended consequences because they're just thinking about how to get reelected right here and right now.)[i] You can invest in stocks, bonds, CD's, real estate, foreign currencies, your own business or, hey—to heck with all that, you could just stick it in a shoe box. To be frank, I don't care.[ii] The only thing I care about it getting accurate information and data in your hands.

As we've seen, the data points to an interesting asset. One that is almost never discussed in the popular media.

If you have been working for any length of time, someone has told you that life insurance was a bad investment at some point. I remember hearing that right out of college. The objective is to create and supervise wealth in the most effective manner for your family. This is certainly not an easy process. But it is most definitely worthwhile.

THE PARADOX OF PAIN

" For most people, the guilt of not growing is easier to bear than the anxiety of continual growth."
UNKNOWN

One of the most important principles to understand when entering this endeavor is the constant awareness of the *'box of pain.'* This principle says that for anything worth doing, there is difficulty involved—usually at the beginning, but often through the entire life of the venture. Anything worthwhile, anything of great importance,

---

[i] Forgive my run-on sentence.

[ii] Actually, I kind of do care. I do want you to make the best decision here. But, for the sake of making a point, I want you to know that it's not going to help or hurt my feelings whether you take into consideration the obvious evidence or not.

takes time, great learning, and usually involves some substantial level of pain or struggle—meaning the venture isn't easy. In fact, imagine now, in the current moment, various personal, professional, financial, and spiritual endeavors that you deem worthwhile—that you deem meaningful. Take a minute or a few and decide for yourself if any of them do not have a *'box of pain.'*

Once you have adequately addressed all possible ventures of worth, you will come to the conclusion that everything worthwhile entails the *'box of pain.'* This very concept explains why so many are not successful. The small box in the upper left-hand corner represents the relative struggle we go through, and the much larger box represents the long-term benefit. Yet, most people flip this equation. They experience the 'guilt of not growing'—in essence, they choose a small amount of short-term comfort (or at least the illusion of comfort) and subconsciously choose a much larger box of long-term struggle. This can be seen in many facets of life depending on the person—from lack of exercise to not growing intellectually to not spending/saving money prudently. Specifically in personal finance, this can be seen in the attempt to avoid new ideas, learning, and analysis.

> *"Make up your mind to act decidedly and take the consequences. No good is ever done in this world by hesitation."*
>
> THOMAS HUXLEY

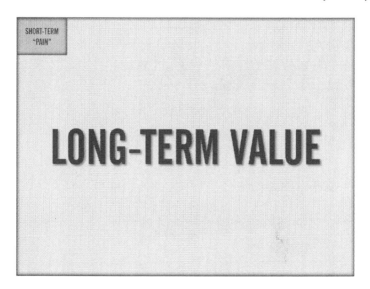

There is only one way to conquer the box of pain: jump in immediately and with everything you have. This journey is not to be taken lightly. You now know more about finance than just about anyone around you. You can analyze situations with vigor and make adequate decisions. You must, though, internalize the fact that the *box of pain* is all around you. It is in the study of finance, the time it takes to build PES, and entire realm of other meaningful endeavors. This is the economic trade-off for anything worth doing. Of course, struggle for the sake of struggle makes no sense. But struggle for a greater purpose is our calling.

G*IVING*

*" How wonderful that no one need wait a single mo-
ment to improve the world. "*

ANNE FRANK

Recently a good friend suggested that I read *The First Thanksgiving* by Robert Tracey McKenzie. He did so after reading a portion of the manuscript of the book you hold in your hands.[iii] As
uncorrelated as they might seem, he inferred that McKenzie's work
went hand-in-hand with the points I have laid out about *how we
think*.

One of the primary points made in *The First Thanksgiving* is that
we often view the past with a partial lens. We look and find what
we, or others, want us to find, and we bend history to meet our
current desires. Although the book is in large part about pilgrims
and America's early settlers, it has great relevance to all that we have
so far discussed and to the culmination—the primary points I mean
to make. Another point of the book is that we often fail to learn the
lessons of history. One of those lessons is that material possessions
and money will not make us happy. History has proven this over
and over again.

Insofar as we believe that we have a purpose on this earth, it is
only logical that we aim to live for that purpose. Whatever financial
wealth we acquire must have a larger impact than to simply allow
our families to lavish in comfort.

One of the tenants of success, as earlier discussed, is to learn to
focus not on ourselves. **We should give selflessly, without expecting *anything* in return.** As difficult as that may be, given our

---

[iii] You're almost done.

natural tendency to focus primarily on ourselves, this is what leads to significance.

24

MOVING FORWARD

" Don't judge each day by the harvest you reap but by the seeds that you plant."
ROBERT LOUIS STEVENSON

" Change your thoughts and you change your world."
NORMAN VINCENT PEALE

I LOVE READING. I CAN'T GET ENOUGH OF IT. This may be a product of the fact that I read only two or three books before my 20th birthday. The only reason I know anything, assuming I do, is because of incessant reading. Experience is invaluable, but it has little context without knowledge.

Something happened my junior or senior year of college: I began reading, and I found that I loved it. Today, I truly believe that anyone who wants to optimize their life must be a reader. At the end of this book (and at *TheFallofLogic.com/Read*), you can find an exhaustive list of books on finance, economics, general business, success, and, equally as important, thinking.[i] When each day concludes, it is perspective that matters. We can only know so much, and we can only do so much. What we learn and how we think are the greatest contributors to both of those—our knowledge and our thoughts. It was only by reading a proverb day and the works of Stephen Covey, Dale Carnegie, and Og Mandino that I was able to realize early in my career the importance of controlling thoughts. You can hear people say that over and over and over again, but it does not register. When you begin to read the logic of the arguments from some of the greatest thinkers of our time, that's when you begin to believe and understand.

The culmination of these words have hopefully had some marginally positive impact on you. My desire is that these methodologies, financially and otherwise, may benefit you for years to come. I do know that they will most assuredly not benefit you unless you act.

BECOMING BETTER

My recommendations are these, if you choose to accept them:

- ***Read at least 1,000 words of financial or business literature per day.*** This should take no longer than twenty

---

[i] Maybe someday they'll make *thinking* an official category.

minutes, but the knowledge you will gain will be price-less. I would recommend sticking with financial litera-ture for the first year, then transitioning to business or other SoE writings.

- ***Exercise at least four days a week.*** While healthy living is not in my SoE, I know how I feel and act when I'm eating right and exercising. I also know how I feel when I don't. Taking care of your body is essential to reaching success in other areas of life.
- ***Sleep at least 7 hours per night.***
- ***Read 1,000 or more words of personal growth and spiritual material each day.***
- ***Pray for at least 10 minutes each day.***
- ***Spend at least one hour of uninterrupted time with your family each day.***
- ***Enhance your SoE, primarily in profitable areas.***
- ***Implement the Private Economic System.***

Doing these things will not make life perfect, and they won't make you impeccably happy. But they will give you the best chance for optimization and impact.

Having read this book in its entirety, you now have more knowledge on financial topics and, more importantly, matters of thought than the vast majority of families. Now is the time. Do not hesitate; act… continue learning… and then act again. The only way forward is to make a decision.

> *"Action is the foundational key to all success."*
> PABLO PICASSO

A Quick Word About

Purple Door Coffee is a specialty espresso bar and coffee shop in Denver, Colorado, that employs teens and young adults who have been homeless and want to leave homelessness behind. I must admit, I am biased. My sister is the co-founder. But the work these guys are doing is amazing. I encourage you to visit them when you're in Denver or give to the cause at PurpleDoorCoffee.com.

Purple Door's Mission

To reclaim and sustain the lives of homeless youth and young adults through supportive and meaningful employment.

Purple Door is committed to creating a loving, Jesus-centered environment, where every single individual is valued no matter what their life has looked like up to this point.

Our name comes from the fact that historically the color purple is the color of royalty, and we truly believe that every person, no matter their station in life, has unsurpassable worth and value and deserves to be treated like royalty.

Purple Door Coffee hopes to be a place of not only employment, but also restoration for those who want to reclaim life.

About Purple Door

Purple Door has now been up and running since April 15th, 2013, but it has been in the works for a long time. Dry Bones Denver has always been about not reinventing the wheel. They have wanted to be an organization that is about meeting unmet needs for the Street Kids of Denver. As they were ministering among friends, they realized that employment and job training was one of the greatest unmet needs present on the streets. This is so key in helping our friends transition off the streets. Some might be able to get a job, but holding it is very difficult for many. Others are not able to be employed because of mistakes in their past.

Dry Bones started dreaming about a café to employ and train friends who were ready for employment and ready to transition away from street life, because of the transferable skills that working in a café environment provides. They have had this dream since 2007. This effort kept getting delayed until Madison started work on it.

When Madison Chandler started a yearlong internship with Dry Bones in 2010, the dream resurfaced. She had decided to take on the dream of starting a coffee shop that will employ and train homeless youth seeking to rebuild their lives. As she started efforts, she remembered a conversation that she had had with Mark Smesrud when they were interns for Dry Bones in the summer of 2009. They had discussed their love of coffee shops and how it would be incredible to combine work at a coffee shop with ministry among the marginalized—particularly Street Kids. While this conversation was very surface level and short-lived, it happened, and we believe for a reason.

Madison contacted Mark about coming to work with Purple Door Coffee a couple of times. He initially said "not now," simply because the timing was never right because of his life situation. Finally, in August of 2011 Madison talked to Mark again about joining the Purple Door Coffee effort, and this time Mark had a peace about it. He spent two months praying and seeking if this was what he was supposed to be doing, and in October of 2011 Mark committed to moving to Denver in January of 2012.

Purple Door took huge leaps forward in July of 2011 when Belay Enterprises began incubating the effort, granting Purple Door Coffee non-profit status and an incredible network of people who knew what they were doing in efforts such as this. Belay is a ministry that partners with area churches to develop businesses that employ and job-train individuals rebuilding lives from addiction, homelessness, prison, and/or poverty. They have been around for 17 years and have had an incredible impact in the city of Denver. Purple Door is so blessed to be a part of what they are doing.

The combination of Belay and Dry Bones has been remarkably beneficial to the progress of Purple Door Coffee, and is a great example of partnership in Kingdom work.

As we continue forward, we look at how God has been so incredibly present and faithful in the entire process, we know that this will continue. We are excited to be a part of what God is up to in the world, and we know that this is only the beginning of the journey. Join us as we continue expanding the story of Purple Door Coffee.

APPENDIX A

Books on *Thinking, How Our Minds Work, and How to Make Better Decisions*

Thinking, Fast, and Slow by Daniel Kahneman

How We Know What Isn't So by Thomas Gilovich

Mistake Were Made (But Not By Me) by Carol Tavris & Elliot Aronson

Predictably Irrational by Dan Ariely

The Invisible Gorilla by Christopher Chabris & Daniel Simons

The Tipping Point by Malcom Gladwell

David and Goliath by Malcom Gladwell

Blink by Malcom Gladwell

What the Dog Saw by Malcom Gladwell

Outliers by Malcom Gladwell

Being Wrong by Kathryn Schulz

A Mind of Its Own by Cordelia Fine

On Being Certain by Robert A. Burton

Why We Make Mistakes by Joseph T. Hallinan

To Sell is Human by Daniel Pink

Drive by Daniel Pink

Blind Spots by Madeleine L. Van Hecke

The Brain That Changes Itself by Norman Doidge

Sway by Ori Brafman & Rom Brafman

Drunk Tank Pink by Adam Alter

My Age of Anxiety by Scott Stossel

The Man Who Mistook His Wife For A Hat by Oliver Sacks

The Talent Code by Daniel Coyle

The Practicing Mind by Thomas M. Sterner

B. *Chase Chandler*

Iconoclast by Gregory Berns
The Paradox of Choice by Barry Schwartz
Incognito by David Eagleman
Decisive by Chip Heath and Dan Heath
Switch by Chip Heath and Dan Heath
Kidding Ourselves by Joseph T. Hallinan
How We Decide by Jonah Lehrer
Everything Is Obvious by Duncan J. Watts
You Are Not So Smart by David McRaney
The Art of Choosing by Sheena Iyengar
Priceless by William Poundstone

APPENDIX B

E D U C A T I O N A L   R E S O U R C E S

The Nash Principles & PES

TheFallofLogic.com
ConsultingByRPM.com
InfiniteBanking.org
NightofClarity.com

General

http://www.investopedia.com/university

Alternative Strategies

tastytrade.com
www.investopedia.com/university/options
www.investopedia.com/university/shortselling/shortselling1.asp

Entrepreneurship

TheLeanStartup.com

Appendix C

Books

It is this author's opinion that each of the following books should be required reading for the person who desires personal financial optimization. However, it is also his opinion that many readers likely maintain busy church, family, business, and social schedules; so the books have been ordered by urgency. (Although, a book not being near the front of the list should not negate its relevance.) He also suggests that if you are single and have no children, you should categorically take advantage of your "leg-up" and have each of these read within the next year. No excuses.[i]

The author does not endorse, condone, or receive revenue from any of the following books. He agrees with much of the content of these recommendations, but fervently disagrees with some. The compiled purpose of the list is not a *"how-to"* or *"must read"* list—rather, it is a *"you should think about this stuff, and study its premise and logical arguments, because this process is really important to your long-term financial wellbeing."* That is, it is focused on and motivated by authenticity, not answers.

The Nash Principles:

Becoming Your Own Banker, R. Nelson Nash
How Privatized Banking Really Works, L. Carlos Lara and Robert P. Murphy
Building Your Warehouse for Wealth, R. Nelson Nash

---

[i] Well, some excuses do indeed count. You know what they are.

Busting the Retirement Myths, Kim Butler
Busting the Financial Planning Lies, Kim Butler
Financial Independence in the 21ˢᵗ Century, Dwayne and Suzanne Burnell
Confessions of a CPA, Bryan Bloom

General Business & Finance:

MONEY Master the Game, Tony Robbins
Backstage Wall Street, Joshua M. Brown

Investing & Valuation:

The Dao of Capital, Mark Spitznagel
The Black Swan, Nassim Nicholas Taleb
Antifragile, Nassim Nicholas Taleb
Why Stocks Go Up and Down, William Pike and Patrick Gregory
Guide to Intangible Asset Valuation, Robert F. Reilly and Robert P. Schweihs
Guide to Investing in Gold and Silver, Mike Maloney

Entrepreneurship

The Lean Startup, Eric Ries
Choose Yourself, James Altucher
Zero to One, Peter Thiel and Blake Masters
The Greatest Salesman in the World, Og Mandino
Who Took My Money, Robert Kiyosaki

How To...

Calculate the Compound Annual Growth Rate (CAGR)

1. Open Microsoft Excel

2. Insert the following terms into your excel document:

B8	▼	:	✕ ✓ *fx*	Future Value	
⬙	A	**B**		C	D
1					
2					
3					
4		Present Value			
5		Payment			
6		ROR (CAGR)			
7		Years			
8		Future Value			
9					
10					
11					
12					
13					

3. Determine which of the variables for which you need to solve. Enter data into all other variables. You must have data for four

of the five variables in order to solve for the fifth variable. In this case, we're solving for the rate or CAGR.

4. Example data:

Be sure to enter your present value and payment as a negative number. In financial calculations, we use negative to indicate money that's 'going away' and positive numbers for money that's 'incoming.'

5. In the cell to the right of *ROR (CAGR)* type *=RATE(*

Then enter the cell numbers of the variables as prompted.

NPER = Years

PMT = Payment.

PV = Present Value

FV = Future Value

Type = 0 (*Type* 0 means 'end of period' and 1 means 'beginning of period.' By using 0 it will assume we saved this money at the end of the year. This is more conservative because we may not always be able to save the entire $6,000 at the beginning of the year.)

3		
4	Present Value	($52,950)
5	Payment	($6,000)
6	ROR (CAGR)	=RATE(C7,C5,C4,C8,0)
7	Years	RATE(nper, pmt, pv, [fv], [type], [guess])
8	Future Value	$234,567
9		
10		

6. This formula gives us the CAGR:

C6   fx   =RATE(C7,C5,C4,C8,0)

	A	B	C	D	E
1					
2					
3					
4		Present Value	($52,950)		
5		Payment	($6,000)		
6		ROR (CAGR)	4.80%		
7		Years	15		
8		Future Value	$234,567		
9					

PERSONAL FINANCE DEFINITIONS

Important and Common Terms:

Qualified Plan - Plans governed by the combination of ERISA and Internal Revenue Code section 401.

Defined Benefit - A qualified plan that has a certain benefit to be paid at some point in the future.

Defined Contribution - A qualified plan that has a specific payment option and limits, but no certain future benefit.

Non-Qualified Plans - Plans not governed by the combination of ERISA and Internal Revenue Code section 401.

Delta - A difference or spread.

Average Annualized Rate of Return - The sum of each yearly rate of return divided by the total number of years.

CAGR - Compound Annual Growth Rate; the actual annualized rate of return of a present value and/or payments, a period of years, and a future ending value. The actual rate of return earned each year.

Gross Rate of Return - Rate of return before calculating the cost of fees and taxes. (Typically calculated as the 'average gross ROR)

Net Rate of Return - Rate of return after calculating the cost of fees and taxes.

Net Net Rate of Return - The rate of return after calculating a current investment vehicle's CAGR, cost of previous and future fees and taxes, and the cost of incurring potential new charges, fees, or taxes by selling and/or moving that asset to another.

The Rule of 72 - 72 can be divided by a CAGR and the answer provides the estimated number of years it will take for an investment to double.

Other Terms: [65]

401(k) - A plan offered by corporations to its employees to set aside tax deferred money for retirement.

403(b) - A plan offered by non-profits and universities to its employees to set aside tax deferred money for retirement.

457 Plans - A plan slightly different from 401(k) in that it is offered to state and governmental employees, but there are never employer matches made.
A through M

Adjustable Rate - A loan in which the interest rate can change during the term of the loan. (Opposite of fixed rate and called variable rate)

Annual Percentage Rate - The yearly cost of the amount financed, including interest and any fees, expressed as a percentage rate. (Also called APR)

Annuities - An insurance industry investment product. These contracts, between an individual and an insurance contract, are set up so that you deposit a sum of money with the insurance company, and they in turn make monthly payments to you.

Application - The process of a borrower asking for the extension of credit from a creditor.

APR - The yearly cost of a credit, including interest, mortgage insurance, and the origination fee (points), expressed as a percentage. (also called Annual Percentage Rate.)

Assets - Any item of economic value owned by an individual.

Bank - Publicly traded corporation, banks are chartered by the state or federal government and offer checking/savings accounts as well as make loans.

Bankruptcy - The condition of being financially insolvent or the administration of an insolvent debtor's property by the court for the benefit of the debtor's creditors.

Chapter 7 - A liquidation proceeding, available to individuals, married couples, partnerships and corporations.

Chapter 13 - A repayment plan for individuals with debts falling below statutory levels, which provides for repayment of some or all of the debts out of future income over 3 to 5 years.

Bonds - A certificate of debt issued by either a corporation or a government.

Borrower - An individual who signs a promissory note and assumes liability to repay under the terms of that note. (Also called a debtor)

Certificate of Deposit (CD) - A deposit account that pays higher interest rate than a savings account.

Charged Off - When a loan becomes uncollectible and is written off, 120 days delinquent for closed-end and 180 days delinquent for open-end loans.

Collateral - Assets pledged by a borrower to secure a loan or other credit, and subject to seizure in the event of default. (Also called security.)

Commercial Credit - A bank loan to a business.

Consumer Credit - A loan from a bank, credit union, or finance company to a person.

Cosigner - An individual other than the borrower who signs a promissory note and thereby assumes equal liability for it.

B. Chase Chandler

Credit - A contractual agreement in which a borrower receives something of value now and agrees to repay the lender at a later date.

Credit Bureau - Agency that collects and sells information about the credit-worthiness of individuals. (Also called credit reporting agency)

Credit Counseling Agency - An agency that offers education, counseling, and budget analysis to consumers.

Credit Repair Organizations Act - A federal law which regulates credit repair businesses.

Credit Report - A report which will contains information about a person's credit history.

Credit Reporting Agency - Agency which collects and sells information about the creditworthiness of individuals. (Also called credit bureau)

Credit Score - A measure of credit risk calculated from a credit report using a standardized formula.

Credit Scoring - A statistical technique used to determine whether to extend credit to a borrower.

Credit Union - Non-profit financial institutions that offer their members check/savings accounts as well as loans.

Creditor - A person or organization which extends credit to others. (Also called lender)

Debt - A liability or obligation in the form of a loan owed by one person to another person and required to be paid by a specified date.

Debt Consolidation - A loan, usually secured with the equity in a home, used to pay off other, higher interest debts resulting in one monthly payment.

Debt Management Program (DMP) - A program where an agency works with a debtor and the debtor's creditors to come up with a repayment plan. The agency receives payment from the debtor and then distributes the money to the creditors. Creditors will occasionally make concessions, such as a reduced interest rate, waiving of fees or re-aging accounts.

Debt Negotiation - An agency negotiates with creditors on a debtor's behalf to reduce the amount of money owed. The agency usually retains a monthly fee, percentage of the money saved or both. The money saved in such a program can be considered taxable income by the IRS. (Also called Debt Settlement)

Debt Settlement - An agency negotiates with creditors on a debtor's behalf to reduce the amount of money owed. The agency usually retains a monthly fee, percentage of the money saved or both. The money saved in such a program can be considered taxable income by the IRS. (Also called Debt Negotiation)

Debtor - An individual who signs a promissory note and assumes liability to repay under the terms of that note. (Also called a borrower)

Delinquent - Failure to make a contractual payment on time.

Disability Insurance - An insurance that will supplement your income should you become unable to work.

Equal Credit Opportunity Act - A federal law prohibiting lenders from discriminating on the basis of the borrower's race, color, national origin, religion, age, sex, marital status, or public assistance program participation.

Fair and Accurate Credit Transactions Act - A federal law which, in part, will reduce identity theft and assist victims in recovering from fraud.

Fair Credit Reporting Act - A federal law designed to promote accuracy and ensure the privacy of the information used in a credit report.

Federal Trade Commission - Also known as the FTC, these government agencies has oversight for the FCRA, ECOA, FACT Act as well as other credit related regulations.

FICO - Fair Isaac Corporation; the inventor of credit scoring models.

Finance Company - A company which makes loans to individuals.

Fixed Rate - A loan in which the interest rate does not change during the entire term of the loan. (Opposite of adjustable rate)

Government Bond - A bond issued by the US Treasury.

Health Insurance - An insurance policy to cover against health claims. There are various types such as HMO, PPO & HSA.

Health Savings Accounts (HSA) - A savings account with tax benefits that can be used for paying medical expenses.

Homeowners Insurance - An insurance to cover the value of real estate. Most mortgage companies require that you insure the value of the home to cover against loss while there is a mortgage in place.

Installment Loans - A loan that is repaid with a fixed number of periodic equal payments.

Interest Rate - The fee charged by a lender to borrower money, expressed as an annual percentage of the principal.

Individual Retirement Accounts (IRA) - A qualified plan account that allows you to personally save for retirement.

Junk Bond - A bond that carries a higher-than-average risk of default and has been given a poor rating by a bond rating company.

Keogh - Retirement accounts for self-employed individuals.

Lender - A person or organization which extends credit to others. (Also called creditor)

Liabilities - The monetary obligations that you owe to others.

Life Insurance - An insurance policy to cover against loss of life. There are various types of polices, such as term and permanent insurance.

Money Market Account - A type of savings account that pays higher interest rates, but requires a minimum balance and restricts the number of withdrawals.

Mortgage - Security agreement where house is pledged for a loan.

Mutual Funds - A fund where people pool together their monies in order to invest together. Typically professionally managed and management fees are charged.

NASDAQ - Largest OTC exchange.

Net Worth - The resulting value between your assets and liabilities.

NYSE - New York Stock Exchange is the largest equity exchange in the world.

Over the Counter (OTC) - The NASDAQ stock exchange is an example of an OTC exchange. Most stocks in the US are traded on the OTC.

Pension Plan - A retirement plan set by an employer for its employees.

Personal Liability Umbrella Insurance - An insurance policy to cover in excess of homeowner or auto insurance policies. Typically used to raise coverage to higher limits.

Promissory Note - A document signed by a borrower promising to repay a loan under agreed-upon terms.

B. Chase Chandler

Pro Bono - Done without compensation for the public good.

Re-aging - Bringing your account current. Bank guidelines vary on their re-aging process. (i.e., some re-aging once in a twelve month period; some once in a re-aging period)

Renters Insurance- An insurance policy that renters can take out to cover the value of their personal belongings while renting a home or apartment.

Revolving Credit - An agreement by a bank to lend a specific amount to a borrower and to allow that amount to be borrowed again once it has been repaid.

Roth IRA - An IRA which you deposit after tax dollars.

Savings Account - A deposit account that pays interest and allows for unlimited deposits and withdrawals.

Secured - Backed by a pledge of collateral. (Opposite of unsecured)

Security - Assets pledged by a borrower to secure a loan. (Also called collateral)

Security Agreement - Loan document pledging asset for a loan.

Simplified Employee Pension (SEP) - A plan for self-employed individuals (and their employees) yet who have less than 25 employees.

Social Security Tax - A tax withheld from your pay to fund the Social Security Retirement System. If you are self-employed, you contribute the full percentage, if you are employed you contribute half and your employer the other half.

Stocks - Instruments that signify ownership in a corporation. There can be different classes such as common stock or preferred.

Truth in Lending - A federal law requiring lenders to fully disclose in writing the terms and conditions of a mortgage, including the annual percentage rate and other charges. (Also called Regulation Z)

U.S. Savings Bonds - Bonds issued by the United States government.

Unsecured - Backed not by collateral but only by the integrity of the borrower.

Variable Rate - A loan in which the interest rate can change during the term of the loan. (Opposite of fixed rate and called adjustable rate)

Will - A legal document which states your wishes for deposition of your belonging upon your death.

Yield - The rate of return on an investment.

Zero-Coupon Bond - Bonds which pay interest only upon their maturity.

ACKNOWLEDGEMENTS

✝

I WANT TO EXTEND A HEARTFELT AND special and sincere and wonderful thank you (seriously… no sarcasm) to my amazing team. I can't pinpoint what I've done right—but I have, only by divine intervention, wound up working with some of the smartest people in the financial and business consulting industry. Jay—you're a remarkable partner. JJ—thank you for thinking outside the box and for blazing a path, a true feat for an attorney. Matt—don't stop being awesome. Finnell—hang in there like a hair in a biscuit. Bradshaw— I still don't know how we got you. Dr. Baber—please quit medicine. Saucer—Roll Tide. I know you still love Nick Saban. Dr. Jolly—thanks for keeping the faith. Jerry—you're youthful spirit breathes life into everyone with whom you come in contact. Glenn and Fields—keep rockin'! A special thank you to Joe Bedwell—a brilliant mentor and wordsmith.

Nelson Nash—many have copied your work, altered it, etc. but you were the one who took us from *zero to one*. Thank you, from the bottom of my heart. To the avant-garde thinkers who have played an integral role in researching and helping to get this message out—Dr. Robert Murphy, Carlos Lara, Patrick Donohoe, Kim Butler, Todd Langford, Barry Dyke—your work is remarkably helpful to those who venture to think outside the box.

Finally, to my family, I'm running out of adjectives. All I can say is I am deeply grateful. Mom and dad—I only hope I can raise children like you. Dr. and Mrs. Phillips—you let me marry your perfect daughter. Your mercy does not go unnoticed.

Most importantly, I thank my wife, Beth. You are stunning in every way. Your faith, love, and patience are astounding. Please keep putting up with me.

Additional Acknowledgements:

To all of my friends, clients, and anyone else who emailed me during the last few months of my completing this work. I'm sorry for neglecting you. Hopefully you've found it worthwhile and will forgive me for my short-term abandonment. My rationalization is that it was for long-term good.

B. Chase Chandler

ABOUT THE AUTHOR

CHASE CHANDLER IS A FINANCIAL AND BUSINESS thought leader. He is the founder of Chandler Advisors, a financial and business consulting firm which focuses on unconventional strategies. Chase speaks around the country about financial, economic, and business topics. Chase holds an undergraduate business degree from Harding University and a Certificate of Financial Management from Cornell University. He has also studied at Pepperdine University and Lipscomb University.

He is the author of three books: *The Wealthy Physician* (2012), *The Fall of Logic* (2014), and *The Wealthy Family* (2015). Mr. Chandler enjoys travel, golf, reading, church, and pretending to be smart. He lives in Nashville, Tennessee with his wife, Beth, and their (soon-to-be) daughter Kate.

B. Chase Chandler

REFERENCES

[1] http://www.newyorker.com/tech/frontal-cortex/why-smart-people-are-stupid

[2] http://www.psychologytoday.com/blog/focus-forgiveness/201307/conscious-the-uncon-scious

[3] Burchard, Brendan (2014). *The Motivation Manifesto*. Hay House.

[4] http://www.merriam-webster.com/thesaurus/greatness

[5] Quote from The Motivation Manifesto by Brendon Burchard

[6] http://columbiadailyherald.com/news/local-news/local-dentist-dies-cycling-accident

[7] https://www.marxists.org/archive/marx/works/subject/quotes/

[8] http://en.wikipedia.org/wiki/Confirmation_bias

[9] http://scienceblogs.com/developingintelligence/2007/05/14/why-the-simplest-theory-is-alm/

[10] http://www.latin-dictionary.net/search/english/aware

[11] http://www.brainpickings.org/2013/05/09/daniel-pink-drive-rsa-motivation/

[12] http://psychcentral.com/blog/archives/2010/04/10/5-reliable-findings-from-happiness-re-search/

[13] http://www.johnmaxwell.com/blog/the-law-of-the-lid

[14] Created by Joseph Luft (1916–2014) and Harrington Ingham (1914–1995), 1955. http://en.wikipedia.org/wiki/Johari_window

[15] http://nypost.com/2014/03/01/americans-have-limited-options-when-it-comes-to-saving-money/

[16] http://www.investopedia.com/terms/f/fiatmoney.asp

[17] http://www.presidency.ucsb.edu/ws/?pid=64935

[18] http://www.coburn.senate.gov/public//index.cfm?a=Files.Serve&File_id=f3c21740-474f-4528-a803-57a2f7974ebb

[19] http://www.nytimes.com/1999/03/21/jobs/the-history-of-retirement-from-early-man-to-aarp.html

[20] http://scholarship.law.georgetown.edu/cgi/viewcontent.cgi?article=1049&context=legal

[21] http://scholarship.law.georgetown.edu/cgi/viewcontent.cgi?article=1049&context=legal

[22] http://www.daveramsey.com/blog/make-12-percent-returns-with-mutual-funds

[23] http://www.daveramsey.com/article/the-12-reality/lifeandmoney_investing/

[24] http://www.forbes.com/sites/johnwasik/2013/06/27/why-mutual-fund-fees-are-too-high/

[25] http://www.marketwatch.com/story/john-bogle-retirement-investors-leave-80-on-the-table-2014-02-06

[26] http://quotes.morningstar.com/chart/fund/chart.action?t=PINVX&region=usa&culture=en-US

[27] http://money.cnn.com/2001/01/04/strategies/q_retire_401k/

[28] http://www.ebri.org/pdf/publications/facts/0205fact.a.pdf

[29] http://www.cbsnews.com/news/401k-founder-my-creation-is-a-monster/

[30] http://www.cbsnews.com/news/401k-founder-my-creation-is-a-monster/
http://blogs.smartmoney.com/encore/2011/11/22/father-of-the-401ks-tough-love/

[31] http://www.dol.gov/ebsa/publications/401k_employee.html
http://www.shrm.org/hrdisciplines/benefits/articles/pages/401k-feeseclined.aspx

[32] http://www.forbes.com/2011/04/04/real-cost-mutual-fund-taxes-fees-retirement-bernicke.html

[33] http://www.bankrate.com/finance/investing/401k-fees-breakdown-7.aspx
http://truckerhuss.com/articles/view_article.cgi?class=articles&article=_pension_benefits/20100201_White_Paper.txt
http://www.shrm.org/hrdisciplines/benefits/articles/pages/turnoverfees.aspx
http://www.demos.org/publication/retirement-savings-drain-hidden-excessive-costs-401ks
http://www.shrm.org/hrdisciplines/benefits/articles/pages/turnoverfees.aspx

[34] http://www.investopedia.com/terms/n/npv.asp

[35] http://www.investopedia.com/terms/n/npv.asp

[36] http://en.wikipedia.org/wiki/Opportunity_cost

[37] http://www.merriam-webster.com/dictionary/debt

[38] http://en.wikiquote.org/wiki/Stephen_Covey

[39] Collins, Daniel. "The Roundabout Path to Profits: Mark Spitznagel on the Dao of Capital." The Roundabout Path to Profits: Mark Spitznagel on the Dao of Capital. 1 Apr. 2014. Web. 27 Jan. 2015. <http://www.futuresmag.com/2014/04/01/the-roundabout-path-to-profits-mark-spitznagel-on>.

[40] Spitznagel, Mark. *The Dao of Capital: Austrian Investing in a Distorted World*. 1st ed. Wiley, 2013. 368. Print.

[41] http://www.nytimes.com/2008/03/27/health/nutrition/27best.html?_r=0

[42] http://www.webmd.com/depression/guide/exercise-depression

[43] http://en.wikipedia.org/wiki/Efficient-market_hypothesis

[44] http://en.wikipedia.org/wiki/Behavioral_economics

[45] http://www.econlib.org/library/Enc/BehavioralEconomics.html

[46] http://www.nytimes.com/2011/10/23/magazine/dont-blink-the-hazards-of-confidence.html?pagewanted=all&_r=1&

[47] http://myinvestingnotes.blogspot.com/2011/08/cycle-of-market-emotions.html

[48] https://www.youtube.com/watch?v=rhJaVEWAG24

[49] Source: Pinnacle Data Corp; http://www.econ.yale.edu/~shiller/data.htm; www.finance.yahoo.com

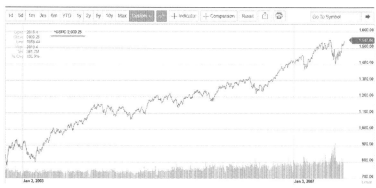

[50] http://video.cnbc.com/gallery/?video=3000210650

[51] http://www.bloomberg.com/news/2011-10-06/black-swan-money-manager-returning-23-anticipating-bear-market.html

[52] http://www.thestreet.com/story/11621555/1/average-investor-20-year-return-astoundingly-awful.html

[53] http://www.thestreet.com/story/11621555/1/average-investor-20-year-return-astoundingly-awful.html

http://www.forbes.com/sites/advisor/2014/04/24/why-the-average-investors-investment-return-is-so-low/

http://www.businessinsider.com/chart-average-investor-returns-2012-12

[54] http://content.time.com/time/magazine/article/0,9171,2099712,00.html

[55] http://www.economist.com/blogs/freeexchange/2014/06/financial-knowledge-and-investment-performance

[56] http://www.ft.com/cms/s/0/abd15744-9793-11e2-b7ef-00144feabdc0.html#axzz3OxMblYVW

[57] Taleb, Nassim Nicholas. *Fooled by Randomness: The Hidden Role of Chance in Life and in the Markets*. 2nd ed. New York: Random House, 2005. Print.

[58] Taleb, Nassim Nicholas. *Fooled by Randomness: The Hidden Role of Chance in Life and in the Markets*. 2nd ed. New York: Random House, 2005. Print.

[59] http://en.wikipedia.org/wiki/History_of_insurance#Life_insurance

[60] http://www.lifehealthpro.com/2013/09/09/a-brief-history-of-life-insurance?t=life-products&page=2

[61] Douglas Doll, *A Brief History of Universal Life*, Society of Actuaries

[62] http://infinitebanking.org/wp-content/uploads/2012/07/BankNotes-Aug-2012.pdf

[63] http://money.cnn.com/2012/03/05/news/economy/national-debt-interest/

[64] http://www.investopedia.com/terms/e/eva.asp

[65] https://financiallit.org/resources/resource-lists/glossary-of-terms/